GMAT Practice Questions

Critical Reasoning

GMAT Free

www.GMATFree.com

CONTENTS

Introduction 1

The Critical Reasoning Strategy 2

Critical Reasoning Practice Questions 3

What's Next? 247

Index of Questions 248

INTRODUCTION

This volume includes practice in Critical Reasoning, one of the three question types on the Verbal section of the GMAT.

The questions in this volume have been designed for realism. Each is benchmarked against a real GMAT question in its format, difficulty, subject matter, and concepts tested. Your practice experience will be most coherent if you work through the questions in order, but you won't suffer terribly by skipping around. Don't concern yourself with the difficulty of individual questions, since the difficulty of even a perfectly normed question is a statistical outcome of a group of test takers. One person's easy question may be another person's difficult question, and *vice versa*. If you master the questions in this book, you will be ready for Critical Reasoning questions on the GMAT.

Every question is repeated on the following page with an explanation. Each explanation emphasizes not a formal method, but rather a realistic expert approach to the question. The Critical Reasoning Strategy, presented on the following page, has been extracted and distilled from a hundreds of examples of how experts actually solve these questions. This method of developing an instructional strategy, based on so-called "cognitive task analysis," cuts out formal multi-step methods, which people struggle to remember and tend to abandon under pressure.

Your guide in this review is Andrew Mitchell, Chief Freedom Officer of GMAT Free LLC, the former Director of GMAT Programs at Kaplan Test Prep, dubbed the "Guru of the GMAT" by Poets & Quants, and cited as a GMAT expert by publications including *The Wall Street Journal*, *The New York Times* and *Bloomberg BusinessWeek*.

As you work through this volume, you are encouraged to join us online. GMAT Free offers a complete, free GMAT course at www.gmatfree.com—registration is optional.

Thank you for your purchase. Let's try some questions...

>> Download the free
CR Strategy Sheets
GMATFree.com/CR-Strategy-Sheets

THE CRITICAL REASONING STRATEGY

You can answer any Critical Reasoning question with this two-step approach:

Step 1: Create and apply a "filter" to evaluate the answer choices. While you read and process the question prompt and question stem, form a conception of what will characterize the correct answer. In order from less specific to more specific, and from easier-to-create to harder-to-create, your filter may be described as:

- **Basic relevance.** After you get an idea of what the prompt is really about, you can evaluate or filter the answer choices based on whether they are truly relevant to the question at hand.

- **Non-contradiction.** You can eliminate answer choices based on whether they contradict the facts of the argument or the main idea of what the answer choices are supposed to answer.

- **Term matching.** Question prompts that present an argument can be divided into "evidence" and "conclusion." By comparing the words on both sides, you can identify terms that are unequal, or poorly "matched," which represent holes in the argument.

- **Critical detail.** You may decide that a question hinges on a critical detail, and you can evaluate the answer choices in their treatment of this detail.

- **Prediction.** You can predict what the correct answer choice will say. In a sense, all filters are predictions, but in some case you'll be able to imagine the correct answer in your mind before turning to the answer choices.

Step 2: Identify "logical proof" of the correct answer. If you can, use a logical test to establish objective grounds that your selected answer is correct, and/or that one or more of the other answer choices cannot be correct. Such tests are not always possible or efficient, but they are decisive. We will refer primarily to two such logical tests:

- **Negation test.** You can often rule an answer choice in or out by testing the impact on the argument of the *negative* of that statement. For example, you may want to show that an answer choice is assumed by the argument in a question. If it is, then negating the answer choice (and accepting that negation as a fact) will contradict or disprove the argument in the question.

- **Analysis by possible/extreme cases.** Sometimes, the statement given by an answer choice will allow for a range of possibilities. If it does, you can try to rule the answer choice in or out by considering some of these possibilities. For example, if an answer choice says that "less than half of the employees at a company have an MBA," you can consider a case in which almost half have an MBA and another case in which no one at all has an MBA. This scrutiny may reveal that an answer choice contradicts the information in the prompt, is not relevant to the argument at hand, or is highly relevant to the argument at hand.

- **Proof by stronger terms.** GMAT questions are often phrased in terms that can be described as logically cautious, or understated. Counterintuitively, it's usually easiest to answer such questions by attempting to answer *more* than the question asks for. For example, if a question asks what would be "useful to know" to evaluate an argument or situation, and you find an answer choice that describes what would be *essential* to know, then you can be certain that you have identified the correct answer choice.

Through practice, you'll use this strategy in natural and nuanced way. For example, your default approach will be to do Step 1, then Step 2, but we'll see that on certain questions it will be feasible or advantageous to use only one step or the other.

CRITICAL REASONING PRACTICE QUESTIONS

Drivers of automobiles over 30 are more likely to purchase music in digital format and are more likely to purchase it in larger amounts than are members of any other demographic group. The popular conception that young people listen to more music in digital format than adults must, therefore, be false.

The argument is flawed primarily because the author

○   fails to distinguish between purchasing and listening
○   does not supply information about drivers of automobiles under 30
○   depends on popular belief rather than on documented research findings
○   does not specify the monetary value of the digital music purchased by any demographic group
○   discusses music in digital format only rather than music sold in any format

Drivers Over 30

Drivers of automobiles over 30 are more likely to purchase music in digital format and are more likely to purchase it in larger amounts than are members of any other demographic group. The popular conception that young people listen to more music in digital format than adults must, therefore, be false.

The argument is flawed primarily because the author

- ○ fails to distinguish between purchasing and listening
- ○ does not supply information about drivers of automobiles under 30
- ○ depends on popular belief rather than on documented research findings
- ○ does not specify the monetary value of the digital music purchased by any demographic group
- ○ discusses music in digital format only rather than music sold in any format

Explanation

Reading the question: we'll start each explanation with a description of how might have approached the question, or what your first impression might have been. These impressions will often be different from the ones you had—that's to be expected—but they give a realistic picture of how an expert engages the question. Throughout the book, we'll refer to the **"stem"** as the final line of text just above the answer choices. Everything above the stem is the **"prompt"** (because it prompts *you,* as if every GMAT question gave you a little poke when you started). We can actually *start* with the question stem. Any order is fair game; you are the ultimately the boss of your GMAT strategy. In 90% or more of Critical Reasoning questions, you'll want to read the prompt and the stem in some order and attempt to create a "filter" (per step one of the strategy) before turning to the answer choices.

Creating a filter: the stem reads, "the argument is flawed primarily because the author…" We can see that our objective is to find a flaw in the argument. Since we have a brief argument, we can employ **term matching** to compare words in the evidence and the conclusion.

Evidence Term	Matches?	Conclusion Term
Drivers of automobiles over 30	≠	Young people
Purchasing	≠	Listening

The argument proceeds as if these terms are equal, but they are not. For example, purchasing and listening are not the same thing, but the argument proceeds as if they are. We now have a way to filter the answer choices: we will look for an answer choice that highlights either mismatch as a flaw.

Applying the filter: Choice (A) does this, so (A) may be our answer. Choice (B) states something that isn't really true; if drivers over 30 buy more, drivers under 30 buy less. Choice (C) contradicts the prompt, which presents us with facts, for the purpose of the argument, so (C) is out. Choice (D) is irrelevant to our understanding of this argument. Choice (E) states something that is true but which is not a flaw of the argument, since the argument is about digital music, not other music. We have opted for one answer choice and against for all the others, so we are done. The correct answer is (A).

Scientists have genetically modified three pigs so that they are thoroughly florescent both in daylight and in darkness. Pigs have been modified in this fashion before, but the scientists who have created the most recent set observe that their technique has improved the odds of successfully modifying a specific embryo and making the adult pig completely florescent. The presence of the green protein will allow genetically modified cells to be tracked if they were transplanted into a human. This will immediately speed scientists' understanding of genetic research for the purpose of improving human health.

Which of the following would be most useful to determine in evaluating the claim above?

- What human diseases the scientists intend to cure with the research enabled by the florescent pig cells
- Whether there is any health risk to the pigs who are rendered florescent
- How quickly the process of rendering pigs florescent can be perfected
- Whether the time saved by being able to detect florescent cells might be offset by the time taken to produce florescent pigs at the improved odds
- How the scientists achieved better results in their most recent technique of creating florescence in the pigs

GLOWING PIGS

Scientists have genetically modified three pigs so that they are thoroughly florescent both in daylight and in darkness. Pigs have been modified in this fashion before, but the scientists who have created the most recent set observe that their technique has improved the odds of successfully modifying a specific embryo and making the adult pig completely florescent. The presence of the green protein will allow genetically modified cells to be tracked if they were transplanted into a human. This will immediately speed scientists' understanding of genetic research for the purpose of improving human health.

Which of the following would be most useful to determine in evaluating the claim above?

- What human diseases the scientists intend to cure with the research enabled by the florescent pig cells
- Whether there is any health risk to the pigs who are rendered florescent
- How quickly the process of rendering pigs florescent can be perfected
- Whether the time saved by being able to detect florescent cells might be offset by the time taken to produce florescent pigs at the improved odds
- How the scientists achieved better results in their most recent technique of creating florescence in the pigs

EXPLANATION

Reading the question: we can begin once again with the question stem, as we did for Drivers Over 30. We don't have to start with the stem on every question, but if it feels counterintuitive to start with the stem first, let's exercise that muscle.

Creating a filter: the stem tells us to choose something that is "useful" to evaluate the argument. Quite often, as we'll discuss more on later questions, the correct answer will be not only "useful," but *essential* to the argument. (This is proof by stronger terms, as mentioned in the Critical Reasoning Strategy.) What's essential to the argument? The language of the argument gets passionate with the phrase "immediately speed understanding." Working back from that phrase, what immediately speeds understanding? The green pig technology makes traceable cells and we are going to transplant those into a human. That's the key connection: 1) the traceable cells and 2) the immediate speeding of understanding. With that connection mind, we can now turn to the answer choices. We'll see, for starters, what answer choices have *anything* to do with 1) the traceable cells and 2) the immediate speeding of understanding. Since we are "filtering" out the irrelevant answer choices, we can think of this as a **basic relevance filter.**

Applying the filter: Choice (A) doesn't pass the filter. Choice (B) is definitely irrelevant to the argument. Skipping down, so is (E). They have no bearing on how the green piggery will help genetic research. Choices (C) and (D), interestingly, both involve time, which pertains to the word "immediately" in the prompt.

Logical proof: we can analyze both (C) and (D) by **extreme cases**; this is step 2 of the Critical Reasoning Strategy presented at the beginning of the book. First, (C). We imagine the technique takes a long time to be perfected—or it's never perfected. That might not matter, if the new technique is already a big improvement. So we're focused on (D). Choice (D) says, if the current pig process churns out completely green pigs only occasionally, we can't benefit much from them. Maybe the new process is much better, but not that good. That would be highly relevant to the argument. The correct answer is (D).

Utility Corp, a company with a specific level of cash in its budget, has been clearing uninhabited land near a national park for the construction of a coal plant. This practice continues even though greater annual profits can be made from a nuclear plant, which will not damage the nearby park, than from a coal plant, which will injure the habitat.

Which of the following, if true, most helps to explain why Utility Corp has been pursuing the less profitable of the two economic activities mentioned above?

- The nearby park is rich with naturally occurring plant life that is important to the survival of various animal species.
- Coal plant operations that are located in uninhabited areas are more profitable than coal plant operations that are located in inhabited areas.
- In certain districts, profits made from coal plant operations are more heavily taxed than profits made from any other industry.
- Some of the energy produced on land near an area such as a national park cannot be delivered cost-effectively to customers.
- The amount of money required to build a nuclear plant is twice as high as the amount needed to begin a coal plant.

ALTERNATIVE PLANTS

Utility Corp, a company with a specific level of cash in its budget, has been clearing uninhabited land near a national park for the construction of a coal plant. This practice continues even though greater annual profits can be made from a nuclear plant, which will not damage the nearby park, than from a coal plant, which will injure the habitat.

Which of the following, if true, most helps to explain why Utility Corp has been pursuing the less profitable of the two economic activities mentioned above?

○   The nearby park is rich with naturally occurring plant life that is important to the survival of various animal species.
○   Coal plant operations that are located in uninhabited areas are more profitable than coal plant operations that are located in inhabited areas.
○   In certain districts, profits made from coal plant operations are more heavily taxed than profits made from any other industry.
○   Some of the energy produced on land near an area such as a national park cannot be delivered cost-effectively to customers.
○   The amount of money required to build a nuclear plant is twice as high as the amount needed to begin a coal plant.

EXPLANATION

Reading the question: we can start yet again with the question stem. We might be motivated to do so by the fact that the question stem can be seen at a glance to have some substantial language in it (it's not just asking for a flaw, as in Drivers Over 30). The stem gives us a specific task: explain why Utility Corp would pursue a less profitable option. A correct answer to this question will clarify the situation without contradicting any of the facts we have so far. For example, maybe the Corp is motivated by something other than greater profits. With that as our filter, a prediction along the lines of "some other motivation," we can turn to the answer choices.

Applying the filter: The answer choices don't match our particular prediction. In fact, the only answer choice that seems relevant to the situation is (E); it's the only one comparing the two options. But choice (E) might, at first, seem to contradict the data—aren't profits from nuclear were greater? Reviewing the question, we see the company has a specific level of cash in its budget, we are told. And there's a high up-front cost to building a nuclear plant, according to (E). So a nuclear plant might be bad for the company's current cash situation, even if it's more profitable in the long run. Choice (E) is a good explanation. Meanwhile, (A) and (D) are focused on the park, which isn't really relevant to the coal vs. nuclear decision. Choice (C) mentions a random detail about coal that hasn't been connected to the coal vs. nuclear question.

Note: in the language of the Critical Reasoning Strategy at the beginning of this book, we started off with a filter than was a "prediction" and we ended up using a filter that was less specific, one of "basic relevance." **It's typical, if our prediction doesn't turn out as planned, to slip back to a less specific filter of the answer choices.** And the various filters can be quite similar, so you don't need to worry too much about which type you are using or whether you switch—at this point, the important thing is to practice having a filter of some sort before you turn to the answer choices.

The correct answer is (E).

Seattle's osprey population has been declining in recent years, primarily because of hunting, both legal and illegal. Osprey prey heavily on salmon, a fish that is prized as food by the coastal population, who had hoped at least that the decline in the osprey population would lead to an increase in salmon for human consumption. Yet the naturally occurring population of salmon has also declined, even though the annual number caught for human consumption has not increased.

Which of the following, if true, most helps to explain the decline in the population of the salmon?

- The decline in the osprey population has meant that fishers can work in some parts of lakes and rivers that were formerly too congested.
- Over the last few years, Seattle's commercial fishing enterprises have increased the number of fishing boats they use.
- A primary predator of salmon is the American eel, on which osprey also prey.
- Many Seattle residents who hunt osprey do so because of the high market price of osprey plumage, not because of the threat osprey pose to the natural salmon population.
- In neighboring stretches of coastline near Seattle, osprey are endangered as a result of extensive hunting.

OSPREY PREY

Seattle's osprey population has been declining in recent years, primarily because of hunting, both legal and illegal. Osprey prey heavily on salmon, a fish that is prized as food by the coastal population, who had hoped at least that the decline in the osprey population would lead to an increase in salmon for human consumption. Yet the naturally occurring population of salmon has also declined, even though the annual number caught for human consumption has not increased.

Which of the following, if true, most helps to explain the decline in the population of the salmon?

○ The decline in the osprey population has meant that fishers can work in some parts of lakes and rivers that were formerly too congested.
○ Over the last few years, Seattle's commercial fishing enterprises have increased the number of fishing boats they use.
○ A primary predator of salmon is the American eel, on which osprey also prey.
○ Many Seattle residents who hunt osprey do so because of the high market price of osprey plumage, not because of the threat osprey pose to the natural salmon population.
○ In neighboring stretches of coastline near Seattle, osprey are endangered as a result of extensive hunting.

EXPLANATION

Reading the question: did you start with the stem on this question? Either way, we discover when we get to the stem that we have to "explain" on this question, just as we did in "Alternative Plants." **"Explain" questions have similar features**:

- The mystery needing explaining has two parts.
- The correct answer...
    - ...usually addresses both parts of the mystery; and
    - ...never contradicts the facts in the prompt.

Creating a filter: in this question, the two parts of the contradiction are delineated by the word "yet." Most "explain" questions have such a division word in the prompt. On one side of the "yet," 1) the osprey have declined. On the other side: 2) their predator, osprey, haven't declined (and we aren't fishing them any more than before). Our filter is to look for an answer choice that addresses both 1) and 2) without contradicting either.

Applying this filter, we can turn to the answers: Choices (A) and (B) irrelevant, because we know fishing isn't the explanation. Choice (C) looks relevant. We'll come back to it. Choice (D) is irrelevant; who cares why we hunt osprey? (E) is similarly irrelevant. Choice (C) is a great explanation. It presents an overlooked effect of the lower number of ospreys. Eels are more populous than ever and gobbling up the salmon, even though there arc fewer osprey. The correct answer is (C).

In a world in which hunger is a problem, genetically modified crops represent a substantial agricultural advance, because they are more resistant to weeds and disease, they produce bigger yields of crops, and they have a longer shelf life. Moreover, although there were concerns about potential human health hazards initially, genetically modified crops have been sold commercially for almost twenty years now; with lots of attention on them, if they created short- or long-term health problems, we would know about it by now.

Which of the following, if true, most weakens the argument stated above?

- There are various ways of producing genetically modified crops, and we are likely develop a new method in the near future which poses new health risks.
- The improved attributes of genetically modified crops have primarily benefitted not the world's hungry, but rather farmers and the owners of corporations.
- Although we have studied the potential health impact of eating GMOs on humans, we have not studied potential disruptions to the ecosystem which would threaten human safety indirectly.
- If companies that produce genetically modified crops discovered a human health hazard of those crops, the companies would have an incentive to downplay or even conceal their findings.
- Places where the winters are cold rarely have a problem of water shortage.

HIDDEN GMOS

In a world in which hunger is a problem, genetically modified crops represent a substantial agricultural advance, because they are more resistant to weeds and disease, they produce bigger yields of crops, and they have a longer shelf life. Moreover, although there were concerns about potential human health hazards initially, genetically modified crops have been sold commercially for almost twenty years now; with lots of attention on them, if they created short- or long-term health problems, we would know about it by now.

Which of the following, if true, most weakens the argument stated above?

○   There are various ways of producing genetically modified crops, and we are likely develop a new method in the near future which poses new health risks.

○   The improved attributes of genetically modified crops have primarily benefitted not the world's hungry, but rather farmers and the owners of corporations.

○   Although we have studied the potential health impact of eating GMOs on humans, we have not studied potential disruptions to the ecosystem which would threaten human safety indirectly.

○   If companies that produce genetically modified crops discovered a human health hazard of those crops, the companies would have an incentive to downplay or even conceal their findings.

○   Places where the winters are cold rarely have a problem of water shortage.

EXPLANATION

Reading the question: let's discuss a new way to attack a question, which is to focus on opinions. Words charged with opinion serve as guideposts to dissect an argument. **Opinion is concentrated in the conclusion of an argument**. When an argument is present, you can often use that fact alone to create a basic relevance filter.

Note: the connection between opinion and conclusion is no GMAT trick; it's more like a law of logic, almost a law of nature. Making an argument is the act of building bridges from things that are initially mutually agreed upon—"facts" or "evidence"—to things that are not initially agreed upon, but which you want ultimately to be agreed upon—and those things are "opinions" or "conclusions." When you catch a whiff of opinion, there likely is an argument present; and if you have an argument, there will absolutely be an opinion inside.

Creating a filter: "substantial" is an opinion word indicating the conclusion of the argument, and pieces of evidence are introduced by "because" and "moreover." Orienting by these words, we can see there are basically two kinds of evidence: a list of virtues of GMOs, and the idea that we would have spotted hazards in GMOs by now, if there were hazards. Both portions are facts, for the purpose of this argument; but the second one is weaker. Maybe we haven't looked in the right places? Or hazards are slow to set in? We'll use those ideas as predictions of the answer and look for something along those lines in the answer choices.

Applying our filter, we find (C) and (D) both roughly fit what we're looking for, and we notice that the other choices, while attacking GMOs, do not attack the *argument*—the connection of facts to opinion. We compare (C) and (D). One must be objectively better. Choice (D), even if true, is somewhat addressed already by the argument; we've put "lots of attention on them"—i.e., from outside of companies, so the secret would have gotten out. And if it's false, it doesn't help the argument much. (C), on the other hand, does help the argument if it's false, and it's closer to what we were thinking: maybe "all our attention" has been in the wrong place. The correct answer is (C).

A small company with a radical four-day work week system is considering changing its policy. Currently, this company requires all employees to arrive at work in the company's office Monday through Thursday; they need not work Friday. The proposed policy would permit each employee every week to choose one day from Monday to Friday not to work.

The adoption of this policy would be most likely to decrease employees' productivity if the employees' job functions required them to

- o work without interruption from other employees
- o consult at least once a day with employees from other companies
- o submit their work for a supervisor's eventual approval
- o interact frequently with each other throughout the entire workday
- o undertake projects that take several days to complete

A small company with a radical four-day work week system is considering changing its policy. Currently, this company requires all employees to arrive at work in the company's office Monday through Thursday; they need not work Friday. The proposed policy would permit each employee every week to choose one day from Monday to Friday not to work.

The adoption of this policy would be most likely to decrease employees' productivity if the employees' job functions required them to

- ○ work without interruption from other employees
- ○ consult at least once a day with employees from other companies
- ○ submit their work for a supervisor's eventual approval
- ○ interact frequently with each other throughout the entire workday
- ○ undertake projects that take several days to complete

EXPLANATION

Reading the question: you're likely to hit cognitive overload while you're practicing and while you sit for the GMAT. That's why it's important to practice with simple methods and focus on ingraining good behaviors in yourself: it's all you can count on when you're tired. Imagine this is such a question: you don't have the energy or patience to strategize and you just read the thing in order. When the adrenaline is pumping, you're going to be fast and linear on some questions. You'll read the prompt, word for word, in order, and then the question stem, and then... **Even when you're tired or rushed, pause and try to make a basic relevance filter before you look at the answer choices.** Make some sort of guess or form some sort of judgment of what's important before turning to the answer choices.

Creating a filter: let's come up with a shred of our own judgment. In the prompt, everyone's extra day off was Friday before, but now they can choose different days. Will it increase their productivity? It's not about time, since the total time worked is the same. So it has to be about something other than time. It could be about how the work time is used, and we guess whether they all need to be doing it on Monday through Thursday for some reason. With that shred of a prediction, we have a basic relevance filter (or more) to apply to the answer choices and find something that would decrease productivity.

Applying the filter: choice (A) would *help* their productivity, because there would be fewer people in the office on average on a given day in the new model. So (A) is out. Choice (B) is irrelevant; we have no information about how they are connected with other companies and whether it matters that our employees are in-office or out of office. Choice (C) is irrelevant, due to the word "eventual"; "eventual" implies that it could wait from one week to the next, so the policy wouldn't matter. Choice (D) looks correct, because, under the new policy, employees will be able to choose different days to be in the office from each other, and so they will tend not to be the office simultaneously as often as before. Choice (E) is irrelevant, because the projects take several days. The correct answer is (D).

In the shipping industry, the amount of time it takes for most of a worker's occupational knowledge and skills to become obsolete has been declining because of the introduction of wearable computing devices, such as smart watches and smart glasses. Given the rate at which wearable computing devices are currently being introduced into shipping, the average worker's old skills become obsolete and new skills are required within as little as two years.

Which of the following plans, if feasible, would allow a company to prepare most effectively for the rapid obsolescence of skills described above?

- ○ The company will develop a program to offer selected employees the opportunity to receive training for three years after they were originally hired.
- ○ The company will increase its investment in wearable computing devices every year for a period of at least two years.
- ○ The company will periodically survey its employees to determine how the introduction of wearable computing devices has affected them.
- ○ Before the introduction of wearable computing devices, the company will institute a training program to inform its employees of the probable consequences of the introduction of wearable computing devices.
- ○ The company will ensure that it can offer its employees any training necessary to meet the requirements of their particular jobs.

In the shipping industry, the amount of time it takes for most of a worker's occupational knowledge and skills to become obsolete has been declining because of the introduction of wearable computing devices, such as smart watches and smart glasses. Given the rate at which wearable computing devices are currently being introduced into shipping, the average worker's old skills become obsolete and new skills are required within as little as two years.

Which of the following plans, if feasible, would allow a company to prepare most effectively for the rapid obsolescence of skills described above?

○   The company will develop a program to offer selected employees the opportunity to receive training for three years after they were originally hired.
○   The company will increase its investment in wearable computing devices every year for a period of at least two years.
○   The company will periodically survey its employees to determine how the introduction of wearable computing devices has affected them.
○   Before the introduction of wearable computing devices, the company will institute a training program to inform its employees of the probable consequences of the introduction of wearable computing devices.
○   The company will ensure that it can offer its employees any training necessary to meet the requirements of their particular jobs.

EXPLANATION

Reading the question: This may be a question in which you find it natural to skip back and forth between the prompt and the stem. Regardless, we'll take our time and read everything before moving on. There is going to be an "obsolescence of skills." How can the company prepare for it? That's going to depend on how exactly it's going to happen. There are two critical details: wearable devices and two years. The answer will be related to or at least accommodate those points. **If you identify one or more details that are critical to the argument or question at hand, you can immediately make those details your filter to evaluate the answer choices.**

Applying our filter to the answer choices, we see that (A) and (B) both have time frames, and hence are at least vaguely connected to "two years." In (A), the training comes too late, so that's wrong. Choice (B) mentions two years, which sounds nice, but the actual measure taken just adds fuel to the fire by getting more wearable devices; there's no remedy offered for the obsolescence of skills. So (B) is out. In (C), a survey might determine the *extent* of the problem, but it doesn't provide a *solution* to the problem. Choice (D) sounds fancier but amounts to the same problem as (C). Finally, (E) gives a rather broad promise: *any* training necessary. Rather unrealistic. But the stem says, "If feasible." If (E) were feasible, it would be able to solve this problem and all kinds of problems. The correct answer is (E).

The Nowka apparel company's design for its new luxury jacket, the Fleecer, included a special design for a synthetic fabric layer that was intended to complement the model's image. The winning bid for supplying this synthetic fabric was submitted by Rainflex. Analysts concluded that the bid would only just cover Rainflex's costs on the fabric, but Rainflex executives claim that winning the bid will actually make a profit for the company.

Which of the following, if true, most strongly justifies the claim made by Rainflex's executives?

- o In any Nowka jacket, the synthetic fabric used in the jacket's hood, if one is present, is of the same make and model as the synthetic fabric of the jacket itself.
- o Rainflex holds exclusive contracts to supply Nowka with the synthetic fabric for a number of other jackets made by Nowka.
- o The production facilities for the Fleecer and those for the synthetic fabric to be supplied by Rainflex are located very near each other.
- o A segment of people who have purchased a carefully designed luxury jacket will replace a worn part of it with a part of exactly the same make and type.
- o When Nowka awarded the fabric contract to Rainflex, the only criterion on which Rainflex's bid was clearly ahead of its competitors' bids was price.

The Nowka apparel company's design for its new luxury jacket, the Fleecer, included a special design for a synthetic fabric layer that was intended to complement the model's image. The winning bid for supplying this synthetic fabric was submitted by Rainflex. Analysts concluded that the bid would only just cover Rainflex's costs on the fabric, but Rainflex executives claim that winning the bid will actually make a profit for the company.

Which of the following, if true, most strongly justifies the claim made by Rainflex's executives?

○ In any Nowka jacket, the synthetic fabric used in the jacket's hood, if one is present, is of the same make and model as the synthetic fabric of the jacket itself.
○ Rainflex holds exclusive contracts to supply Nowka with the synthetic fabric for a number of other jackets made by Nowka.
○ The production facilities for the Fleecer and those for the synthetic fabric to be supplied by Rainflex are located very near each other.
○ A segment of people who have purchased a carefully designed luxury jacket will replace a worn part of it with a part of exactly the same make and type.
○ When Nowka awarded the fabric contract to Rainflex, the only criterion on which Rainflex's bid was clearly ahead of its competitors' bids was price.

EXPLANATION

Reading the question: as we did in Shipping Skills, we can focus on the opinion first. We might get the idea from the stem, which mentions a "claim," an opinion-charged word, or from the appearance of the word "claim" in the prompt itself. "Rainflex executives claim." We'll work back from there. They want to do some bid even though the bid will just cover costs on the fabric. They evidently think there is some other way to make a profit from the bid. So our correct answer may indicate a way to get profit from the bid even though the dollar amount won in the bid is not high. And the answer choice must somehow discuss profit or have implications for profit to be of basic relevance.

Applying the filter: Choice (A) doesn't lead to profits, since the jacket's size, number of flaps, et cetera, are already included in the (high) cost. Choice (B) is relevant to profit, but it says that Rainflex *already* has the contracts. If this contract in question were unprofitable but led to later profitable work, that would be a great answer, but that's not what (B) is saying. So (B) is out. Choice (C) reduces a cost for Rainflex, which is consistent with our filter, but that doesn't help it profit when the bid is too low to cover even the fabric cost. Choice (D) is similar to (B): it gives us an ongoing stream of business. If these jackets last forever but need the lining replaced, and Rainflex gets some or all of that, maybe it can profit. Choice (D) is stated in modest terms, but it's relevant and points to a source of profit, whether large or small. Choice (E) is unrelated to whether there is a way for Rainflex to profit from *this deal*, although it has implications for Rainflex's business overall.

Logical proof: now that we have done a few examples of creating and applying filters to the answer choices, we'll start incorporate the second step of the Critical Reasoning Strategy described at the front of this book: establishing logical proof. One method to establish logical proof of an answer. We can do this for (D). In one case, imagine that buyers of the jacket purchase so many pieces of fabric of these jackets that they are ultimately paying the initial price of the jacket many times over. In that case, the fabric company could indeed make a profit on these jackets. On the other hand, if we *negate* (D), we are saying there are *no* further sales of this jacket through replacement. That would *weaken* the conclusion. We can see that choice (D) describes something that is material (so to speak) to the argument. The correct answer is (D).

In most countries, lower taxes stimulate economic growth, which is an increase of the capacity of an economy to produce goods and services. In the nation of Tattua, economic growth is significantly higher than it is in the nation of Hothal. Clearly, therefore, Tattua's industries must, on the whole, be further advanced technologically than Hothal's are.

The argument is most vulnerable to which of the following criticisms?

- ○ It offers a conclusion that is no more than a paraphrase of one of the pieces of information provided in its support.
- ○ It presents as evidence in support of a claim information that is inconsistent with other evidence presented in support of the same claim.
- ○ It takes one possible cause of a condition to be the actual cause of that condition without considering any other possible causes.
- ○ It takes a condition to be the effect of something that happened only after the condition already existed.
- ○ It makes a distinction that presupposes the truth of the conclusion that is to be established.

In most countries, lower taxes stimulate economic growth, which is an increase of the capacity of an economy to produce goods and services. In the nation of Tattua, economic growth is significantly higher than it is in the nation of Hothal. Clearly, therefore, Tattua's industries must, on the whole, be further advanced technologically than Hothal's are.

The argument is most vulnerable to which of the following criticisms?

○   It offers a conclusion that is no more than a paraphrase of one of the pieces of information provided in its support.
○   It presents as evidence in support of a claim information that is inconsistent with other evidence presented in support of the same claim.
○   It takes one possible cause of a condition to be the actual cause of that condition without considering any other possible causes.
○   It takes a condition to be the effect of something that happened only after the condition already existed.
○   It makes a distinction that presupposes the truth of the conclusion that is to be established.

EXPLANATION

Reading the question: As in Drivers Over 30, here we have a couple short statements of evidence and then a statement of opinion—a conclusion. Here, the conclusion statement is introduced by the word "clearly," which is almost invariably used when a statement *isn't* clear, in which case that statement is an opinion. These brief arguments resemble syllogisms. The most famous syllogism is: "All men are mortal. Socrates is a man. Therefore, Socrates is mortal." **When you confront a syllogistic or pseudo-syllogistic argument, you can build your filter using term matching.**

Creating a filter: as in Drivers over 30, we can match terms by sketching or imagining a table:

Evidence Term	Matches?	Conclusion Term
Tattua's economy	≈	Tattua's industries
Hothal's	=	Hothal's
Economic growth, "capacity of an economy to produce goods and services"	≠	"technologically advanced"

The worst mismatch of terms here is the last one. The argument appears to equate economic growth and technological advancement. Or, possibly, it assumes that advanced tech is the cause of the economic growth and not something else, like lower taxes. Either one of these views is not stated or supported in the argument as it stands, so we have found a major weakness in the argument.

Applying the filter: The key is that there could be something else that has caused economic growth. That notion is conveyed by answer choice (C). Choice (A) isn't true; the conclusion is not a paraphrase, since, as we've said, it comes out of nowhere with the new terms "technology" and "advancement." Similarly, choice (B) is off because the argument is missing connections, not offering contradictory connections. Skipping to choice (E): this answer choice, like (A), would require mentioning "technological advancement" earlier in the argument. Similarly, (D) means there is a logical loop, but tech advancement is not referred to earlier. Note that, given the format of the answer choices, a logical test such as the negation test is not possible, so we have had to rely solely on our filter to get to the answer. The correct answer is (C).

Archeologists have discovered ancient coins in near Antioch, Syria from a variety of neighboring countries dating to the time of the Roman Empire. They have inferred that the Roman Empire established the Antioch as a center of trade, or at least a hub through which trade routes of many countries passed.

Which of the following would, if true, most significantly strengthen the archeologists' inference?

○ Situated at the crossing of both north-south and east-west trade routes, Antioch was perfectly positioned to be a commercial center.
○ A historian's journal reveals that, when Alexander the Great visited Antioch, he made a dedication speech at a temple in which he referred to Antioch as "the commercial jewel of the Empire, Syrian-born."
○ During the Empire, the Romans saw fit to build great temples, a forum, a theater, baths, aqueducts, and other public buildings in Antioch.
○ There were virtually no coins from neighboring countries found in Antioch that dated to the time prior to the advent of the Roman Empire in the city.
○ Archeologists also found a record of a gold wire-fashioner's guild, dated from the same time as the coins, which had detailed notations of the shipments coming and going from Antioch to a number of nearby countries.

Archeologists have discovered ancient coins in near Antioch, Syria from a variety of neighboring countries dating to the time of the Roman Empire. They have inferred that the Roman Empire established the Antioch as a center of trade, or at least a hub through which trade routes of many countries passed.

Which of the following would, if true, most significantly strengthen the archeologists' inference?

○ Situated at the crossing of both north-south and east-west trade routes, Antioch was perfectly positioned to be a commercial center.
○ A historian's journal reveals that, when Alexander the Great visited Antioch, he made a dedication speech at a temple in which he referred to Antioch as "the commercial jewel of the Empire, Syrian-born."
○ During the Empire, the Romans saw fit to build great temples, a forum, a theater, baths, aqueducts, and other public buildings in Antioch.
○ There were virtually no coins from neighboring countries found in Antioch that dated to the time prior to the advent of the Roman Empire in the city.
○ Archeologists also found a record of a gold wire-fashioner's guild, dated from the same time as the coins, which had detailed notations of the shipments coming and going from Antioch to a number of nearby countries.

EXPLANATION

Reading the question: we find an extremely brief argument. We can compare with Taxes and Growth: both questions present arguments, and both arguments are brief. The argument in Taxes and Growth has a structure more like a syllogism, so this question may not be quite so perfect for term matching as Taxes and Growth, but we can still try term matching. Term matching is viable on some level whenever you have an argument with evidence and a conclusion.

Creating a filter: the key terms in this argument are "coins," in the evidence, and "trade center," in the conclusion. The argument's purpose is to establish a connection between these two concepts, so the answer choice that most strengthens our connection between "coins" and "trade center" will be the correct answer. With that criterion as our filter, we can head to the answer choices.

Applying our filter, we can examine each choice in turn first for whether it has to do with the linkage of 1) coins and 2) trade center. Which answer choices mention both the coins and the trade center? None of them! Taking a step back and looking at basic relevance, we can see that choices (D) and (E) are most relevant. If we can logically prove one, we'll have our answer.

Logical proof: If we accept the negation of (D) as fact, then there *were* coins predating the Roman Empire in the area. This fact would destroy the argument, because in that case coins would not be proof that Romans established the center of trade. Since accepting the negation of (D) destroys the argument, accepting (D) itself strengthens the argument: it patches a critical weakness in the argument. How about (E)? Choice (E) is tricky, because it gives strength to the conclusion of the argument. It introduces a new piece of evidence supporting that conclusion, and that does strengthen the conclusion. But it is less material to the argument given, which involves the connection between coins and the conclusion drawn from the coins found. Choice (D) "passes" the negation test and (E) does not. Therefore, the correct answer is (D).

Callers to a customer help line frequently complained about the quality of service. Seventy percent of survey respondents cited the services agents' lack of knowledge of how to solve the problems they were calling about. To address the problem, management decided that each service agent should go through regular training. Each agent spent half a day each week in sessions covering how to respond to callers' problems. Nevertheless, after three months of training, the rate of caller complaints has not decreased.

Which of the following, if true, most helps to explain why the training failed to achieve its goal?

- The training program created significant additional cost in running the help line.
- Taking service agents out of the group answering calls at any given time causes the average wait time of callers to rise.
- The ongoing training does not cover all possible caller problems.
- The proportion of repeat callers to the help line is low, so callers have no way of observing that service agent knowledge has improved.
- The company providing the help line has lost customers due to their dissatisfaction with the quality of service, both before and after the regular training began.

Callers to a customer help line frequently complained about the quality of service. Seventy percent of survey respondents cited the services agents' lack of knowledge of how to solve the problems they were calling about. To address the problem, management decided that each service agent should go through regular training. Each agent spent half a day each week in sessions covering how to respond to callers' problems. Nevertheless, after three months of training, the rate of caller complaints has not decreased.

Which of the following, if true, most helps to explain why the training failed to achieve its goal?

○ The training program created significant additional cost in running the help line.
○ Taking service agents out of the group answering calls at any given time causes the average wait time of callers to rise.
○ The ongoing training does not cover all possible caller problems.
○ The proportion of repeat callers to the help line is low, so callers have no way of observing that service agent knowledge has improved.
○ The company providing the help line has lost customers due to their dissatisfaction with the quality of service, both before and after the regular training began.

EXPLANATION

Reading the question: the prompt doesn't presents not an argument, but rather a situation. We're presented with only facts and no opinion. So it makes sense when we get to the question stem and see that we're asked to "explain."

Creating a filter: as we discussed in Osprey Prey, since we are explaining, we should identify a "mystery" with two parts. The correct answer will probably address both parts of the mystery, without contradicting any of the facts given. The mystery's two parts are that 1) the team has been trained, but 2) complaints are still high. A possible explanation is that there is a "new problem." For example, maybe the training was conducted in an insulting manner and drove away some of the best agents, so the remaining agents are knowledgeable but defective in some new way. We'll look for something like this in the answers... a "new problem."

Applying the filter: Choice (A) presents a new problem, but not one that would affect customer complaints. So (A) is out. Choice (B) presents a new problem: increased wait time. It's not just an explanation; it's an explanation that describes how the action in part 1) above could generate the problem in part 2) above. So (B) is in. Choice (C) is relevant, and plausible, but it doesn't generate a new problem, as we're looking for. Also, agents wouldn't have to be trained in every conceivable problem in order to be much better trained and for complaints to go down. In other words, it says something about part 1) of our mystery, but doesn't establish any connection to part 2). So (C) is out. Choice (D) fails to connect to part 2); if the help team is better trained, they should rate higher. Choice (E) also fails to connect to part 2); in fact, losing unhappy customers would be a reason to think complaints would go down. The correct answer is (B).

Springfield's city council wants to minimize the city's average yearly expenditures on its parking meters and so is considering replacing the coin-operated meters currently in use with roadside kiosks at which parking slips can be purchased via credit card. Since many of the coin-operated meters require replacement, the costs associated with the conversion to credit card kiosks would be minimal.

Which of the following would it be most useful to know in determining whether switching to roadside kiosks would be likely to help minimize Springfield's yearly maintenance costs?

- ○ Whether the expected service life of roadside kiosks is at least as long as that of the currently used coin-operated meters
- ○ Whether any cities have switched from coin-operated meters in their parking meters to new devices other than roadside kiosks
- ○ Whether the company from which Springfield currently buys coin-operated meters for traffic signals also sells roadside kiosks
- ○ Whether Springfield's city council plans to increase the number of paid parking spaces in Springfield
- ○ Whether the crews that currently replace coin-operated meters in Springfield know how to replace the existing fixtures with roadside kiosks

EXPIRING METERS

Springfield's city council wants to minimize the city's average yearly expenditures on its parking meters and so is considering replacing the coin-operated meters currently in use with roadside kiosks at which parking slips can be purchased via credit card. Since many of the coin-operated meters require replacement, the costs associated with the conversion to credit card kiosks would be minimal.

Which of the following would it be most useful to know in determining whether switching to roadside kiosks would be likely to help minimize Springfield's yearly maintenance costs?

○ Whether the expected service life of roadside kiosks is at least as long as that of the currently used coin-operated meters
○ Whether any cities have switched from coin-operated meters in their parking meters to new devices other than roadside kiosks
○ Whether the company from which Springfield currently buys coin-operated meters for traffic signals also sells roadside kiosks
○ Whether Springfield's city council plans to increase the number of paid parking spaces in Springfield
○ Whether the crews that currently replace coin-operated meters in Springfield know how to replace the existing fixtures with roadside kiosks

EXPLANATION

Reading the question: we are thinking about switching meter types to save money. The switching costs are "minimal," so basically zero. However, we don't know why the new meters are expected to be less costly; the argument doesn't seem to say that.

Creating a filter: Supposing that a prediction of the correct answer doesn't come to mind, we can simply look for something that is of basic relevance, something that gets to the heart of the question, which meter type costs more on an ongoing basis?

Applying the filter: which answer choices touch on this question? Choice (A) may. Choice (B) does not. Choice (C) does not, especially since we've been told the setup cost is minimal. Choice (D) does not. Choice (E) doesn't address what we were looking for, the ongoing costs of one meter type relative to another. We have been told the costs of switching are "minimal," and that would appear to include bringing in a new crew, training the crew, and so on. So, given the facts, choice (E) is much less substantial than it sounds. Choice (A) is the only contender left.

Logical proof: we can confirm (A) by analysis by extreme cases. In fact, **you can usually apply analysis by extreme cases to answer choices that begin with the word "whether."** Consider one case: if the new meter type died out much, much faster than the other, it would surely be more expensive over time. We are guaranteed that switchover costs are minimal by the data given, but we are not guaranteed anything about ongoing replacement. On the other hand, in a different case, if the new meter died much, much *slower* than the old meters, then it would be *less* expensive over time. Since these two cases yield different answers to the question of minimizing yearly costs, answer choice (A), indeed, states something that is "useful" and indeed important to know in order to answer the question of yearly costs. The correct answer is (A).

Which of the following most logically completes the passage?

In cars, airbags provide good protection for the chest and head, but little or no protection for legs. A study of injuries resulting from car accidents showed that a large proportion were caused by blows to the legs. Therefore, if air bags protected this area, the risk of serious injury in car accidents would be greatly reduced, especially since _____.

- ○ among the drivers included in the study's sample of injuries, only a very small proportion had been wearing an air bag at the time of their accident
- ○ even those drivers who drive cars with air bags have a poor understanding of the degree and kind of protection that air bags afford
- ○ an air bag that included protection for the legs would have to be somewhat larger and more expensive than current air bags
- ○ although the bones in the legs are large, severe impacts in that area are very likely to cause serious injury, such as compound fracture
- ○ drivers generally remain in their seat when they crash, which reduces the likelihood of severe impacts to the legs

Auto Body

Which of the following most logically completes the passage?

In cars, airbags provide good protection for the chest and head, but little or no protection for legs. A study of injuries resulting from car accidents showed that a large proportion were caused by blows to the legs. Therefore, if air bags protected this area, the risk of serious injury in car accidents would be greatly reduced, especially since _____.

- among the drivers included in the study's sample of injuries, only a very small proportion had been wearing an air bag at the time of their accident
- even those drivers who drive cars with air bags have a poor understanding of the degree and kind of protection that air bags afford
- an air bag that included protection for the legs would have to be somewhat larger and more expensive than current air bags
- although the bones in the legs are large, severe impacts in that area are very likely to cause serious injury, such as compound fracture
- drivers generally remain in their seat when they crash, which reduces the likelihood of severe impacts to the legs

Explanation

Reading the question: we have a novel task in this question: we will complete the passage! The answer choices, as you can see, are not of a format such that they can be negated or analyzed by cases. Questions that ask for you for a logical continuation tend to have this problem, so, **on logical continuation questions, the second step of the Critical Reasoning Strategy will usually not be possible (e.g., the answer choices cannot be negated), and you'll have to answer the question using only a filter.**

Creating a filter: We are putting something in the blank that will complete the idea that bigger airbags that go down and cover the legs will reduce serious injuries. There is already evidence on the table; what's missing? We gravitate to the charged word "serious." The study cited in the prior sentence says "a large proportion" of accidents, but says nothing about their seriousness. So, what's missing and could go in the blank would be first of all, that the air bags will work in the leg area, and secondly, something about the seriousness of the accidents. That's our filter.

Applying the filter: Which answer choices fit either of these categories? Choices (A) through (C) do not. Choice (D) does. Choice (E) might. We take a closer look at (E). (E) discusses the likelihood of severe accidents in general, but it doesn't help us figure out whether specifically the accidents that have been happening and that an air bag will stop are severe. Back to (D). Choice (D) basically tells us, "Leg injuries are serious." This fills in one of the key missing pieces of the argument. The correct answer is (D).

Recently, scientists determined that great white sharks can live over 70 years, much longer than had been previously thought. They made the discovery by examining the layers of different colors that accumulated on the shark's teeth over the years. In the 1950s, atomic bomb testing produced unusually large amounts of carbon-14, which fell from the atmosphere into the ocean and accumulated as a distinctive layer on the shark's teeth corresponding to a known period in time. Perplexingly, even though great white sharks live longer than had been expected, some parties maintain that based on the new findings, the great white sharks must be protected from overfishing.

Which of the following, if true, best resolves the discrepancy identified above?

○ Great white sharks need to be protected from overfishing because they are dying rapidly due to poisoning by carbon-14.
○ Great white sharks were determined to live longer than had been previously thought based on the discovery of a carbon-14-rich layer within older sharks' teeth.
○ Great white sharks are evidently endangered and therefore need to be protected from overfishing.
○ Some great white sharks may have rich layers of carbon-14 from other sources, depending on their migration patterns.
○ Great white sharks' longer lifespan implies that they mature more slowly and reproduce more slowly than had previously been assumed.

Recently, scientists determined that great white sharks can live over 70 years, much longer than had been previously thought. They made the discovery by examining the layers of different colors that accumulated on the shark's teeth over the years. In the 1950s, atomic bomb testing produced unusually large amounts of carbon-14, which fell from the atmosphere into the ocean and accumulated as a distinctive layer on the shark's teeth corresponding to a known period in time. Perplexingly, even though great white sharks live longer than had been expected, some parties maintain that based on the new findings, the great white sharks must be protected from overfishing.

Which of the following, if true, best resolves the discrepancy identified above?

○ Great white sharks need to be protected from overfishing because they are dying rapidly due to poisoning by carbon-14.
○ Great white sharks were determined to live longer than had been previously thought based on the discovery of a carbon-14-rich layer within older sharks' teeth.
○ Great white sharks are evidently endangered and therefore need to be protected from overfishing.
○ Some great white sharks may have rich layers of carbon-14 from other sources, depending on their migration patterns.
○ Great white sharks' longer lifespan implies that they mature more slowly and reproduce more slowly than had previously been assumed.

EXPLANATION

Reading the question: We have a long prompt and a short stem, so we check the stem. It says "resolve a discrepancy." That's the same as "explain." As discussed in Osprey Prey and Caller Complaints, since we are explaining, we should identify the two parts of the so-called "discrepancy." The correct answer will need to address both parts, without contradicting any of the facts given.

Creating a filter: "Perplexingly" is an important word, because it allows us to parse the prompt into two parts. The second, shorter part is that sharks must be protected from overfishing. Why is that perplexing? Because of whatever the main point of the first part is: sharks live longer than expected. We'll look for something that connects logically to both parts: 1) sharks live longer than expected, and 2) they must be protected.

Applying the filter: (A) doesn't connect to the sharks' age. Choice (B) just restates part of the prompt. Choice (C) just restates the other part of the prompt. Choice (D) doesn't connect to either portion of the discrepancy. Choice (E) touches on both parts: it says that if sharks are older than we thought, there are fewer of them than we thought. That's a good reason to protect them from overfishing.

Logical proof: A logical proof is not always possible on "explain" questions, but we can use the negation test to confirm (E), in this case. Suppose that sharks reproduced more *quickly* than had previously been assumed: that would *lessen* the need to protect sharks. Since the negation would add to the mystery and contradict the opinion of "some parties," we have confirmation the non-negated (E) would, indeed, resolve the mystery. The correct answer is (E).

Pundit: **Many people blame the construction of retail locations by major corporations for the decline in locally owned bookstores over the past ten years.** Yet clearly, online sales of books have also played an important role in this decline. In the past ten years, sales by online retailers of books have risen sharply, and surveys of consumer behavior have indicated that many purchasers of books online, if convenient online options had not been available to them, would otherwise have purchased books at a local bookstore.

In the pundit's argument, the portion in boldface plays which of the following roles?

- ○ It is the main conclusion of the argument.
- ○ It is a finding that the argument seeks to explain.
- ○ It is an explanation that the argument concludes is correct.
- ○ It provides evidence in support of the main conclusion of the argument.
- ○ It introduces a judgment that the argument opposes.

LOCAL BOOKSTORES

Pundit: **Many people blame the construction of retail locations by major corporations for the decline in locally owned bookstores over the past ten years.** Yet clearly, online sales of books have also played an important role in this decline. In the past ten years, sales by online retailers of books have risen sharply, and surveys of consumer behavior have indicated that many purchasers of books online, if convenient online options had not been available to them, would otherwise have purchased books at a local bookstore.

In the pundit's argument, the portion in boldface plays which of the following roles?

- O   It is the main conclusion of the argument.
- O   It is a finding that the argument seeks to explain.
- O   It is an explanation that the argument concludes is correct.
- O   It provides evidence in support of the main conclusion of the argument.
- O   It introduces a judgment that the argument opposes.

EXPLANATION

Reading the question: this question has a novel characteristic, boldfaced text. The question stem asks for the role of the boldfaced text, and the answer choices are stated in general, logical terms, not in terms of the specifics of the argument. Indeed, all boldfaced text questions have these properties:

1.   A prompt that contains one or more arguments;

2.   A question stem that asks for the role of the boldfaced statements;

3.   Answer choices that are stated in general, logical terms.

On boldfaced questions, you don't need to evaluate the argument. Rather, summarize the role of the boldfaced statements and how the boldfaced statements are related to the non-boldfaced statements, and look for your summary in the answer choices.

Creating a filter: we have multiple arguments here. Opinion-charged words can be our guides. The phrase "many people blame" kicks off one argument. Then, the phrase, "yet clearly," kicks off an opposing viewpoint. On the basis of those observations alone, we can construct a filter to evaluate the answer choices. The boldfaced sentence gives the opinion of many people, and then the rest of the prompt is the pundit's counterargument.

Applying the filter: matching our prediction with the answer choices, we find that it's present in (E). The correct answer is (E).

In recent years, some painters of graffiti have been winning recognition as artists. But since graffiti is vandalism, painting graffiti is inherently an act of rebellion and lawbreaking. For this reason, painting graffiti is not art.

Which of the following is an assumption that supports drawing the conclusion above from the reason given for that conclusion?

○ Some graffiti is painted in remote places, where it will not be used by any law enforcer or anyone else.
○ Some painters of graffiti are more concerned than others with the illegal nature of the paintings they produce.
○ Painters of graffiti should be more concerned with the illegality of their paintings than they currently are.
○ An object is not an art object if its maker might be motivated primarily by questions of whether or not creating that object is permissible.
○ Artists are not concerned with the monetary value of their products.

GRAFFITI ART

In recent years, some painters of graffiti have been winning recognition as artists. But since graffiti is vandalism, painting graffiti is inherently an act of rebellion and lawbreaking. For this reason, painting graffiti is not art.

Which of the following is an assumption that supports drawing the conclusion above from the reason given for that conclusion?

○ Some graffiti is painted in remote places, where it will not be used by any law enforcer or anyone else.
○ Some painters of graffiti are more concerned than others with the illegal nature of the paintings they produce.
○ Painters of graffiti should be more concerned with the illegality of their paintings than they currently are.
○ An object is not an art object if its maker might be motivated primarily by questions of whether or not creating that object is permissible.
○ Artists are not concerned with the monetary value of their products.

EXPLANATION

Reading the question: we are presented with a thin argument. The first sentence gives an introduction and the second two sentences are argument. Since we have a pseudo-syllogistic argument, as we did in Drivers Over 30 and Taxes and Growth, we can analyze the argument using term matching:

Evidence Term	Matches?	Conclusion Term
Painters of graffiti	≈	Painting graffiti
Since graffiti is vandalism, painting graffiti is inherently an act of rebellion and lawbreaking	N/A	
Rebellion and lawbreaking	≠	Not art

The missing connection is between "lawbreaking" and what constitutes art. The author assumes that you can be an artist only if you're not a lawbreaker. The clause, "painting graffiti is inherently an act of rebellion and lawbreaking," may sound like an opinion, but it's a piece of evidence in this argument.

Applying our filter: answer choices (A) through (D) all touch on both graffiti and the law in some fashion. The one that matches our expectation most closely is (D). It doesn't use the word lawbreaking, but it hits on the key matter, the conditional definition of art: it's not art if the maker is a rebel.

Logical proof: we can prove our answer using the second step of the Critical Reasoning Strategy, logical proof. We apply the negation test. If the statement in choice (D) *not* true—it's art regardless of whether the creator is a rebel or whether it's legal or why it's done—then the argument in the prompt crumbles. That's proof that the argument assumes the statement in choice (D). The correct answer is (D).

An online media company plans to increase its share of market by deeply discounting its subscription prices for the next two months. The discounts will cut into profits, but because they will be heavily advertised, the company expects that they will attract buyers away from rival providers of similar media. The company foresees that, in the longer term, customers initially attracted by the discounts will remain loyal subscribers.

In assessing the plan's chances of achieving its aim, it would be most useful to know which of the following?

○ Whether the company's competitors are likely to respond by offering deep discounts on their own subscriptions
○ Whether the advertisements will be created by the company's current advertising agency
○ Whether some of the company's subscription options will be more deeply discounted than others
○ Whether the company will be able to cut costs sufficiently to maintain profit margins even when the discounts are in effect
○ Whether an alternative strategy will enable the company to enhance its profitability while holding a constant or diminishing share of the market

SUBSCRIPTION PLAN

An online media company plans to increase its share of market by deeply discounting its subscription prices for the next two months. The discounts will cut into profits, but because they will be heavily advertised, the company expects that they will attract buyers away from rival providers of similar media. The company foresees that, in the longer term, customers initially attracted by the discounts will remain loyal subscribers.

In assessing the plan's chances of achieving its aim, it would be most useful to know which of the following?

○   Whether the company's competitors are likely to respond by offering deep discounts on their own subscriptions
○   Whether the advertisements will be created by the company's current advertising agency
○   Whether some of the company's subscription options will be more deeply discounted than others
○   Whether the company will be able to cut costs sufficiently to maintain profit margins even when the discounts are in effect
○   Whether an alternative strategy will enable the company to enhance its profitability while holding a constant or diminishing share of the market

EXPLANATION

Reading the question: the prompt describes a plan of action, and **a plan of action can be thought of as argument saying, "Let's do this; it's a great idea and will work."** We have a case of understated terms, "most useful to know," so we'll be able to prove the correct answer by stronger terms.

Creating a filter: the "great idea" in this plan is to slash prices, take losses, and win customers for the long term. What would be most useful to know? Something that is important to the plan—critical, even. We can imagine some things we'd need to know to determine whether the plan will work. For example: 1) whether we are really getting customers and/or 2) whether we are really earning back money from them over time and/or 3) whether there is some big unidentified side effect or problem that we are missing.

Applying the filter: (A) is relevant; if competitors also slash, our plan might not work. Then, per our prediction 1) above, we might not actually get more customers. We'll keep (A) in. Choice (B) is not relevant; we have no reason to think ads are better in-house or out-of-house. Choice (C) is not relevant to whether the plan will work; whatever product or service we're pricing low is what's supposedly going to win the customers and those customers are the ones we're going to have to keep and win back profits from. Choice (D) contradicts the information we've been given; it is explicitly part of the plan that we suffer losses in the short term. Choice (E) is irrelevant; whether a different plan might work is relevant to what plan might be best, but it's not relevant to whether this plan specifically will work, which is the question at hand.

Logical proof: we're left only with (A). As we saw in Expiring Meters, when answer choices are phrased with the word "whether," we can use analysis by extreme cases to give logical proof to our answer. In one case, if competitors *don't* lower their prices, even raise their prices to very high levels, we have further reason to think that lowering prices will bring in customers. In another case, if competitors lower their prices below ours, then we have good reason to think our plan *won't* work. Evidently choice (A) highlights something important to the plan. The correct answer is (A).

Through Topeka airport, consumer travel by plane is just voluminous enough for the commercial airlines to make modest profits. The size of the city's population is stable and is not expected to increase much. Yet there are investors ready to double the number of flights to and from the airport within ten years, and they are predicting solid profits both for themselves and for the established airlines.

Which of the following about the city of Topeka, if true, most helps to provide a justification for the investors' prediction?

- o Over the next ten years, people in their middle-aged years, the prime traveling age, will be a rapidly growing proportion of the city's population.
- o As distinct from the existing flights, most of the flights being planned would be run at "very early" morning times, in hopes of stimulating interest in those schedules.
- o Spending on train and bus travel to and from Topeka has been increasing modestly each year for the past ten years.
- o The average number of seats per flight is lower among existing routes than it is among routes still in the planning stages.
- o The sale of snacks and drinks in-flight accounts for a steadily growing share of most airlines' profits.

Topeka Flights

Through Topeka airport, consumer travel by plane is just voluminous enough for the commercial airlines to make modest profits. The size of the city's population is stable and is not expected to increase much. Yet there are investors ready to double the number of flights to and from the airport within ten years, and they are predicting solid profits both for themselves and for the established airlines.

Which of the following about the city of Topeka, if true, most helps to provide a justification for the investors' prediction?

- Over the next ten years, people in their middle-aged years, the prime traveling age, will be a rapidly growing proportion of the city's population.
- As distinct from the existing flights, most of the flights being planned would be run at "very early" morning times, in hopes of stimulating interest in those schedules.
- Spending on train and bus travel to and from Topeka has been increasing modestly each year for the past ten years.
- The average number of seats per flight is lower among existing routes than it is among routes still in the planning stages.
- The sale of snacks and drinks in-flight accounts for a steadily growing share of most airlines' profits.

Explanation

Reading the question: If the Subscription Plan question was fresh in your mind, you might have noticed in your approach to this question that it presents something similar: a plan, or what we could call an argument about the future. And the prompt, though not rich with argument, does contain the opinion of the investors. However, our filter below will end up closer to that for an "explain" question. Don't let that bother you: questions frequently can be categorized in one or more ways. After all, there aren't official categorizations to these questions.

Creating a filter: the critical detail here is that we are expecting the airport traffic to grow even though the city population will not increase. For example, tourism to the city might be expected to grow. That way, the population doesn't grow, but flights grow. That's the key detail: we need a situation in which 1) we do not require the population of the city does not grow and 2) the traffic through the airport will increase. As in an explain question, the correct answer should address both.

Applying the filter: choice (A) matches our filter; since, 1) the number of people is not increasing, but 2) the travel per person is increasing. Choice (B) misses the target; even if the airport stimulated interest in early morning flights, would people necessarily fly more overall, or just shift their flight preferences? Choice (C) doesn't connect to 1) or 2). Choice (D) is tempting. If flights in the future have more seats, they might be more profitable. But this explanation fails to connect both 1) and 2): if the population isn't growing, why should double the number of flights be profitable? Choice (E) is also out, as it also fails to explain how we can profitably double flights. We're left with (A).

Logical proof: we can apply the negation test to choice (A). If the percentage of the population of prime traveling age went *down* in the future, we would have a good reason to doubt the plan. Choice (A), indeed, is material to the argument. The correct answer is (A).

A major car company experienced a drop in sales in the month following the publication of a widely read review of the latest model, which asserted the new model was of low quality. The company also received numerous complaints from consumers who had read the review. The company, nevertheless, insists that negative reactions to the review had nothing to do with the company's subsequent drop in sales.

Which of the following, if true, most strongly supports the company's position?

- ○ Other major car companies reported similar reductions in sales during the same month.
- ○ The consumers who registered complaints with the network were commercial clients that remained regular buyers of the company's cars.
- ○ Major car companies publicly attribute drops in sales to the car models' quality only when they receive complaints about quality.
- ○ This was not the first time a model of car from this company had been negatively reviewed and had inspired consumers to complain to the company.
- ○ Most car buyers rely on reviews of new models as their primary source of information regarding their purchase decision.

CAR REVIEW

A major car company experienced a drop in sales in the month following the publication of a widely read review of the latest model, which asserted the new model was of low quality. The company also received numerous complaints from consumers who had read the review. The company, nevertheless, insists that negative reactions to the review had nothing to do with the company's subsequent drop in sales.

Which of the following, if true, most strongly supports the company's position?

○ Other major car companies reported similar reductions in sales during the same month.
○ The consumers who registered complaints with the network were commercial clients that remained regular buyers of the company's cars.
○ Major car companies publicly attribute drops in sales to the car models' quality only when they receive complaints about quality.
○ This was not the first time a model of car from this company had been negatively reviewed and had inspired consumers to complain to the company.
○ Most car buyers rely on reviews of new models as their primary source of information regarding their purchase decision.

EXPLANATION

Reading the question: this prompt, much like Topeka Flights, exhibits some of the features of an argument but is more like an "explain" question. If you are studying with GMAT books and materials from other sources, be aware that most of them overemphasize the importance of arguments in Critical Reasoning. Arguments are certainly essential to Critical Reasoning, but actual questions often focus on other aspects of reasoning.

Note: we can take the opportunity to highlight the fact that, **if you are stumped by a prompt or can't create a filter, you can try going straight to the negation test.** We need to understand the essence of the prompt—sales are down, reviews are negative, and there are complaints from people who have read the review—but from there we can move straight to the answer choices.

Logical proof: we're asked for an answer that strengthens, so the correct answer, when negated, will weaken or destroy the argument. Choice (A): if other companies did *not* report similar reductions in sales, it wouldn't strongly weaken the argument; there are still a variety of possible problems at this company. So choice (A) is not highly material to the situation. Choice (B): if the complainers *did not* remain regular buys of the cars, then they probably dropped the product. That would weaken the claim, because in that case the review did ultimately cause the drop-off in sales. So choice (B) is probably our answer. Choice (C), when negated, doesn't lead to anything sensible. Choice (D): suppose this *was* the first time this company had been in a situation like this. That wouldn't help us determine either way whether the company's claim is accurate. Choice (E), if negated, would indicate that car buys do *not* rely on reviews. That statement strongly strengthens the carmaker's argument, so Choice (E), when *not* negated, strongly *weakens* the argument—and we want a strengthener. So choice (E) is exactly wrong. Only one answer choice passed the negation test. The correct answer is (B).

Consultant: Advertising in videos purchased for download has shown promise as a way to activate consumers with a specific product message. Because the long-term impact on brand perception have yet not been shown, however, I do not recommend its use at this time.

Client: Your position is inconsistent with your usual practice. You suggest many forms of advertising that have a potential negative brand impact, so concern about long-term brand impact cannot be the real reason you will not recommend this form of advertising.

The client's argument is flawed because it fails to consider that

o   in the long-term, downloaded videos might have a negative effect on perceptions of a company's brand
o   it is possible that the consultant does not believe that advertisements in downloaded videos have been conclusively shown to be effective
o   if the client does not advertise in any medium, his product may lose its position in the market
o   the long-term impact on brand perception of an advertisement can take some time to manifest itself
o   known risks can be weighed against known benefits, but unknown risks cannot

Consultant: Advertising in videos purchased for download has shown promise as a way to activate consumers with a specific product message. Because the long-term impact on brand perception have yet not been shown, however, I do not recommend its use at this time.

Client: Your position is inconsistent with your usual practice. You suggest many forms of advertising that have a potential negative brand impact, so concern about long-term brand impact cannot be the real reason you will not recommend this form of advertising.

The client's argument is flawed because it fails to consider that

- in the long-term, downloaded videos might have a negative effect on perceptions of a company's brand
- it is possible that the consultant does not believe that advertisements in downloaded videos have been conclusively shown to be effective
- if the client does not advertise in any medium, his product may lose its position in the market
- the long-term impact on brand perception of an advertisement can take some time to manifest itself
- known risks can be weighed against known benefits, but unknown risks cannot

EXPLANATION

Reading the question: the substance of this question is to keep track of the points of view and then critique the latter one. The consultant says, roughly, that advertising in videos has shown promise, but we don't recommend it. The client says, roughly, you recommend other things like this, so that can't be right.

Creating a filter: Term matching works here. The client is equating "many forms of advertising that have a potential brand impact" with the subject of their discussion, "advertising in videos purchased for download." But these terms are not quite the same, and, quite possibly, there is a significant difference between these two forms of advertising.

Applying the filter: We'll go out of order. Choice (B) doesn't compare the types of advertising or discuss brand impact, so it's out. Same for choice (C). Choices (A) and (D) are inconsistent with the prompt. They both state something that has already been stated or implied by the consultant and acknowledged by the client. We are left with (E). Can we find grounding in (E)? In this case, the "known risks" are the bad brand ads the consultant has suggested in the past and which the client is bringing up. "Unknown risks" are the bad brand from advertising in videos purchased for download. The client is equating these two things, whereas the consultant is distinguishing them. In fact, (E) fulfilled our prediction, since it touched on the difference we came up with in term matching.

Logical proof: We can apply the negation test to choice (E). If we accept the negation of (E) as fact, then the known risks and the unknown risks *could* be weighed against each other. In that case, the two types of ads would be comparable, and the client wouldn't be making a mistake at all. The correct answer is (E).

Plan: Wishing to reduce the number of citizens without health insurance, the government of Patrio decided last year to run an extensive advertising campaign that targeted young people and which described the importance of choosing and enrolling in a health insurance plan.

Result: The percentage of young people enrolled in a health insurance plan has not increased.

Further information: Most young people in Patrio saw and remembered the advertising. Moreover, surveys revealed that more young people after the campaign believed that it was important to choose and enroll in a health insurance plan.

In light of the further information, which of the following, if true, does most to explain the result that followed implementation of the plan?

○   Most young people in Patrio already were enrolled in a health insurance plan before the advertising campaign began.
○   All young people found it inconvenient to have to choose a plan before enrolling in health insurance.
○   Young people did not learn through the advertising campaign how to choose a plan, and they did not know where else to find that information.
○   Young people increased in number proportionally to other groups in Patrio over the last year.
○   Most young people found the health insurance plans available to be unaffordable.

Plan: Wishing to reduce the number of citizens without health insurance, the government of Patrio decided last year to run an extensive advertising campaign that targeted young people and which described the importance of choosing and enrolling in a health insurance plan.

Result: The percentage of young people enrolled in a health insurance plan has not increased.

Further information: Most young people in Patrio saw and remembered the advertising. Moreover, surveys revealed that more young people after the campaign believed that it was important to choose and enroll in a health insurance plan.

In light of the further information, which of the following, if true, does most to explain the result that followed implementation of the plan?

○ Most young people in Patrio already were enrolled in a health insurance plan before the advertising campaign began.
○ All young people found it inconvenient to have to choose a plan before enrolling in health insurance.
○ Young people did not learn through the advertising campaign how to choose a plan, and they did not know where else to find that information.
○ Young people increased in number proportionally to other groups in Patrio over the last year.
○ Most young people found the health insurance plans available to be unaffordable.

EXPLANATION

Reading the question: There are various pieces to this argument. The question stem orients us, because it tells us to "explain." That means that we'll need a "mystery" with two parts, and that the correct answer will touch on both parts.

Creating a filter: The two pieces of our mystery are 1) the percentage enrolled in the program hasn't increased, even though 2) the campaign appeared to work... Youngsters *remembered* the advertising. Further, the campaign convinced them of the importance to having a plan. Perhaps there is some other consideration that hasn't been included here, an overlooked problem? We'll look for an "overlooked problem" but above all expect the correct answer to touch on both 1) and 2).

Applying the filter: We'll go out of order. Choice (A) is not an overlooked problem and doesn't connect to 2); it doesn't address why the plan seemed to work. Choice (D) is not an overlooked problem and doesn't connect to 1) or 2). Choices (B), (C), and (E) are all pretty good options. Choice (B) presents an overlooked problem, and it connects to 1). However, it doesn't connect to 2); even if the plan is inconvenient, if the percentage who thought it was important went up, why didn't enrollment go up? They decided that it was important, so they should have done it anyway. So (B) is out. Choice (E) is similar to (B); it presents a disadvantage with the plan, hammering on 1), but fails to connect well to 2). For example, (E) says "most," not "all," so it suggests that *some* youngsters could afford the plan. Given that fact, even then the percentage enrolled should have gone up somewhat. Finally, choice (C) connects to both 1) and 2). The outreach could appear to work but fail to increase enrollment if the youngsters never learned how to enroll. The correct answer is (C).

An online retailer that makes its deliveries through a private shipping company has determined that, unlike before, now it can profitably begin making deliveries seven days a week, not just six days a week. Delivering a given number of shipments within a narrower window of time tends to be more cost effective, because, on average, delivery trucks will be able to exploit economies in their driving routes and will incur lower average shipping costs per dollar of delivered goods per hour. Nevertheless, the retailer expects profits to rise with the change.

Which of the following, if true, provides the best reason for the expectation?

○ Due to trends in retail, the average volume occupied in a delivery truck by a single shipment has increased.
○ Due to a shift in consumer sentiment, the additional purchases that customers will be inclined to make by receiving their items marginally faster will outweigh the loss of savings of spreading shipments over a greater number of days.
○ Due to mismanagement at the shipping company, most of the cost savings made possible by delivering over six days rather than seven are not captured.
○ The expanded delivery timetable will attract new customers to the retailer and it will drive away no customers at all.
○ Due to reorganization at both the shipping company and the retailer, the trucks' delivery routes will have to be redesigned in the near future anyway, so the retailer can make the change in timetable now without incurring any one-time costs related to the change in operations.

SUNDAY DELIVERY

An online retailer that makes its deliveries through a private shipping company has determined that, unlike before, now it can profitably begin making deliveries seven days a week, not just six days a week. Delivering a given number of shipments within a narrower window of time tends to be more cost effective, because, on average, delivery trucks will be able to exploit economies in their driving routes and will incur lower average shipping costs per dollar of delivered goods per hour. Nevertheless, the retailer expects profits to rise with the change.

Which of the following, if true, provides the best reason for the expectation?

○ Due to trends in retail, the average volume occupied in a delivery truck by a single shipment has increased.
○ Due to a shift in consumer sentiment, the additional purchases that customers will be inclined to make by receiving their items marginally faster will outweigh the loss of savings of spreading shipments over a greater number of days.
○ Due to mismanagement at the shipping company, most of the cost savings made possible by delivering over six days rather than seven are not captured.
○ The expanded delivery timetable will attract new customers to the retailer and it will drive away no customers at all.
○ Due to reorganization at both the shipping company and the retailer, the trucks' delivery routes will have to be redesigned in the near future anyway, so the retailer can make the change in timetable now without incurring any one-time costs related to the change in operations.

EXPLANATION

Reading the question: If and when we get confused by this prompt or any prompt, we can start with the simplest part and work from there. We'll use this approach in Reading Comprehension. For example, "exploiting economies in driving routes" may be unclear, but delivering on seven days rather than six is clear. So we start with increased delivery time. That tends to be less cost effective, because of some details about how the deliveries are done, but the company "expects profits to rise with the change."

Creating a filter: We could treat this as an explain question, but here's a little trick: **When we have an argument that profits will go up, we can break it into two logical pieces: i) revenues go up and/or ii) costs go down.** In this case, the delivery cost is not going down—could the new model bring down some other cost (probably not)? Or increase revenues (more likely)?

We apply the filter, looking for some other cost going down, or revenues going up. Choice (A) doesn't give us that; it's good news for the retailer, but this change has already taken effect, so it's already built into the "before" part of the "before-and-after" comparison that the company is making. Choice (B) gives us what we're looking for: it describes increased revenues, and even revenues that exceed costs. Choice (B) passes the filter. Choice (C) does not give us a rising revenue or lowering cost. Choice (D) is similar to (A), but inferior, because this retailer could have more customers without making more revenue, or they might make a little more revenue but not enough to profit more. Choice (E) basically says there are no one-time costs to the shift, but that doesn't explain why the difference between revenues and costs will increase with the change; it still could be less profitable over time after change on a marginal basis.

Logical proof: if we accept the negation of (B), then consumer purchases will *not* increase sufficiently to increase profits. That fact would highly damage the argument, so (B) itself, indeed, supports the argument. The correct answer is (B).

At a large, popular restaurant, a reduction of 25 percent in the number of patrons each night would allow the management to get rid of the common long lines of people waiting to eat dinner. A second, partner restaurant, a 25 minute drive away, would, if refurbished, be an attractive alternative for half of the patrons who visit the first restaurant. Nevertheless, a waiter at the restaurant is confident that refurbishing the partner restaurant would not end the long lines at the original location.

Which of the following, if true, most helps to justify the waiter's position?

- ○ Refurbishing the second restaurant would require not only redecorating and new furniture, but also the creation of a menu suitable to that location's chef, which would be a substantially different menu from that of the original location.
- ○ A third location, next door to the first one, would be a perfectly attractive alternative to patrons of the first location, if minor adjustments to the storefront were made.
- ○ The second restaurant is located on a relatively undeveloped property which might be home to other attractive businesses—especially if traffic to the restaurant there were to grow.
- ○ If a patron has to wait to be seated at a given restaurant, there is an increased chance that that same person will not return again to the restaurant.
- ○ The first restaurant is inside the same shopping mall as a popular movie theater.

SECOND RESTAURANT

At a large, popular restaurant, a reduction of 25 percent in the number of patrons each night would allow the management to get rid of the common long lines of people waiting to eat dinner. A second, partner restaurant, a 25 minute drive away, would, if refurbished, be an attractive alternative for half of the patrons who visit the first restaurant. Nevertheless, a waiter at the restaurant is confident that refurbishing the partner restaurant would not end the long lines at the original location.

Which of the following, if true, most helps to justify the waiter's position?

○ Refurbishing the second restaurant would require not only redecorating and new furniture, but also the creation of a menu suitable to that location's chef, which would be a substantially different menu from that of the original location.
○ A third location, next door to the first one, would be a perfectly attractive alternative to patrons of the first location, if minor adjustments to the storefront were made.
○ The second restaurant is located on a relatively undeveloped property which might be home to other attractive businesses—especially if traffic to the restaurant there were to grow.
○ If a patron has to wait to be seated at a given restaurant, there is an increased chance that that same person will not return again to the restaurant.
○ The first restaurant is inside the same shopping mall as a popular movie theater.

EXPLANATION

Reading the question: devouring the prompt, we learn about a popular restaurant, a partner restaurant, and an opining waiter. We're told that, if we can divert 25% of folks to restaurant #2, we get rid of the lines at restaurant #1. The question is, can we do it by improving the look of restaurant #2? The opining waiter says no. And our job is to justify the opining waiter's opinion.

Creating a filter: we can try using a basic relevance filter. Namely, which answer choice supports the waiter's opinion that the refurbishing won't work?

Applying the filter: Answer choice (A) is irrelevant to whether or not restaurant #2 can attract people away. Choice (B) doesn't matter: whether hypothetical restaurant #3 could draw people away doesn't impact whether restaurant #2 could draw people away. Choice (C) doesn't matter: it concerns what would happen *after* the plan worked, and we are concerned with *whether* it would work. Choice (D) tells us that lines ultimately lose customers. Maybe so, but restaurant #1 is good enough that even with the loss, the lines stay long. And it doesn't have anything to do with whether restaurant #2 can draw away patrons from #1. So (D) is out. What about (E)? We're wondering whether we can draw enough people to restaurant #2. Maybe the movie theater is enough of a magnet that they don't want to go over to #2. And we note, reviewing the prompt, maybe they don't want to drive. They have already parked for the movie, for example. It's the only option with a basic relevance to the waiter's position.

Logical proof: We can use the negation test to justify choice (E). If you negate directly, you get "The first restaurant is *not* inside the same shopping mall as a popular movie theater." That seems quite irrelevant. But in general, **if a negated statement doesn't seem to make sense, you can try a more general or more specific version of the statement to see its impact on the argument.** For example, "The first restaurant is *not* near any other customer attraction that would pull customers near restaurant #1 and make them want to stay nearby." Whether that statement is true makes a critical difference in the waiter's argument. The correct answer is (E).

A quark-gluon plasma, a hypothesized phase of quantum chromodynamics of interest to physicists, is hypothesized to exist at conditions of extremely high temperature or density that never naturally occur on Earth. The conditions engendering quark-gluon plasma were thought to have occurred in the first hundred microseconds or so of the universe. It follows that physicists will never be able to observe quark-gluon plasma.

Which of the following, if true, most seriously weakens the argument above?

- ○ So-called quark stars are hypothesized to exist of extremely dense matter.
- ○ The temperature of quark-gluon plasma is believed to be 4 billion degrees Celsius.
- ○ The existence of the quark-gluon plasma was first hypothesized on the basis of observations by physicists.
- ○ High temperatures and densities not usually found on Earth can be created in particle accelerators.
- ○ A quark-gluon plasma is thought to consist of asymptotically free quarks and gluons, which are several of the basic building blocks of matter.

Rare Plasma

A quark-gluon plasma, a hypothesized phase of quantum chromodynamics of interest to physicists, is hypothesized to exist at conditions of extremely high temperature or density that never naturally occur on Earth. The conditions engendering quark-gluon plasma were thought to have occurred in the first hundred microseconds or so of the universe. It follows that physicists will never be able to observe quark-gluon plasma.

Which of the following, if true, most seriously weakens the argument above?

- So-called quark stars are hypothesized to exist of extremely dense matter.
- The temperature of quark-gluon plasma is believed to be 4 billion degrees Celsius.
- The existence of the quark-gluon plasma was first hypothesized on the basis of observations by physicists.
- High temperatures and densities not usually found on Earth can be created in particle accelerators.
- A quark-gluon plasma is thought to consist of asymptotically free quarks and gluons, which are several of the basic building blocks of matter.

Explanation

Reading the question: the subject matter of this prompt can be daunting. However, the *structure* of this prompt is not so forbidding; it's a brief argument, and in fact it resembles some of the other pseudo-syllogistic arguments that we have seen, even Drivers Over 30. So we can analyze the argument and build a filter using term matching, even if we don't fully understand all the terms involved.

Evidence Term	Matches?	Conclusion Term
Quark-gluon plasma	=	Quark-gluon plasma
Conditions that never naturally occur on earth	≠	Will never be observed

The key term mismatch is in the second row of this table. Saying these conditions "never naturally occur on Earth" is not quite the same as saying that these conditions will never be observed. Maybe these conditions could occur artificially. It's not a physics point: **term matching can help you identify logical leaps in an argument even if you don't understand all the terms involved**. For example, since we note that the argument is consistent in referring to "quark-gluon plasmas" in the evidence and in the conclusion, we don't worry about the definition of that term.

Applying the filter: In the answer choices, (D) hits right on the answer. The other answer choices give facts that don't have anything to do with how the pieces of the argument are connected; for example, they don't discuss high temperature or density. Actually, (A) does, and (A) is next best after (D). But (A) leaves open whether quark stars exist or not and whether physicists can observe what's going on in them.

Logical proof: We can confirm our answer with the negation test. If high temperatures and densities not usually found on Earth could *not* be created in particle accelerators, that fact would *strengthen* the argument considerably: in that case, it would appear more likely that scientists *can't* observe this phenomenon. The correct answer is (D).

Female cowbirds sing a variety of types of songs, demonstrating a wide range of vocal capabilities. Basing their judgment on the fact that different local populations of cowbirds of the same species sing in styles particular to their populations, ornithologists have concluded that the cowbirds' singing styles are culturally acquired, rather than genetically transmitted.

Which of the following, if true, would most strengthen the conclusion drawn by the ornithologists?

○   There are more similarities than differences among the songs.
○   Younger female cowbirds are not proficient at singing and have been observed watching their mothers sing for years before themselves starting to sing.
○   The songs of one species of cowbird lack the vocal range and ornamentation characteristic of the songs of all other species of cowbird.
○   Local populations of cowbirds seldom come into contact with each another.
○   It is well known that the mating dances of some birds are learned rather than transmitted genetically.

COWBIRD SONGS

Female cowbirds sing a variety of types of songs, demonstrating a wide range of vocal capabilities. Basing their judgment on the fact that different local populations of cowbirds of the same species sing in styles particular to their populations, ornithologists have concluded that the cowbirds' singing styles are culturally acquired, rather than genetically transmitted.

Which of the following, if true, would most strengthen the conclusion drawn by the ornithologists?

○ There are more similarities than differences among the songs.
○ Younger female cowbirds are not proficient at singing and have been observed watching their mothers sing for years before themselves starting to sing.
○ The songs of one species of cowbird lack the vocal range and ornamentation characteristic of the songs of all other species of cowbird.
○ Local populations of cowbirds seldom come into contact with each another.
○ It is well known that the mating dances of some birds are learned rather than transmitted genetically.

EXPLANATION

Reading the question: the question gives us a fact of introduction, a clause of evidence, and a clause of conclusion. We need to strengthen the conclusion. However, **the easiest way to strengthen an argument is first to weaken it.** The strengthener will patch a key area of weakness.

Creating a filter: since we are working with an argument, we can use term matching:

Evidence Term	Matches?	Conclusion Term
Female cowbirds	≈	Cowbirds
Styles are particular to local populations	≠	Styles are culturally, not genetically, acquired

The key connection of this argument is in the second line. It's that behaviors specific to local populations must be cultural, not genetic. That is what makes or breaks this argument: the bond between "local population behavior" and "cultural rather than genetic factors." We'll look for these points in the answer choices.

Applying the filter: The promising choices are (B) and (E), both of which hit on the idea of "cultural, not genetic." Choice (A) doesn't touch on either key point, so it's out. Choice (C) talks about species, not populations, and if it's relevant to the cultural vs. genetic question at all, it would weigh in on the wrong side, for genetics. Choice (D) is neutral to the argument: a lack of contact doesn't help us differentiate between behaviors and genes, since both behaviors and genes are isolated in their own ways. Choice (E) concerns mating dances, and we have no evidence connecting mating dances and singing styles, so it doesn't strengthen the conclusion about singing styles. That leaves us with choice (B).

Logical proof: we can use the negation test to confirm choice (B). If younger cowbirds never interacted with their parents, or if they were born knowing how to sing, the argument would be greatly weakened: singing would appear to be genetically acquired. Therefore, the un-negated form of (B) is indeed a strengthener. The correct answer is (B).

Which of the following most logically completes the argument?

A particular computer virus frequently infects personal computers through an email message. Even though virus-scanning software installed on a computer is designed to identify and alarm the user of a virus infection on that computer shortly after it occurs, this particular virus is rarely observed by virus-scanning software. This fact, however, does not mean that the computer's security systems have blocked installation of the virus, because _____.

- ○ shortly after it appeared on the Internet, hackers modified the virus in a way that made it more effective
- ○ the virus was able to replicate itself and then send itself to people in the victim's address book
- ○ even after the virus had stopped spreading, the backdoors created during the initial infections remained active
- ○ the virus was able to disable virus-scanning software and pose as a virus-removal tool
- ○ the virus also altered the victim's operating system in a way that made it difficult to shut down the computer without cutting off power to the system

Which of the following most logically completes the argument?

A particular computer virus frequently infects personal computers through an email message. Even though virus-scanning software installed on a computer is designed to identify and alarm the user of a virus infection on that computer shortly after it occurs, this particular virus is rarely observed by virus-scanning software. This fact, however, does not mean that the computer's security systems have blocked installation of the virus, because _____.

○ shortly after it appeared on the Internet, hackers modified the virus in a way that made it more effective
○ the virus was able to replicate itself and then send itself to people in the victim's address book
○ even after the virus had stopped spreading, the backdoors created during the initial infections remained active
○ the virus was able to disable virus-scanning software and pose as a virus-removal tool
○ the virus also altered the victim's operating system in a way that made it difficult to shut down the computer without cutting off power to the system

EXPLANATION

Reading the question: We have seen a fill-in-the-blank question before, in "Auto Body." Such questions may be phrased with or without a printed line signifying the blank. As we discussed in Auto Body, what goes in the blank should be a logical continuation of the prompt. Logical tests tend not to be possible on this type of question, so we will rely on our filter, ideally a prediction.

Creating a filter: how can we predict what goes in the blank? It must not contradict what has come before and it should finish the expression of the idea. The key is that the virus is on the computer even though the scanning software hasn't detected it. We could imagine that there is a defect in the scanner, or an ingenious design to the virus. Note that you are not expected to know anything about IT security for this question. **Critical Reasoning questions are designed *not* to require any outside knowledge.** Outside knowledge may still be useful, inevitably, and that's why the questions cover a range of topics. We could decide on the prediction, "The virus has outsmarted the security systems," as our filter.

Applying the filter: Do any answer choices match our prediction? Choice (A) somewhat does, but rather vaguely. Choice (B) doesn't address why the virus wasn't detected. Choice (C) also doesn't seem to address why the virus wasn't detected, though we might be able to read something into the term "backdoor." Choice (D) would definitely constitute outsmarting the security system. Choice (E) involves outsmarting, but not in a way that would necessarily obscure detection. We're left with (D). We confirm the logic: the correct answer must give an explanation for how a virus might have gone undetected by security systems. Choice (D) is the only option. Choice (C) sounds close, but we presume that many viruses possess backdoors and are detected. The correct answer is (D).

For similar homes and comparable residents, home insurance for theft has always cost more in Springfield than in Shelbyville. Police studies, however, show that homes owned by Springfield residents are, on average, slightly less likely to be robbed than homes in Shelbyville. Clearly, therefore, insurance companies are making a greater profit on home theft insurance in Springfield than in Shelbyville.

In evaluating the argument, it would be most useful to compare

- the population density of Springfield with the population density of Shelbyville
- the cost of compensating theft losses in Springfield with the cost of compensating theft losses in Shelbyville
- the rates Springfield residents pay for auto insurance with the rates paid for auto insurance by residents of Shelbyville
- the condition of Springfield's roads and streets with the condition of Shelbyville's roads and streets
- the cost of home theft insurance in Springfield and Shelbyville with that in other cities

NEIGHBORING INSURANCE

For similar homes and comparable residents, home insurance for theft has always cost more in Springfield than in Shelbyville. Police studies, however, show that homes owned by Springfield residents are, on average, slightly less likely to be robbed than homes in Shelbyville. Clearly, therefore, insurance companies are making a greater profit on home theft insurance in Springfield than in Shelbyville.

In evaluating the argument, it would be most useful to compare

○ the population density of Springfield with the population density of Shelbyville

○ the cost of compensating theft losses in Springfield with the cost of compensating theft losses in Shelbyville

○ the rates Springfield residents pay for auto insurance with the rates paid for auto insurance by residents of Shelbyville

○ the condition of Springfield's roads and streets with the condition of Shelbyville's roads and streets

○ the cost of home theft insurance in Springfield and Shelbyville with that in other cities

EXPLANATION

Reading the question: we can use opinion-charged words to identify the pieces of the argument here. "Clearly" introduces the conclusion. The word "however" also is a clue: it tells us that the first sentence is a data point, not just filler. The logical structure is: A is true, but B is true, therefore C is true. A is the difference in cost in home insurance between these two cities, B is the rate of theft. The argument is not too strong.

Creating a filter: as the page summarizing the Critical Reasoning Strategy mentions, **a prediction of the correct answer, even a vague or unrealistic prediction, is most powerful filter to evaluate answer choices.** Predicting isn't always easy, but on this question, there are many reasons why insurance companies might have to pay more for losses in Springfield than in Shelbyville. Maybe the thieves in Springfield are more skilled and they manage to steal more per theft than in Shelbyville. That possibility is unlikely to be an answer choice, but we can still use it: "thieves in Springfield are more skilled and steal more."

Applying the filter, we evaluate the answer choices. Choice (B) is actually pretty close to our prediction. Choice (C) involves auto rates, which wouldn't shed light on this question without further information. (D) and (E) also involve comparisons with other things that we know nothing about, so they cause problems rather than solve problems. Back to (A), we can see it doesn't directly concern whether companies profit more from fewer thefts. Notice that our prediction was quite different from choice (B), but it was similar enough to help us spot (B) quickly.

Logical proof: we can use analysis by extreme cases to establish that choice (B) is correct. If the losses per theft were *identical* in Shelbyville and in Springfield, the conclusion would be true and the argument would stand; if they were *wildly different*, the conclusion could be false. The correct answer is (B).

The value of gold has crashed; will it ever return to its previous high within the next year? Even at around $60, the value of gold is still up over 100 percent since it matched its last all-time high in the low $30 range just two months ago. One trend is clear, at $60 or at $250, the ecosystem of watching and trading gold continues to expand. Within the next year, without a doubt, **more portfolios will include gold, more companies will be created to serve people who consider trading gold, and more people will buy gold.** Clearly, it can be concluded that **gold will go up.**

In the argument given, the two portions in boldface play which of the following roles?

o   The first is a prediction that, if accurate, would provide support for the main conclusion of the argument; the second is that main conclusion.
o   The first is a prediction that, if accurate, would provide support for the main conclusion of the argument; the second is a conclusion drawn in order to support that main conclusion.
o   The first is an objection that the argument rejects; the second is the main conclusion of the argument.
o   The first is an objection that the argument rejects; the second presents a conclusion that could be drawn if that objection were allowed to stand.
o   The first is a claim that has been advanced in support of a position that the argument opposes; the second is a claim advanced in support of the main conclusion of the argument.

The value of gold has crashed; will it ever return to its previous high within the next year? Even at around $60, the value of gold is still up over 100 percent since it matched its last all-time high in the low $30 range just two months ago. One trend is clear, at $60 or at $250, the ecosystem of watching and trading gold continues to expand. Within the next year, without a doubt, **more portfolios will include gold, more companies will be created to serve people who consider trading gold, and more people will buy gold.** Clearly, it can be concluded that **gold will go up.**

In the argument given, the two portions in boldface play which of the following roles?

○ The first is a prediction that, if accurate, would provide support for the main conclusion of the argument; the second is that main conclusion.
○ The first is a prediction that, if accurate, would provide support for the main conclusion of the argument; the second is a conclusion drawn in order to support that main conclusion.
○ The first is an objection that the argument rejects; the second is the main conclusion of the argument.
○ The first is an objection that the argument rejects; the second presents a conclusion that could be drawn if that objection were allowed to stand.
○ The first is a claim that has been advanced in support of a position that the argument opposes; the second is a claim advanced in support of the main conclusion of the argument.

EXPLANATION

Reading the question: we have boldface in this question, as we did in Local Bookstores. As we discussed in that question, boldface questions have a prompt that contains one or more arguments, a question stem that asks for the role of the boldfaced statements, and answer choices that are stated in general, logical terms. We'll build a filter by analyzing how the various sentences are related and then predicting a general, logical statement.

Creating a filter: The last sentence is definitely a conclusion. We look for other instances of opinion assertion. Starting with the beginning, we see that the tone is casual, but mostly we have fact and filler. The long boldfaced sentence is a prediction: "within the next year." Since it is about the future, it's an opinion, not a fact. In arguments, a phrase like, "without a doubt," tends to mean the opposite of its denotation—it's highlighting an opinion. So the first boldfaced sentence is an opinion about the future and the second one is the author's conclusion, drawn in part on the basis of that opinion. That's our prediction.

Applying the filter: Since the second part of our prediction is simpler, we eliminate answer choices based on that part first. On those grounds, choices (B), (D), and (E) are out, and (A) and (C) are left. Choice (A) matches our prediction for the first part and (C) does not. The correct answer is (A).

The rate of smoking, globally, is higher now than ever before. In fact, 20% more people smoke today than did 20 years ago. In the nation of Patrio, 20% of people smoke; in Paisi, 25%. And in the last twenty years, the number of people who smoke increased by 13% in Kokua and 27% in Kappa.

Which of the following conclusions can most properly be drawn from the information above?

- ○ There are more smokers in Paisi than in Patrio.
- ○ There were fewer smokers in Kappa twenty years ago then there are in Paisi today.
- ○ The world's population is less than 120% of its value 20 years ago.
- ○ The average rate of smoking in any of the world's countries must be at least 13%.
- ○ At no point over the last 20 years was the world's smoking rate less than 13% below the rate 20 years ago.

SMOKING BY NATION

The rate of smoking, globally, is higher now than ever before. In fact, 20% more people smoke today than did 20 years ago. In the nation of Patrio, 20% of people smoke; in Paisi, 25%. And in the last twenty years, the number of people who smoke increased by 13% in Kokua and 27% in Kappa.

Which of the following conclusions can most properly be drawn from the information above?

○   There are more smokers in Paisi than in Patrio.
○   There were fewer smokers in Kappa twenty years ago then there are in Paisi today.
○   The world's population is less than 120% of its value 20 years ago.
○   The average rate of smoking in any of the world's countries must be at least 13%.
○   At no point over the last 20 years was the world's smoking rate less than 13% below the rate 20 years ago.

EXPLANATION

Reading the question: this prompt is not quite like any we've seen so far, in that it presents statistics and no argument. This setup is perfect for proof by stronger terms: the conclusion that is "most properly drawn" will be one that *must* be drawn—in other words, the answer choice that *must be true*. We can head straight to the answer choices to establish that proof.

Logical proof: first, must (A) be true? No; we are given only percentages, not numbers, and we have no way of inferring numbers. We could have a case in which Paisi's population is very, very small. So (A) is out. Must choice (B) be true? No; these two countries are mentioned in different facts that remain unconnected. It could be that Paisi is very, very small and Kappa is very, very big. Skipping (C) for a moment, we can quickly knock out (D) and (E) also by analysis by cases: we can imagine different cases for countries that haven't been mentioned, or years that haven't been mentioned, and that data could diverge wildly or not at all and still leave the above true.

We're left with (C). Must (C) be true? In the prompt, we have that 20% more people smoke than 20 years ago. Also, the first sentence says that the rate is higher than ever before. Combining them, say the population 20 years ago was 100, and x% of them smoked, which is $100x$ people. Today, the number of people that smoke is $1.2(100x)$. But the rate of smoking now is x or greater ("higher than ever before"), meaning that $1.2(100x)$ divided by the current population is greater than or equal to x:

$$\frac{1.2(100x)}{P} \geq x$$

Multiplying both sides by P and dividing both sides by x, we have:

$$1.2(100) \geq P$$

Indeed, today's population P can be no greater than the population of 20 years ago, which we had picked to be 100 but could have left as a variable. Here we used a technique that is common in GMAT Problem Solving: **when working with percentages, try assuming a total value of 100 to make your line of reasoning more concrete.** The correct answer is (C).

Which of the following most logically completes the argument below?

Crops can be purged of insects by introducing insects sterilized artificially by radiation; the sterilized male insects of a particular species are released to mingle with a natural population and mate with females who fail to have offspring, thereby inhibiting the ability of the local population of that species to reproduce. A new technique of sterilizing the medfly makes the sterilized male medflies exceptionally attractive to the females, so that a local population can be wiped out completely. But complete extermination might bring new risks. A farmer who considers his plot exceptionally attractive to medflies might think that his plot is the perfect case in which to use the new, more powerful, sterilized insect technique, but he should consider that _____.

- ○ he might produce an overly abundant crop, driving down his own prices and profit
- ○ perhaps the risk that the new insect sterilization does not work at all, since it has been less proven through practice, is not worth the additional benefit, at this point
- ○ releasing radiated insects into the wild could have effects on the environment, and possibly the farmer's crop, that would be impossible to trace
- ○ his plot, already exceptionally abundant, might already produce more crops than he can sell at ideal prices, and the additional cost of the new technique would be wasted
- ○ his plot might be exceptionally attractive also to another species of insect for which no sterilized insect method exists and which might thrive on the plot once the competing medflies have been eliminated

STERILIZED INSECTS

Which of the following most logically completes the argument below?

Crops can be purged of insects by introducing insects sterilized artificially by radiation; the sterilized male insects of a particular species are released to mingle with a natural population and mate with females who fail to have offspring, thereby inhibiting the ability of the local population of that species to reproduce. A new technique of sterilizing the medfly makes the sterilized male medflies exceptionally attractive to the females, so that a local population can be wiped out completely. But complete extermination might bring new risks. A farmer who considers his plot exceptionally attractive to medflies might think that his plot is the perfect case in which to use the new, more powerful, sterilized insect technique, but he should consider that _____.

○   he might produce an overly abundant crop, driving down his own prices and profit
○   perhaps the risk that the new insect sterilization does not work at all, since it has been less proven through practice, is not worth the additional benefit, at this point
○   releasing radiated insects into the wild could have effects on the environment, and possibly the farmer's crop, that would be impossible to trace
○   his plot, already exceptionally abundant, might already produce more crops than he can sell at ideal prices, and the additional cost of the new technique would be wasted
○   his plot might be exceptionally attractive also to another species of insect for which no sterilized insect method exists and which might thrive on the plot once the competing medflies have been eliminated

EXPLANATION

Reading the question: this question, like Auto Body and Expert Virus, asks us for a logical continuation of the prompt. Our completion must be in line with both the facts and the relevant opinions in the prompt.

Creating a filter: we pay special attention to the emotionally charged phrases "perfect case" and "he should consider." The "perfect case" describes the viewpoint of the farmer, while "he should consider" describes the viewpoint not of the farmer, but of the author of the paragraph. From those two fragments alone, we can infer that what goes in the blank will be a reason the new technique might not work or be so good for this farmer. Can we be more specific? Indeed: the author says "there are risks." So the correct answer will probably highlight a risk that the farmer may have overlooked.

Applying the filter: choice (A) gives a risk, though it is not exactly a continuation of the passage, since it brings in new concepts, prices and profit. Choice (B) contradicts the data we have been given, which tells us that the technique will do what it's designed to do. Choice (C) describes a new risk, so it passes the filter. Choice (D), like (B), contradicts data we are given to work with, namely, that the farmer considers his plot ideal. Choice (E) describes a risk of this new technique, so it passes the filter.

Logical proof: we are down to choices (C) and (E). Can we establish that one is better? Yes: the author says that "*complete extermination* might bring new risks." Choice (E) is specifically a risk of *complete extermination*, whereas (C) is not. **When you're trying to decide between two answer choices, look for a critical detail that makes one objectively superior to the other.** The correct answer is (E).

Citizen: at our city's airport, we have invested time and money in security checkpoints that are a waste of time. We train and staff security staff for the purpose of searching incoming automobiles, but we search fewer than five percent of those automobiles. We might as well disband the security checkpoints. The cost is wasted, and there is a ninety-five percent chance that an illegal substance would get through the checkpoint anyway.

Council member: Even if we granted that those odds didn't justify the costs—which I disagree with— you seem not to recognize that the presence of the checkpoint itself deters some people who would bring in illegal substances from doing so.

The council member responds to the citizen's argument by

- ○ rejecting the citizen's argument while proposing that the percentage of incoming automobiles that are checked should be raised
- ○ casting doubt on whether the citizen has correctly understands the chances that an illegal substance could pass through the checkpoint
- ○ objecting to the approach the citizen has used to argue against the checkpoints
- ○ defending the current system and further pointing out a benefit of the system that the citizen has failed to mention
- ○ shifting the discussion from the argument at hand to an attack on the personal qualities of the citizen

SECURITY CHECKPOINTS

Citizen: at our city's airport, we have invested time and money in security checkpoints that are a waste of time. We train and staff security staff for the purpose of searching incoming automobiles, but we search fewer than five percent of those automobiles. We might as well disband the security checkpoints. The cost is wasted, and there is a ninety-five percent chance that an illegal substance would get through the checkpoint anyway.

Council member: Even if we granted that those odds didn't justify the costs—which I disagree with—you seem not to recognize that the presence of the checkpoint itself deters some people who would bring in illegal substances from doing so.

The council member responds to the citizen's argument by

○ rejecting the citizen's argument while proposing that the percentage of incoming automobiles that are checked should be raised
○ casting doubt on whether the citizen has correctly understands the chances that an illegal substance could pass through the checkpoint
○ objecting to the approach the citizen has used to argue against the checkpoints
○ defending the current system and further pointing out a benefit of the system that the citizen has failed to mention
○ shifting the discussion from the argument at hand to an attack on the personal qualities of the citizen

EXPLANATION

Reading the question: the citizen makes a fairly thin argument, and the council member makes a good point in response. We're asked how the council member responds. We can see at a glance that the answer choices are of the general, logical type. **It's often worth glancing at the answer choices to check their format, though you want to construct a filter before evaluating them.** To match the answer choices, we'll make a general, logical prediction of the answer.

Creating a filter: we can make the following prediction of the correct answer. The citizen is assessing the value of this security program too narrowly, and the council member points out a benefit of the program the citizen hadn't considered. That's the filter: "benefit overlooked."

Applying the filter: Do any answer choices fit our prediction? Choice (A) is far off from our prediction. Choice (B) misses the main thrust of pointing out a benefit the citizen hadn't considered. And the council member says, "even if we granted that those odds didn't justify the costs," so with his main point he is specifically *not* arguing about the odds, as (B) indicates. Choice (C) and (E) are far off from our prediction. Choice (D) is close to our prediction, so we are left with (D).

Logical proof: we generally can't make a logical proof of our answer to a logical continuation question, but we can confirm our answer, in this case, by mapping the generalities of the answer choice back to specifics in the prompt. The council member definitely "defends the current system," and he does "point out a benefit of the system that the citizen has failed to mention"—it's that the mere presence of the checkpoint deters some people who might not have been caught. The correct answer is (D).

Last year the rate of unemployment was 8.2 percent, but this year it has been 7 percent. We can conclude that unemployment is on a downward trend and the rate will be even lower next year.

Which of the following, if true, most seriously weakens the conclusion above?

- The unemployment figures were computed on the basis of a representative sample of economic data rather than all of the available data.
- This year a temporary government spending project depressed the unemployment rate by 0.8 percent.
- Increases in hiring would cause companies to be more productive, netting them earnings that would allow them to hire yet further.
- The 8.2 percent rate of unemployment last year represented a two-year high.
- The unemployment rate is a measure only of those individuals without employment who are looking for jobs.

UNEMPLOYMENT TREND

Last year the rate of unemployment was 8.2 percent, but this year it has been 7 percent. We can conclude that unemployment is on a downward trend and the rate will be even lower next year.

Which of the following, if true, most seriously weakens the conclusion above?

○   The unemployment figures were computed on the basis of a representative sample of economic data rather than all of the available data.
○   This year a temporary government spending project depressed the unemployment rate by 0.8 percent.
○   Increases in hiring would cause companies to be more productive, netting them earnings that would allow them to hire yet further.
○   The 8.2 percent rate of unemployment last year represented a two-year high.
○   The unemployment rate is a measure only of those individuals without employment who are looking for jobs.

EXPLANATION

Reading the question: this is a weak argument, and we're asked to weaken it, so it will end up in shambles. We can create a filter by making a prediction of the answer. Perhaps unemployment for this population fluctuates from year to year around some level, so it's not down, it's basically the same within the envelope of fluctuation. We can use that expectation to filter the answer choices.

Applying the filter: choice (A) would strengthen the argument, so it's out. Choice (B) bears some similarity to our prediction, so it passes the filter. Choice (C) presents a hypothetical that does not shed light on the truth of the current situation, so it's irrelevant. Choice (D) doesn't especially weaken the argument; the rate could still be on a downward trend, given (D). Choice (E) is a definition of the unemployment rate that doesn't shed light on whether it's truly downward-trending. That leaves us with choice (B).

Logical proof: We can confirm choice (B) with the negation test. What if this year a temporary government spending project *increased* the unemployment rate by 0.8 percent? Then we have a reason to believe that the rate will go down in the future, when the temporary project effect is gone. So the negation of (B) would *strengthen* the argument, so (B) itself does weaken the argument. The correct answer is (B).

Counterfeit DVDs containing high-quality illegal copies of popular movies have proliferated in recent years and are sold at much lower prices than authorized DVDs, robbing the movies' rights holders of royalties on sales and diverting profits from production companies. To help track the distribution and sale of counterfeit DVDs, a government agency plans to produce informational brochures about the consequences and risks of counterfeiting; they also request sellers and consumers to report any counterfeit DVDs they encounter.

Which of the following, if true, would provide most support for the notion that the agencies' plan will have its intended effect?

○ Many counterfeit DVDs are of low quality, and high-quality and low-quality DVDs are difficult to distinguish at the time of purchase.
○ All popular movies that are available in a given market as counterfeit DVDs are available as authorized DVDs.
○ Most sellers of counterfeit DVDs would defend movie artists' rights if they had a mechanism to do so.
○ There are other, greater threats to the piracy of movies, such as online downloads of illegal video files of those movies.
○ Vendors of authorized DVDs tend to have more repeat customers than the vendors of counterfeit DVDs.

COUNTERFEIT DVDs

Counterfeit DVDs containing high-quality illegal copies of popular movies have proliferated in recent years and are sold at much lower prices than authorized DVDs, robbing the movies' rights holders of royalties on sales and diverting profits from production companies. To help track the distribution and sale of counterfeit DVDs, a government agency plans to produce informational brochures about the consequences and risks of counterfeiting; they also request sellers and consumers to report any counterfeit DVDs they encounter.

Which of the following, if true, would provide most support for the notion that the agencies' plan will have its intended effect?

- O Many counterfeit DVDs are of low quality, and high-quality and low-quality DVDs are difficult to distinguish at the time of purchase.
- O All popular movies that are available in a given market as counterfeit DVDs are available as authorized DVDs.
- O Most sellers of counterfeit DVDs would defend movie artists' rights if they had a mechanism to do so.
- O There are other, greater threats to the piracy of movies, such as online downloads of illegal video files of those movies.
- O Vendors of authorized DVDs tend to have more repeat customers than the vendors of counterfeit DVDs.

EXPLANATION

Reading the question: In this question we have a plan. The government will distribute brochures to fight counterfeiting. As we've seen before, a plan is like an argument with the main idea, "These actions are going to have this effect." We see that we want to choose an answer that strengthens the plan. To strengthen, we first weaken.

Creating a filter: **To weaken a "plan" argument, imagine a situation in which all of the steps of the plan are completely or mostly fulfilled, but somehow the effect doesn't occur.** We imagine that the brochures are printed and a brochure lands in the hands of every seller and consumer. We can imagine, even further, that everyone actually *reads* the brochure (which is imagining a lot). But it's easy to imagine that the plan won't have its effect even then. Maybe, even if everyone gets and reads a brochure; people won't care. The flaw in the argument is that maybe people won't care. So a great way to strengthen the argument would be to establish that people *will* care.

Applying the filter: Choice (C) matches our prediction. Choices (A), (B), and (D) have little to do with whether the plan will work. Choice (E) *might* weaken the argument, as more fleeting relationships might make it more difficult to target people to give the brochure to and might make it more difficult to report vendors. So (E) is out, and we're left with only (C).

Logical proof: we can confirm that (C) is correct either by the negation test or by analysis by cases. If sellers were unbelievably passionate to defend movie artists' rights, that attitude would indeed strengthen the plan. And if, on the other hand, they didn't care about defending rights—or wanted to defraud artists— then the plan would face a major hurdle. Choice (C) is indeed material to the plan. The correct answer is (C).

Bovine spongiform encephalopathy (BSE) is a disease in cattle that can spread to humans through the consumption of beef. A government ministry plans to reassure consumers of beef that sufficient controls are in place at farms to render nonexistent the risk of contracting BSE from beef. Prohibitions against cattle's eating other cattle brain tissue and regulations on the treatment of cattle waste have been put in place and dramatically reduced BSE cases. But diagnosis of BSE is difficult: it has an incubation period of months to years, during which there are no symptoms. At present, there is virtually no way to detect BSE reliably except by examining post-mortem brain tissue. And beef is known to be produced and sold from cattle that have not undergone testing.

Which of the following, if performed by the government ministry, could logically be expected to overcome the problem with their plan to reassure consumers of beef?

○   Publishing educational material explaining that the threat of BSE has been dramatically reduced
○   Requiring all beef that has not been directly tested for BSE to be labelled as such
○   Investing in techniques, which have shown substantial promise, to detect BSE in bovine blood
○   Exacting steep fines from vendors of beef sold from cows whose brain tissue has not been tested
○   Quarantining all cattle from farms at which any case of BSE has been detected until the threat has been conclusively eradicated

BSE and Beef Customers

Bovine spongiform encephalopathy (BSE) is a disease in cattle that can spread to humans through the consumption of beef. A government ministry plans to reassure consumers of beef that sufficient controls are in place at farms to render nonexistent the risk of contracting BSE from beef. Prohibitions against cattle's eating other cattle brain tissue and regulations on the treatment of cattle waste have been put in place and dramatically reduced BSE cases. But diagnosis of BSE is difficult: it has an incubation period of months to years, during which there are no symptoms. At present, there is virtually no way to detect BSE reliably except by examining post-mortem brain tissue. And beef is known to be produced and sold from cattle that have not undergone testing.

Which of the following, if performed by the government ministry, could logically be expected to overcome the problem with their plan to reassure consumers of beef?

○ Publishing educational material explaining that the threat of BSE has been dramatically reduced
○ Requiring all beef that has not been directly tested for BSE to be labelled as such
○ Investing in techniques, which have shown substantial promise, to detect BSE in bovine blood
○ Exacting steep fines from vendors of beef sold from cows whose brain tissue has not been tested
○ Quarantining all cattle from farms at which any case of BSE has been detected until the threat has been conclusively eradicated

Explanation

Reading the question: Since the prompt is lengthy and chunky-looking, we might drift down to the question stem. Laziness can be a force for good. From the question stem, we see this question has a touch of complexity: there is a plan, and there is a problem with the plan, and we're asked for a solution. The stem also pretty much tells us what the plan is.

Creating the filter: We go read the prompt, looking for more about the plan and the identification of the problem. The problem starts with the word "but": there is a long incubation period, and furthermore we sell beef without testing it. Two solutions that spring to mind involve having a time machine or testing the beef. Testing the beef is probably too obvious, but it's better than the time machine, so we'll take that and go to the answer choices.

Applying the filter: (A) doesn't match our filter. (B) is related to testing. (C) is a new form of testing that sounds promising. (D) is actually similar to our prediction. (E) is not about testing, but seems logical. We can try to make our filter more specific. The right answer must relate definitively to the *plan* and overcoming the problem with the plan. The plan is to "reassure consumers" that controls are in place. We realize that (C), (D), and (E) could all happen without consumers having any idea that the measures had been taken. (B) is the only one that reassures consumers at all, regardless of the fact it's a less complete solution to BSE. The correct answer is (B).

Recently in our county, sales of beer have suffered a significant decline in restaurants, nightlife establishments, and retail stores. During this same time, the sheriff's office has initiated a new and well-funded campaign against the short-term dangers and long-term health risks caused by alcohol consumption. Therefore, the decrease in beer consumption has been caused by consumers' awareness of the dangers and risks of alcohol consumption.

Which of the following, if true, most seriously calls into question the explanation above?

- On average, people in the town consume 30 percent less beer today than they did two years ago.
- Heavy beer drinkers may have withdrawal symptoms, such as anxiety, that create other difficulties in their lives.
- Sales of beer in different channels, such as in restaurants and in bars, have not all declined at the same rate.
- The sheriff's campaign has been negative in tone and has largely relied on local TV advertising employing scare tactics.
- Although beer consumption has without a doubt decreased, wine consumption in the town has significantly increased.

SHERIFF VS. BEER

Recently in our county, sales of beer have suffered a significant decline in restaurants, nightlife establishments, and retail stores. During this same time, the sheriff's office has initiated a new and well-funded campaign against the short-term dangers and long-term health risks caused by alcohol consumption. Therefore, the decrease in beer consumption has been caused by consumers' awareness of the dangers and risks of alcohol consumption.

Which of the following, if true, most seriously calls into question the explanation above?

○ On average, people in the town consume 30 percent less beer today than they did two years ago.
○ Heavy beer drinkers may have withdrawal symptoms, such as anxiety, that create other difficulties in their lives.
○ Sales of beer in different channels, such as in restaurants and in bars, have not all declined at the same rate.
○ The sheriff's campaign has been negative in tone and has largely relied on local TV advertising employing scare tactics.
○ Although beer consumption has without a doubt decreased, wine consumption in the town has significantly increased.

EXPLANATION

Reading the question: we like the prompt, because it's not just an argument; it's a causal argument. **When you spot a causal argument, you can filter for the possibility of an alternate cause.** The logic of the argument is: X causes Y. An alternate possibility is that Z causes Y, so you can think of a preloaded filter for causal arguments as "looking for a Z."

Applying the filter: On to the answer choices. Choice (A) either strengthens the argument or is irrelevant. (B) gives a reason why beer drinkers might keep drinking beer, but it doesn't shed light on what has caused this particular sequence of events, so it doesn't weaken the argument and is not the correct answer. Choice (C) says that not all the rates of decline are the same. That's not so hard to believe. Bars could be down 10% and stores could be down 12% and it could all be due to the sheriff's campaign, so Choice (C) does not weaken the argument and is therefore not the correct answer. Choice (D) might reflect negatively on the sheriff, but it doesn't mean that the sheriff's campaign hasn't caused the change. Choice (E) matches our filter. The fact that wine is up gives an alternate cause for beer's decline; it's a shift in the taste of the local population. We have, in other words, "found a Z," an alternate explanation for Y. Note that the fact people are drinking more wine indicates specifically that they are not swayed by the campaign about risks of alcohol. The correct answer is (E).

Which of the following best completes the passage below?

In a price war, each of multiple suppliers of highly competitive products and services repeatedly lowers its price to avoid being undercut and thereby losing sales and customers to its competitors. Due to these competitive pressures, the companies involved generally reduce their prices far more than they otherwise would, even to the point where none of the companies is able to make a profit on sales. A price war is usually detrimental to all companies involved, who will profit from reasonable but higher costs, but at the same time a company cannot always afford to let a competitor lower price without matching or lowering beyond that price.

Assuming that none of the competitors can be knocked out of the market, it should be expected that _____.

- ○ in a competitive market, each company will attempt to avoid a price war by setting prices low and being prepared to raise them as circumstances require
- ○ in a competitive market, each company will wish to avoid a price war but be prepared to be the first company to lower price
- ○ each company in a competitive market will attempt to signal to its competitors that does not want a price war but will not necessarily allow competitors to undercut its price
- ○ each company in a competitive market will attempt to signal to its competitors that does not want a price war at any cost, even if competitors undercut its price
- ○ each company in a competitive market will attempt to create an atmosphere of complete uncertainty as to whether it will lower prices, for example, by establishing discounts that are marketed as temporary but which may in effect be permanent

PRICE WARS

Which of the following best completes the passage below?

In a price war, each of multiple suppliers of highly competitive products and services repeatedly lowers its price to avoid being undercut and thereby losing sales and customers to its competitors. Due to these competitive pressures, the companies involved generally reduce their prices far more than they otherwise would, even to the point where none of the companies is able to make a profit on sales. A price war is usually detrimental to all companies involved, who will profit from reasonable but higher costs, but at the same time a company cannot always afford to let a competitor lower price without matching or lowering beyond that price.

Assuming that none of the competitors can be knocked out of the market, it should be expected that _____.

○ in a competitive market, each company will attempt to avoid a price war by setting prices low and being prepared to raise them as circumstances require
○ in a competitive market, each company will wish to avoid a price war but be prepared to be the first company to lower price
○ each company in a competitive market will attempt to signal to its competitors that does not want a price war but will not necessarily allow competitors to undercut its price
○ each company in a competitive market will attempt to signal to its competitors that does not want a price war at any cost, even if competitors undercut its price
○ each company in a competitive market will attempt to create an atmosphere of complete uncertainty as to whether it will lower prices, for example, by establishing discounts that are marketed as temporary but which may in effect be permanent

EXPLANATION

Reading the question: this prompt defines price wars; then it discusses how they are generally bad for everyone involved, but it can be easy to get dragged into one. Supposing that we're not sure how to predict the blank, we can use a basic filter. In this case, we can attempt to eliminate answer choices that contradict the facts of prompt or are contrary to the spirit of what is said.

Applying the filter: Choice (A) contradicts the prompt because the prompt says companies would prefer high prices, not low prices. So (A) is out. Choice (B) seems contradictory with itself, not to mention the prompt: if you want to avoid it, why would you start it? Choice (C) is definitely not contradictory with the prompt and sounds correct. Choice (D) contradicts what we have been told—namely that, although these wars are undesirable, you "cannot always afford to let a competitor lower price without matching or lowering beyond that price." So (D) is out. Choice (E) does not obviously contradict the prompt, so far as we can see. That leaves us with (C) and (E).

Logical proof: Is (C) objectively better? It boils down to whether it's more logical to be confusing or clear to your competitors. If (C) happens, the companies are likely to avoid a price war: this is what they want, we are told. If (E) happens, it will be easy for them to slip into a price war, through semi-accident: we are told they do not want this. The correct answer is (C).

Although a direct survey has yet to be produced, clearly the growing popularity of tablet computers in our country is leading to diminished levels relative to decades past of using that old-fashioned handheld device—that is, reading books. For example, one third of adults in our country now own tablet computers. And even as far back as eight years ago, before tablets had even hit the market, only about half of adults in our country answered affirmatively to a survey question that they happened to be reading a book or novel at the present time.

Each of following would be useful to determine in order to evaluate the argument EXCEPT

- ○ Whether the proportion of adults in our country in decades past currently reading a book or novel was more or less than half
- ○ Whether some factor or factors other than tablet computer usage might have led to lower the reading of books and novels
- ○ Whether the times of day and situations in which people use tablet computers are the same as those in which they previously read books or novels
- ○ Whether the surveyed populations in both studies accurately represent the populations of the country as a whole
- ○ Whether and in what percentage adults in our country currently happen to be reading a book or a novel entirely or partly on a cell phone

TABLETS VS. BOOKS

Although a direct survey has yet to be produced, clearly the growing popularity of tablet computers in our country is leading to diminished levels relative to decades past of using that old-fashioned handheld device—that is, reading books. For example, one third of adults in our country now own tablet computers. And even as far back as eight years ago, before tablets had even hit the market, only about half of adults in our country answered affirmatively to a survey question that they happened to be reading a book or novel at the present time.

Each of following would be useful to determine in order to evaluate the argument EXCEPT

- ○ Whether the proportion of adults in our country in decades past currently reading a book or novel was more or less than half
- ○ Whether some factor or factors other than tablet computer usage might have led to lower the reading of books and novels
- ○ Whether the times of day and situations in which people use tablet computers are the same as those in which they previously read books or novels
- ○ Whether the surveyed populations in both studies accurately represent the populations of the country as a whole
- ○ Whether and in what percentage adults in our country currently happen to be reading a book or a novel entirely or partly on a cell phone

EXPLANATION

Reading the question: we see that the prompt is longish and there's the word "EXCEPT" in the question stem. "Except" questions require close evaluation of the answer choices. Going thoroughly at first will help us ultimately finish swiftly. By the way, in case you ever wondered why the EXCEPT and other words on test are in CAPS: there is no special meaning to the capitalization; the test-makers are just trying to help you read the question correctly.

Creating a filter: The word "clearly" hints that our conclusion lies in the first sentence. It's that tablet reading is supplanting book reading. Not a great argument, though. One piece of evidence is the proportion of tablet ownership, and the other is a prior proportion of folks currently reading a book. The two proportions are not connected in any way by the argument: that would be the clearest way to strengthen it... showing that people move from one category to another. It would also be nice to know that the proportion of book readers has decreased. It would also be nice to know that people are using their tablets for reading—not for other purposes or just letting them collect dust. We can use these expectations as our filter. Choices that match these expectations will *not* be the correct answer, since we have the word "except."

Applying the filter: Choice (A) describes something relevant to the argument, since the argument compares present reading levels to past levels. So (A) is *not* the answer. Choice (B) describes something useful to know—we could have coincidence without causation—so it is not the correct answer. Choice (C) matches one of our predictions—maybe tablet reading isn't really taking away from book reading. So (C) is out. Choice (D) concerns sample representativeness, an important point which pops up with some regularity on the GMAT. Choice (E) sounds relevant at first, but it has a defect: it mentions cell phones, not tablets. Reading on cell phones is relevant to reading, but it has not been connected to the present argument about whether tablet reading is supplanting book reading. The correct answer is (E).

Which of the following best completes the passage below?

The movie production company's estimate of financial losses due to the illegal download of movies cannot be correct, because it's a measure of the wrong phenomenon. Most of illegal downloading of movies is done exclusively by people who have a passing interest in the movies but no intention of buying them, as he appears to assume. Thus, the loss to the industry is

- o   nothing but harmless downloading done because the files are free
- o   better measured in terms of rentals than purchases
- o   smaller than his estimate
- o   actually equal to the total market value of those downloaded copies times the number of people actually interested in buying them
- o   actually equal to the difference between this year's sales and a particular previous year's sales, adjusted for inflation

Pirating Losses

Which of the following best completes the passage below?

The movie production company's estimate of financial losses due to the illegal download of movies cannot be correct, because it's a measure of the wrong phenomenon. Most of illegal downloading of movies is done exclusively by people who have a passing interest in the movies but no intention of buying them, as he appears to assume. Thus, the loss to the industry is

o   nothing but harmless downloading done because the files are free
o   better measured in terms of rentals than purchases
o   smaller than his estimate
o   actually equal to the total market value of those downloaded copies times the number of people actually interested in buying them
o   actually equal to the difference between this year's sales and a particular previous year's sales, adjusted for inflation

Explanation

Reading the question: We have a question of logical continuation: we will complete the passage. Therefore, we'll predict something before checking out the answers.

Creating a filter: We learn from the prompt that movie pirates generally have no real interest in the movies... thus, the loss to the industry is "less than it would appear, because only a fraction of the apparent losses represent what would have been purchases." Not a pretty wording in our prediction there, but that's of no consequence.

Applying the filter: What prompts match? Choice (C) does. Choice (D) is related to what we said, though it's hyper-specific. Choice (D) also misses how the estimate in question is wrong—it doesn't even mention whether it's high or low, the critical piece of the picture. The correct answer is (C).

In the city of North Haverbrook, where a new tourism industry is growing, hotels have been booked to capacity and forced to turn away potential visitors with increasing frequency. The number of desired room bookings is expected to increase by 25 percent within the next four years. Meanwhile, the local chamber of commerce believes that the establishment of new hotels will increase booking capacity by only 3 percent per year. Nevertheless, the chamber believes that this growth in the hotel industry will be sufficient to ensure that North Haverbrook's hotels do not turn away more potential bookings than they presently do.

Which of the following, if true, provides the strongest grounds for the officials' prediction?

o   Visitors to North Haverbrook can easily stay in nearby South Haverbrook, where hotel capacity exceeds demand by 15 percent.
o   Many of the new visitors to North Haverbrook are campers, and there is ample excess capacity to camp in North Haverbrook's park.
o   Many of the new visitors are students who intend to save costs by sleeping several people to a room.
o   Many of the new visitors to North Haverbrook will visit at times of year other than the two peak months.
o   Visitors to North Haverbrook can reach the city only by cable car up a mountain, and the capacity of the cable car traffic will grow even more slowly than that of the hotel rooms.

HAVERBROOK HOTELS

In the city of North Haverbrook, where a new tourism industry is growing, hotels have been booked to capacity and forced to turn away potential visitors with increasing frequency. The number of desired room bookings is expected to increase by 25 percent within the next four years. Meanwhile, the local chamber of commerce believes that the establishment of new hotels will increase booking capacity by only 3 percent per year. Nevertheless, the chamber believes that this growth in the hotel industry will be sufficient to ensure that North Haverbrook's hotels do not turn away more potential bookings than they presently do.

Which of the following, if true, provides the strongest grounds for the officials' prediction?

o   Visitors to North Haverbrook can easily stay in nearby South Haverbrook, where hotel capacity exceeds demand by 15 percent.
o   Many of the new visitors to North Haverbrook are campers, and there is ample excess capacity to camp in North Haverbrook's park.
o   Many of the new visitors are students who intend to save costs by sleeping several people to a room.
o   Many of the new visitors to North Haverbrook will visit at times of year other than the two peak months.
o   Visitors to North Haverbrook can reach the city only by cable car up a mountain, and the capacity of the cable car traffic will grow even more slowly than that of the hotel rooms.

EXPLANATION

Reading the question: although the question stem isn't really phrased as such, the prompt has the structure of an "explain" question. There are two facts seemingly in contradiction, and we must choose the statement that accommodates and reconciles them.

Creating a filter: How could 1) a 3% increase in capacity be sufficient when 2) room bookings go up 25%? Supposing that we don't have a prediction, we can turn to the answer choices and look for choices that don't contradict the facts and address both 1) and 2).

Applying the filter: choice (A) contradicts the prompt; the whole point is that we won't have to turn anyone away. Same with (B): *room bookings* are supposed to go up 25%, not just visitors, so (B) is either contradictory or irrelevant. Choice (E) is irrelevant to the comparison of demand and capacity in the hotel rooms.

Logical proof: so we're left with (C) and (D). We can examine cases to elucidate what they mean and which is correct. Choice (D) would be wrong if we were told that the peak booking or simultaneous booking is up 25 percent... but we are not told that. Does (C) have a problem? Yes, it does: we are talking about room bookings, not the number of people. So (C) is actually irrelevant; it can be true and the number of room bookings is still going up 25%. So the explanation is that capacity doesn't need to grow as fast as the bookings because the bookings will show up at times with excess capacity, not the busy times. The correct answer is (D).

Contrary to earlier predictions, demand for wine has not increased in recent years. Yet, even though prices and production amounts have also been stable during the last three years, wine producers last year increased their profits by more than 10 percent over the previous year's level.

Any of the following statements, if true about last year, helps to explain the rise in profits EXCEPT:

o   Consumers in many countries increased their home stockpiles of bottles of wine, yet their overall consumption of wine decreased.
o   Wine producers have saved money on wages by switching from paying laborers an hourly wage to paying them by the amount harvested.
o   The price of oil, the major energy source used by wine producers in harvesting their crops, dropped by over 20 percent.
o   Many small wine producers joined together to form an association of wine producers and began to buy supplies at low group rates.
o   Rainfall in wine-producing regions was higher than it had been during the previous year, allowing the growers to save money on expensive artificial irrigation.

WINE PROFITS

Contrary to earlier predictions, demand for wine has not increased in recent years. Yet, even though prices and production amounts have also been stable during the last three years, wine producers last year increased their profits by more than 10 percent over the previous year's level.

Any of the following statements, if true about last year, helps to explain the rise in profits EXCEPT:

- Consumers in many countries increased their home stockpiles of bottles of wine, yet their overall consumption of wine decreased.
- Wine producers have saved money on wages by switching from paying laborers an hourly wage to paying them by the amount harvested.
- The price of oil, the major energy source used by wine producers in harvesting their crops, dropped by over 20 percent.
- Many small wine producers joined together to form an association of wine producers and began to buy supplies at low group rates.
- Rainfall in wine-producing regions was higher than it had been during the previous year, allowing the growers to save money on expensive artificial irrigation.

EXPLANATION

Reading the question: this prompt may be puzzling at first. However, regardless of whether we can think of an explanation easily, we can see that we have to "explain" in this question. That means that the correct answer will link to two pieces: 1) demand for wine has not increased, and 2) prices and production amounts are stable, but profits are up. The "except" indicates that four answer choices will explain this, and one will fail to explain it.

Creating a filter: we already have a filter, which is linking to points 1) and 2) that we've just identified. Further, we can briefly imagine some broad possibilities. Some other costs may have gone down; taxes could have been erased; maybe people switched from cheaper wines to more expensive wines (we're not sure whether this one is allowed by the information, but it does occur to me). Broadly, we want to increase profits and/or decrease costs, without challenging the information given.

Applying the filter: We dislike (A), so we skip it. This is an EXCEPT question, so we are keeping our filter basic and skipping anything that's not simple on the first pass. Choice (B) decreases a cost, so it's a good explanation, so it's not the answer. Same with choice (C): it's a valid explanation, so it's an invalid answer choice. Ditto for (D). Same for (E). Choices (B) through (E) all involve costs going down, so the correct answer must be (A). On further scrutiny, choice (A) just adds to the mystery, since the overall consumption of wine has decreased. It doesn't explain the mystery, so it's the correct answer. The correct answer is (A).

Which of the following most logically completes the argument below?

A non-profit organization is deciding whether to deliver and administer a limited quantity of a new vaccine for malaria, a mosquito-borne disease, to Country A or Country B, two countries with equal populations that are evenly distributed geographically and equally at risk of malaria. The expected rate of success per administration is expected to be the same in each country, but the non-profit organization has limited time to administer the drug and is uncertain of reaching either population in its entirety. Country B is smaller. Therefore, administering the vaccine to Country B will be more effective than administering to Country A, since _____.

- ○ the sparser population density of Country A would not be compensated for by more efficient transportation in-country
- ○ vaccines in Country A would have to be administered earlier in order to take effect at the necessary rate than in Country B
- ○ the vaccine is more suited to the equally distributed terrain and even temperatures of Country B
- ○ the vaccine will have wider uses in Country B than in Country A
- ○ administering the malaria vaccine will be a superior use of time over administering vaccines for other diseases

VACCINE ADMINISTRATION

Which of the following most logically completes the argument below?

A non-profit organization is deciding whether to deliver and administer a limited quantity of a new vaccine for malaria, a mosquito-borne disease, to Country A or Country B, two countries with equal populations that are evenly distributed geographically and equally at risk of malaria. The expected rate of success per administration is expected to be the same in each country, but the non-profit organization has limited time to administer the drug and is uncertain of reaching either population in its entirety. Country B is smaller. Therefore, administering the vaccine to Country B will be more effective than administering to Country A, since _____.

- ○ the sparser population density of Country A would not be compensated for by more efficient transportation in-country
- ○ vaccines in Country A would have to be administered earlier in order to take effect at the necessary rate than in Country B
- ○ the vaccine is more suited to the equally distributed terrain and even temperatures of Country B
- ○ the vaccine will have wider uses in Country B than in Country A
- ○ administering the malaria vaccine will be a superior use of time over administering vaccines for other diseases

EXPLANATION

In our initial approach, we can see that we have a question asking for a logical continuation. The most important material seems to start with the phrase "uncertain of reaching either population in its entirety." That morsel, plus the fact Country B is smaller, gives a good reason to administer in Country B; it's otherwise equal, but denser (we might guess we are assuming they have equal populations?), so we can administer more efficiently.

Applying the filter: Choice (A) talks about population density, so it passes the filter. Choice (C) also seems related, because it involves country size, but it's in fact introducing a completely new idea. So it's not a logical continuation, as the blank demands; what goes in the blank doesn't fit as a completely new reason, but will have identifiable logical grounding in what has come earlier in the prompt. Choice (A) is the only relevant candidate in this respect. We confirm the logic. They are basically still talking about how Country B is smaller. Not only is that country smaller, but while Country A's transportation is a little better, which would help administration of the vaccine, it's not better enough to outweigh the fact that Country B is smaller and there is a population density favoring administration. Answer choice (A) is a logical continuation indeed. The correct answer is (A).

Which of the following most logically completes the argument?

The city is threatened by an impending tropical storm, which is expected to raise the water outside the city to levels approaching the height of the protective barrier along the coast. Three teams of engineers and oceanographers have independently predicted the maximum water level will reach 89%, 83%, and 88% of the height of the protective barrier. The city is sufficiently safe, provided that
_____.

- ○ we take additional, sufficient steps to safeguard the city
- ○ the uncertainty of the predictions is sufficiently small relative to the difference between the predicted water level and the barrier's height
- ○ no additional independent prediction yields a value of 95% or higher
- ○ the three teams of engineers and oceanographers have based their predictions on similar assumptions
- ○ the three teams of engineers and oceanographers have based their predictions on dissimilar assumptions

IMPENDING STORM

Which of the following most logically completes the argument?

The city is threatened by an impending tropical storm, which is expected to raise the water outside the city to levels approaching the height of the protective barrier along the coast. Three teams of engineers and oceanographers have independently predicted the maximum water level will reach 89%, 83%, and 88% of the height of the protective barrier. The city is sufficiently safe, provided that _____.

- ○ we take additional, sufficient steps to safeguard the city
- ○ the uncertainty of the predictions is sufficiently small relative to the difference between the predicted water level and the barrier's height
- ○ no additional independent prediction yields a value of 95% or higher
- ○ the three teams of engineers and oceanographers have based their predictions on similar assumptions
- ○ the three teams of engineers and oceanographers have based their predictions on dissimilar assumptions

EXPLANATION

Reading the question: since we must make a logical continuation, we try to predict the answer. The only prediction that springs to mind is a simplistic one: "The city is sufficiently safe, provided that *their predictions are correct*." That is our predicted answer about their predictions about the storm. **Even a simple or obvious prediction can be used as a basic relevance filter.**

Applying the filter: choices (B) through (E) are all relevant to the basic question of the correctness of the prediction. One is objectively best, while the rest are objectively not best. (B) seems best, so we can attempt to establish logical proof for (B).

Logical proof: we can confirm answer choice (B) by analysis by cases. Imagine that each team gave a certainty of plus or minus *50%* the height of the wall. In that case, the city is *not* sufficiently safe. On the other hand, if the certainty is plus or minus 1%, the city is safe. Choice (B) must be right. Similar analysis of choices (C), (D), and (E) shows that they are not material to the argument in such a way. The correct answer is (B).

Adjusting the supply of money and increasing government spending are the two methods available to the country of Paisi to stimulate its economy. While both methods can create economic growth, increased government spending brings unemployed resources into use, producing extra output and income and benefiting the economy in the long run. Therefore, by increasing spending, the government of Paisi will do the most that it can do to stimulate its economy.

Which of the following is an assumption on which the argument depends?

- There are substantial government works projects that have yet to be done, such as the building of roads and infrastructure.
- The government of Paisi would not be forced to increase spending by a specific amount on a specific timetable.
- The government of Paisi could opt to take no action at all.
- Adjusting the supply of money could not be used effectively in conjunction with increasing government spending.
- The economy requires stimulation measures more than other measures, such as steps to stabilize the economy.

METHODS OF STIMULATION

Adjusting the supply of money and increasing government spending are the two methods available to the country of Paisi to stimulate its economy. While both methods can create economic growth, increased government spending brings unemployed resources into use, producing extra output and income and benefiting the economy in the long run. Therefore, by increasing spending, the government of Paisi will do the most that it can do to stimulate its economy.

Which of the following is an assumption on which the argument depends?

○ There are substantial government works projects that have yet to be done, such as the building of roads and infrastructure.
○ The government of Paisi would not be forced to increase spending by a specific amount on a specific timetable.
○ The government of Paisi could opt to take no action at all.
○ Adjusting the supply of money could not be used effectively in conjunction with increasing government spending.
○ The economy requires stimulation measures more than other measures, such as steps to stabilize the economy.

EXPLANATION

Reading the question: the question is asking for an "assumption." We parse by looking for opinion. Here, the opinion is indicated by "therefore": the conclusion is the last sentence. The argument is that, of two ways to stimulate the economy, increasing spending is a better way of stimulating the economy. The middle sentence gives the sole piece of evidence for this conclusion. We fixate on the phrase "the long run," a critical detail. The argument depends on the idea that long-run benefits are important enough to be a decisive way of determining which option here is better.

Applying the filter: Choices (B) and (E) both concern the timetable or long-run versus short-run, but our prediction isn't helping us evaluate them quickly. We can switch to the negation test.

Logical proof: negating (A), say there were *not* substantial work projects. That is harmful, but there might be other ways to stimulate spending. So (A) is out. On to (B): what if increasing spending *had* to be done on a specific timetable? That would not necessarily be a problem. So (B) is out. In (C), whether or not the government has to stimulate the economy is a separate question from what the best way to do it is. Choice (E) is irrelevant. The argument concerns only the best way to stimulate, not whether to stimulate or how important it is to stimulate. So (E) is out. That leaves us with choice (D). We can apply the negation test to (D). What if both methods could be used together? The prompt does not specify that these two measures are mutually exclusive. That appears to be an assumption. And if they aren't mutually exclusive, the government might not be doing the so-called "most that it can do" by just stimulating. The correct answer is (D).

A production facility that requires its air to be free of particulate matter requires staff and visitors to enter the production floor by way of a single hallway that is interrupted at each of three points by a changing room. In each room, an entrant must change into a new lab jacket, a hat, and new clean shoe coverings after the room is blasted with air. The facility intends to speed up the process of entering the production facility by replacing the three rooms with two changing rooms of a new design whose method of blasting air is effective enough to maintain the required air quality.

Which of the following would be most important to know in determining whether the production facility's plan, if implemented, is likely to achieve its goal?

- ○ Whether the initial cost of the replacement and the additional cost of maintaining the new rooms over time is less than the additional earnings generated from time saved in the new process
- ○ Whether the time it will take to make the installation is worth the time that the installation will save
- ○ Whether the air blasting technique takes equal time in the current design of room and in the new design
- ○ Whether yet another air blasting technique would eliminate the need to wear lab jackets, hats, and clean shoe coverings
- ○ Whether staff and visitors also exit the production floor through the same changing rooms

Changing Rooms

A production facility that requires its air to be free of particulate matter requires staff and visitors to enter the production floor by way of a single hallway that is interrupted at each of three points by a changing room. In each room, an entrant must change into a new lab jacket, a hat, and new clean shoe coverings after the room is blasted with air. The facility intends to speed up the process of entering the production facility by replacing the three rooms with two changing rooms of a new design whose method of blasting air is effective enough to maintain the required air quality.

Which of the following would be most important to know in determining whether the production facility's plan, if implemented, is likely to achieve its goal?

- Whether the initial cost of the replacement and the additional cost of maintaining the new rooms over time is less than the additional earnings generated from time saved in the new process
- Whether the time it will take to make the installation is worth the time that the installation will save
- Whether the air blasting technique takes equal time in the current design of room and in the new design
- Whether yet another air blasting technique would eliminate the need to wear lab jackets, hats, and clean shoe coverings
- Whether staff and visitors also exit the production floor through the same changing rooms

Explanation

Reading the question: this prompt gives us a plan. As we've discussed, a plan is like an argument in which the conclusion is, "This thing is going to work." We're switching from three little cleaning rooms to two, with a more vigorous blasting of air. And as we've discussed before, since we have answer choices that start with "whether," we will be able to evaluate by analysis of extreme cases. But we can start with a basic relevance filter. The "goal" of the plan is to "speed up the process of entering the production facility." Let's filter based on which answer choices are relevant to that goal.

Applying the filter: choice (A) does not pass the filter; the cost is irrelevant to whether or not the plan will *work* as proposed to speed up entry. Choice (B) concerns saving time, but it's still fails to pass the filter, because the objective of the plan is to speed up entering the production facility, not save all time for everyone on the planet in every conceivable way. Choice (C) has some potential. We consider one case: the time in the extra-blasty room is the same as the current room. It doesn't alone guarantee that the plan will work, but it doesn't ruin the plan. But if the air blasting in the new room takes a really long time, that will outweigh the time saved in changing jacket, hat, and shoe coverings only twice rather than three times. So (C) is in and is a good candidate for the right answer. Choice (D) is out, because while it might impact whether this plan is the best plan, it doesn't impact whether this plan will work, which is what we are after. Choice (E) sounds possibly relevant, but isn't as grounded in the argument as (E). For all we know, exiting interferes in no way with entry, so (E) is not necessarily relevant to achieving the goal.

Logical proof: we have already established logical proof of (C) through analysis by cases. **Logical proof does not have to come last,** and you may often naturally find yourself alternating between applying a filter and using the negation test. You just want to be careful not to forget about your filter, as people often do when they dig into the answer choices. Another caveat: matching against a prediction or basic relevance is much faster than applying the negation test. The correct answer is (C).

Although computers can improve hand-eye coordination and spatial reasoning, computer games are a cause of poor literacy in children. After-school hours spent playing computer games are hours not spent reading. Therefore, children who spend most of their spare time playing these games have less experience reading than other children have.

The argument depends on which of the following assumptions?

- ○ Passive activities such as watching television and listening to music do not hinder the development of reading skills in children.
- ○ Most children who play video games do not have other opportunities other than after-school hours in which they might focus on reading.
- ○ Children who do not spend most of their after-school hours playing computer games spend at least some of that time reading.
- ○ Formal instruction contributes little or nothing to children's acquisition of reading skills.
- ○ The mental skills developed through playing computer games do not contribute significantly to children's intellectual development.

GAMES AND LITERACY

Although computers can improve hand-eye coordination and spatial reasoning, computer games are a cause of poor literacy in children. After-school hours spent playing computer games are hours not spent reading. Therefore, children who spend most of their spare time playing these games have less experience reading than other children have.

The argument depends on which of the following assumptions?

○ Passive activities such as watching television and listening to music do not hinder the development of reading skills in children.
○ Most children who play video games do not have other opportunities other than after-school hours in which they might focus on reading.
○ Children who do not spend most of their after-school hours playing computer games spend at least some of that time reading.
○ Formal instruction contributes little or nothing to children's acquisition of reading skills.
○ The mental skills developed through playing computer games do not contribute significantly to children's intellectual development.

EXPLANATION

Reading the question: Since this prompt gives us a brief, pseudo-syllogistic argument, it's perfect for term matching. Here, we should we term match between the third sentence and the first two sentences. We can see this because the conclusion comes after the word "therefore," in the last sentence. Meanwhile, the first two sentences are evidence.

Evidence Term	Matches?	Conclusion Term
Children	=	Children
Hours not spent reading	=	Less experience reading
After-school hours	≠	Most of their spare time

The mismatch is in the final row: the phrase "after-school hours" does not necessarily equal "most of their spare time," given the weekend, or hours before school or on summer break. So we predict that's the answer: it has something to do with the mismatch between free time and after-school time.

Applying the filter: Choices (B) and (C) both are close to the filter.

Logical proof: We can analyze (B) by cases. Video game players might have other opportunities to read, such as on the weekend, but even if they read all weekend, if the other kids read all weekend, too, the video game players are reading less. So (B) isn't critical. We can confirm choice (C) by the negation test. If the other kids are *not* reading during after-school hours, then the video game players are not falling behind on a second of reading relative to the other kids when they play video games. The correct answer is (C).

A "vice tax" can suppress demand for a product or service that is not wholly in the public's favor by making it more expensive. The country of Balbonia wished to duplicate Geraldia's success in using a vice tax to reduce the sales of nicotine products, such as cigarettes. When Balbonia introduced the same tax into its market, however, demand for nicotine products remained undiminished, even though the currency-adjusted prices of nicotine in Balbonia rose to levels equivalent to those in Geraldia.

Which of the following, if true, most helps to explain the contrasting impact of the two instances of vice tax described above?

○   Balbonia has a much greater variety of nicotine products and makers of those products than does Geraldia, including electronic cigarettes.
○   It required a different tax rate and tax structure in Balbonia to achieve the same effective nicotine product prices as were present in Geraldia.
○   Geraldia has laws restraining the marketers of nicotine products from increased advertising of their products, while Balbonia does not.
○   Smokers of cigarettes in Balbonia have more of an ingrained habit of smoking after dinner than do smokers in Geraldia.
○   Vice taxes were far more prevalent in Balbonia than in Geraldia even prior to the introduction of the nicotine vice tax in Balbonia.

BALBONIA'S VICE TAX

A "vice tax" can suppress demand for a product or service that is not wholly in the public's favor by making it more expensive. The country of Balbonia wished to duplicate Geraldia's success in using a vice tax to reduce the sales of nicotine products, such as cigarettes. When Balbonia introduced the same tax into its market, however, demand for nicotine products remained undiminished, even though the currency-adjusted prices of nicotine in Balbonia rose to levels equivalent to those in Geraldia.

Which of the following, if true, most helps to explain the contrasting impact of the two instances of vice tax described above?

○ Balbonia has a much greater variety of nicotine products and makers of those products than does Geraldia, including electronic cigarettes.
○ It required a different tax rate and tax structure in Balbonia to achieve the same effective nicotine product prices as were present in Geraldia.
○ Geraldia has laws restraining the marketers of nicotine products from increased advertising of their products, while Balbonia does not.
○ Smokers of cigarettes in Balbonia have more of an ingrained habit of smoking after dinner than do smokers in Geraldia.
○ Vice taxes were far more prevalent in Balbonia than in Geraldia even prior to the introduction of the nicotine vice tax in Balbonia.

EXPLANATION

Reading the question: We inhale the prompt. The vice tax has worked in G country, but not in B country, even though the tax did affect the price of nicotine products as planned. Why?, we are asked.

Creating a filter: the question rules out price as an explanation, so the explanation is something other than price. Maybe people in B country love their nicotine products more and are unperturbed by the new prices. Maybe people in B country are richer, although that does touch on pricing in some ways. We imagine that B country is more nicotine-demanding. We can think of our filter for the correct answer is "demand, not price."

Applying the filter: choice (A) doesn't touch on demand, and the tax effects should be unrelated to the variety of products, if they are taxed equally, which we're led to believe. So (A) is out. Choice (B) is out; the mechanism to achieve the effect is irrelevant if the price effect is equal, which we're led to believe. Choice (C) is close to our filter, since it touches on the subject of demand. Prices in B country are up, but increased advertising could help with demand. Choice (D) also concerns demand, so it passes the filter. Choice (E) is out; we don't see any reason to think other vice taxes would affect this vice tax. That leaves us with choices (C) and (D).

Logical proof: we'll find an objective difference between (C) and (D). The prompt has a dramatic phrase: demand for nicotine products remained undiminished. Abundant advertising, in (C), could explain why demand was undiminished across the board—in basically all nicotine-buying and -consuming situations. After-dinner smoking, in (D), could explain why *some* nicotine consumption would survive, but it doesn't explain demand going completely undiminished. The correct answer is (C).

Two fitness experts have developed a remarkable exercise system that appears to yield immediate and prolonged improvements to a person's physical and mental health. In careful testing, they have found that the system is accessible to people of different ages and fitness levels. Furthermore, since the system involves unusual techniques, custom pieces of small equipment, and natural dietary supplements, the system would take years for competitors to replicate. And when they tested the system during a two-month trial, potential customers stated emphatically that they would pay the stated prices to continue in the system and that they preferred it over other forms of exercise. All evidence indicates that the new exercise system will have successful launch in the market.

Which of the following would it be most useful to determine in order to evaluate the argument?

- Whether the system is more effective than other systems
- Whether the system is sufficiently difficult for serious athletes
- Whether it will be easy to get people to try the system
- Whether competitors will be able to offer a virtually identical system at lower cost
- Whether the cost of providing the system to a customer is high relative to its market price

NEW EXERCISE SYSTEM

Two fitness experts have developed a remarkable exercise system that appears to yield immediate and prolonged improvements to a person's physical and mental health. In careful testing, they have found that the system is accessible to people of different ages and fitness levels. Furthermore, since the system involves unusual techniques, custom pieces of small equipment, and natural dietary supplements, the system would take years for competitors to replicate. And when they tested the system during a two-month trial, potential customers stated emphatically that they would pay the stated prices to continue in the system and that they preferred it over other forms of exercise. All evidence indicates that the new exercise system will have successful launch in the market.

Which of the following would it be most useful to determine in order to evaluate the argument?

- ○ Whether the system is more effective than other systems
- ○ Whether the system is sufficiently difficult for serious athletes
- ○ Whether it will be easy to get people to try the system
- ○ Whether competitors will be able to offer a virtually identical system at lower cost
- ○ Whether the cost of providing the system to a customer is high relative to its market price

EXPLANATION

Reading the question: we see a long prompt, and a short stem, so we check out the stem. The phrase "most useful to determine" allows us to create a filter immediately. **The phrasing of Critical Reasoning questions tends to be understated. When you are asked what "may be true," look for what *must* be true. When you're asked what would be "useful to determine," look for what is *critical* to determine.** This is proof by stronger terms, as mentioned in the Critical Reasoning Strategy.

Note: You may be wondering why the question would ask for something "useful," if the answer is something "critical." The reason is that the test maker uses understated language as a cautious practice to ensure that the correct answer is objectively correct. Something "critical to know" is certainly "useful to know." For this exact reason, when you see understated language, you are not guaranteed that the correct answer will be more critical, but if you find a critical answer choice, you'll know it's correct.

Applying the filter, we look for a choice that *must* be true. (A) is out; we are told the system is effective, and people like it, and it's accessible. And they would pay for it! So it doesn't matter whether or not it's more effective. The prompt even tells us people *prefer it to other forms of exercise.* So (A) is out. (B) seems irrelevant; the system doesn't have to be for everyone in order to launch well. It's accessible to various types of people and they like it and so on. (B) is out. Choice (C) looks promising. Choice (D) contradicts the evidence. We're told it will take competitors a long time to copy this system, and we aren't concerned with the long term—we are talking about a "launch." Choice (E) is out, since the prompt doesn't say anything about cost. We're left with (C).

Logical proof: Is choice (C) critical? We can analyze by cases. What if it's hard to get people to try the new system? We could see that being an issue. But do we have objective backing in the prompt? Yes: we are told that potential customers liked the product "when they tried it during a two-month trial." What if they don't like the product yet after a month? Or more to the point, if it takes two months to like the product, and we are having trouble getting people to try it at all, that will impede the launch. The correct answer is (C).

Organic fertilizers are made from mineral deposits along with bone meal, plant meal, or composted manure, while synthetic fertilizers are made by processing raw materials. The numeric ratio listed on a fertilizer, whether it's organic or synthetic, indicates the proportions of the nutrients inside. For example, a bag of fertilizer labeled "4-8-6" contains 4 pounds of nitrate, 8 pounds of phosphate, and 6 pounds of potash. A 100-pound bag of 4-8-6 organic fertilizer and a 100-pound bag of 4-8-6 synthetic fertilizer may differ in other respects, but not in the amount of nutrients they deliver into your soil.

Which of the following, if true, most strengthens the argument above?

○ Organic fertilizers are produced with an equivalent bag size and nutrient ratio for every synthetic fertilizer bag size and nutrient ratio that is produced.
○ The mechanisms by which organic and synthetic fertilizers are absorbed in soil are not substantially different.
○ The total number of pounds of organic nitrate, phosphate, and potash delivered into soil each year in organic fertilizer equals the total number of pounds of each delivered in synthetic fertilizer.
○ A variety of different tests conducted last year found that levels of nutrients or contaminants other than nitrate, phosphate, and potash in distinct soils that had been treated with a volume of 4-8-6 synthetic fertilizer were no higher than those in samples treated with a volume of 4-8-6 organic fertilizer.
○ The design and the use of organic fertilizer are in no way motivated by a desire to deliver a different amount of nutrients into soil for a given nutrient ratio.

ORGANIC FERTILIZER

Organic fertilizers are made from mineral deposits along with bone meal, plant meal, or composted manure, while synthetic fertilizers are made by processing raw materials. The numeric ratio listed on a fertilizer, whether it's organic or synthetic, indicates the proportions of the nutrients inside. For example, a bag of fertilizer labeled "4-8-6" contains 4 pounds of nitrate, 8 pounds of phosphate, and 6 pounds of potash. A 100-pound bag of 4-8-6 organic fertilizer and a 100-pound bag of 4-8-6 synthetic fertilizer may differ in other respects, but not in the amount of nutrients they deliver into your soil.

Which of the following, if true, most strengthens the argument above?

○   Organic fertilizers are produced with an equivalent bag size and nutrient ratio for every synthetic fertilizer bag size and nutrient ratio that is produced.
○   The mechanisms by which organic and synthetic fertilizers are absorbed in soil are not substantially different.
○   The total number of pounds of organic nitrate, phosphate, and potash delivered into soil each year in organic fertilizer equals the total number of pounds of each delivered in synthetic fertilizer.
○   A variety of different tests conducted last year found that levels of nutrients or contaminants other than nitrate, phosphate, and potash in distinct soils that had been treated with a volume of 4-8-6 synthetic fertilizer were no higher than those in samples treated with a volume of 4-8-6 organic fertilizer.
○   The design and the use of organic fertilizer are in no way motivated by a desire to deliver a different amount of nutrients into soil for a given nutrient ratio.

EXPLANATION

First impressions: this argument looks long and appears to involve some obscure definition. We can check the question stem: we're asked to strengthen the argument. We can focus on the elements of opinion. The last sentence is the opinion, whereas the first three sentences give facts.

Creating a filter: The key is that the "amount of nutrients" is the same between organic and synthetic fertilizer. Why? Because they are both 4-8-6, meaning they have the same proportions of nutrients. These terms have been matched by the argument. Is the "amount of nutrients" delivered the same because the proportions are the same? Is there any way these things could be different? We'll take that idea our filter for basic relevance.

Applying the filter, we eliminate (A), (C) and (E), and keep (B) and (D). Choices (A), (C) and (E) are irrelevant comparisons—they have no bearing on whether these two fertilizers work identically. Choice (D) starts to get after the same considerations, but it discusses contaminants and nutrients other than the ones at hand, and it doesn't say that the levels are equal, only "no higher" in synthetics. So (D) is not material to the claim in the prompt.

Logical proof: using the negation test, we can see that the negated (B) weakens the argument. If the mechanisms by which organic and synthetic fertilizers are absorbed in soil *are* substantially different, then the argument is flawed and the conclusion may be incorrect. The non-negated (B) therefore patches a weakness of the argument and does, in fact, strengthen the argument. The correct answer is (B).

A group of scientists have studied schizophrenics in an isolated community in Costa Rica with the objective of learning about the causes of schizophrenia worldwide. A flaw in this strategy is that schizophrenia is characterized by impaired emotional responses, and the way emotional responses are learned may differ across cultures of the world. It might even be fair to say that, on what is now a largely interconnected planet, a schizophrenic in an isolated community is a schizophrenic of no practical interest.

Which of the following, if true, would most weaken the argument made above about the group's approach?

o   All schizophrenics have certain features in common which, if studied, would help scientists to learn about the causes of schizophrenia in general.
o   Living in an urban environment during childhood or as an adult doubles the risk of schizophrenia in an individual.
o   To understand schizophrenia, it is necessary to learn about not just impaired emotional responses, but also paranoid beliefs, hallucinations, and disorganized thinking.
o   The group of scientists will not draw conclusions about schizophrenics as a whole from their findings in the isolated community.
o   Of the schizophrenics present in the isolated community, more than half have travelled abroad in their adulthood.

ISOLATED SCHIZOPHRENICS

A group of scientists have studied schizophrenics in an isolated community in Costa Rica with the objective of learning about the causes of schizophrenia worldwide. A flaw in this strategy is that schizophrenia is characterized by impaired emotional responses, and the way emotional responses are learned may differ across cultures of the world. It might even be fair to say that, on what is now a largely interconnected planet, a schizophrenic in an isolated community is a schizophrenic of no practical interest.

Which of the following, if true, would most weaken the argument made above about the group's approach?

○ All schizophrenics have certain features in common which, if studied, would help scientists to learn about the causes of schizophrenia in general.
○ Living in an urban environment during childhood or as an adult doubles the risk of schizophrenia in an individual.
○ To understand schizophrenia, it is necessary to learn about not just impaired emotional responses, but also paranoid beliefs, hallucinations, and disorganized thinking.
○ The group of scientists will not draw conclusions about schizophrenics as a whole from their findings in the isolated community.
○ Of the schizophrenics present in the isolated community, more than half have travelled abroad in their adulthood.

EXPLANATION

Reading the question: this question contains opinions, so we can digest it by finding and categorizing opinions. We've got a plan and a criticism of the plan, so there are two bodies of opinion: what the scientists think, and what the author thinks.

Creating a filter: more specifically, we are asked to weaken what the author thinks—we are weakening the criticism of the plan. The gist of this criticism is the second sentence; the final sentence is mostly puffery. The essence of sentence #2 is that, since emotional responses differ by geography, scientists will not find the causes of schizophrenia in a concentrated area. We could attack this view primarily by asserting that, even though emotional aspects of schizophrenia might differ by geography, the *causes* of schizophrenia don't. So we predict that the correct answer choice, a weakening statement, will be like, "even though emotional aspects of schizophrenia might differ by geography, the *causes* of schizophrenia don't."

Applying the filter: choice (A) is similar to our expectation, while choice (B) is not. Choice (C) is similar, but it fails to connect to or mention the causes of schizophrenia. Choice (D) weakens the wrong thing—it weakens the scientists' view that their plan will work. Choice (E) disputes the evidence, not the argument, and it doesn't dispute the evidence well, since it concerns adulthood and the evidence concerns childhood, presumably.

Logical proof: we are left with (A), which we can confirm through the negation test. If there are *no* common features linked to the causation of the disease, the scientists' plan would surely fail. Therefore, the statement in (A) is material to both the plan and the criticism of the plan. The correct answer is (A).

Known to be antisocial birds, cuckoos are solitary animals that practice brood parasitism, whereby they plant their young in another bird's nest through deception and subterfuge so that the host bird will take on the burden of raising the cuckoo's offspring. However, the ani species of cuckoo is highly social; anis congregate with others of their kind and often trust humans. Scientists attribute the anis' more social behavior to communal living conditions that do not require antisocial behavior of the birds.

Which of the following, if true, most strongly supports the scientists' explanation of anis' more social behavior?

- The degree to which a bird is social or antisocial is species-dependent and therefore primarily genetic.
- The more social species of cuckoo nest communally; a number of females lay their eggs in the nest and usually share the responsibility of incubation and feeding.
- The majority of cuckoos are monogamous, having only one mate.
- In some cuckoo communal living environments, female cuckoos take multiple males as mates.
- Cuckoos tend to show flexibility in prey and foraging techniques.

SOCIAL CUCKOOS

Known to be antisocial birds, cuckoos are solitary animals that practice brood parasitism, whereby they plant their young in another bird's nest through deception and subterfuge so that the host bird will take on the burden of raising the cuckoo's offspring. However, the ani species of cuckoo is highly social; anis congregate with others of their kind and often trust humans. Scientists attribute the anis' more social behavior to communal living conditions that do not require antisocial behavior of the birds.

Which of the following, if true, most strongly supports the scientists' explanation of anis' more social behavior?

○   The degree to which a bird is social or antisocial is species-dependent and therefore primarily genetic.
○   The more social species of cuckoo nest communally; a number of females lay their eggs in the nest and usually share the responsibility of incubation and feeding.
○   The majority of cuckoos are monogamous, having only one mate.
○   In some cuckoo communal living environments, female cuckoos take multiple males as mates.
○   Cuckoos tend to show flexibility in prey and foraging techniques.

EXPLANATION

Reading the question: the prompt leaves some questions unanswered. Cuckoos usually are antisocial parasites. But ani cuckoos are social—are they parasites? The answer to that question doesn't leap out. Furthermore, there is the question of the "living conditions"—what are they?

Creating the filter: of these questions, the most important, we can conjecture, is what exactly these living conditions are. The parasite business is irrelevant, perhaps, and we are talking about the question of antisocial versus social, which will depend on the living conditions. Clarifying that would add further "support" to the "scientists' explanation." So we can use "living conditions" as a basic relevance filter.

Applying the filter: choice (A) gives us genes, not living conditions, so it doesn't pass the filter. Choice (B) looks relevant—it discusses living conditions and resolves the mystery about whether ani cuckoos are parasites. So (B) stays in. Choice (C) appears to be true of all cuckoos, so it does nothing to explain the difference among them. Choice (C) is out. Ditto for (D) and (E). We're left with (B) only.

Logical proof: when you're reasonably certain on a question or running behind on time, you'll want to skip the logical proof step. **Applying the negation test whenever possible on Critical Reasoning questions may be too time-consuming; you can skip it selectively to balance time management and accuracy.** However, we can apply the negation test to (B). Say that ani cuckoos did *not* nest communally. In such a case, they might well be brood parasites, like other cuckoos. And in such a case, their living conditions, so far as we know, would not be communal. The negation of (B) would severely weaken the argument, so (B) strengthens the argument. The correct answer is (B).

If the city goes on polluting the air at present rates, air quality and visibility over the city will begin to suffer, rainwater may be polluted, and the city will contribute to the global problem of greenhouse emissions. Taxing every polluting commercial establishment per volume of polluted air or per particulate volume of greenhouse emissions will induce businesses to reduce the amount of pollution they emit; this charge will therefore protect the city's air.

Which of the following is an assumption made in drawing the conclusion above?

- Businesses will reduce the amount of pollution they emit by reducing the number of products they build.
- The tax will not significantly affect the commercial health of most businesses, even if their factories do not reduce the amount of pollution they emit.
- The tax will not induce businesses to dispose of their greenhouse gas pollution covertly.
- The quality of the air is an important issue for most of the city's residents.
- Polluted air could be purified and cleaned of greenhouse gasses through technology installed at company factories at the point of emission.

TAXING POLLUTION

If the city goes on polluting the air at present rates, air quality and visibility over the city will begin to suffer, rainwater may be polluted, and the city will contribute to the global problem of greenhouse emissions. Taxing every polluting commercial establishment per volume of polluted air or per particulate volume of greenhouse emissions will induce businesses to reduce the amount of pollution they emit; this charge will therefore protect the city's air.

Which of the following is an assumption made in drawing the conclusion above?

○ Businesses will reduce the amount of pollution they emit by reducing the number of products they build.
○ The tax will not significantly affect the commercial health of most businesses, even if their factories do not reduce the amount of pollution they emit.
○ The tax will not induce businesses to dispose of their greenhouse gas pollution covertly.
○ The quality of the air is an important issue for most of the city's residents.
○ Polluted air could be purified and cleaned of greenhouse gasses through technology installed at company factories at the point of emission.

EXPLANATION

Reading the question: the prompt concerns a plan, and we need to find an assumption in the plan. Plans tend to have lots of assumptions, but they can be difficult to think of. We tax polluters, so they pollute less—no assumption jumps out. Without a specific prediction, therefore, we can apply a basic filter to each answer choice: does it have any relevance to whether the plan will work?

Applying the filter: We test the choices for relevance to the plan. In choice (A), reducing pollution is part of our conclusion, but the "number of products" need not be part of it. Choice (B) is not critical to the argument; it doesn't say or claim or require that businesses will *like* the tax or even survive it. Choice (C) looks relevant. Choice (D) is irrelevant to whether the tax will work. And choice (E) is not required for the plan to work, as we can see by a negation test: say there *isn't* a way to purify gasses at the point of emission. They could still pollute less, by producing less, or by capturing the air and shipping it into space in sealed containers, or whatever. So choice (E) is out.

Logical proof: We're left with (C), so we apply the negation test. Negating it, we get, "The tax *will* induce businesses to dispose of their greenhouse gas pollution covertly." That statement, if true, deals a severe blow to the argument. The plan won't achieve its aim if polluters continue to pollute covertly. Choice (C) is indeed critical. The correct answer is (C).

The more incentives there are for financial institutions to provide home mortgages, the more mortgage options financial institutions will provide to cater to different circumstances, and the odds that a potential home buyer is able to purchase a home are increased when more mortgage options are available. Therefore, by increasing incentives to financial institutions to provide home mortgages, the government can create circumstances that are more helpful for home buyers.

If the statements above are true, which of the following must be true?

o   The providers of mortgages can be of most help to potential home buyers by providing numerous financing options.
o   The higher are the odds that a potential home buyer can purchase a home, the more numerous are mortgage options provided to that potential home buyer.
o   If incentives to financial institutions to provide home mortgages are increased, the odds are increased that a potential home buyer will be able to purchase a home.
o   The more the government provides incentives to financial institutions to provide home mortgages, the greater are the odds that home buyers will pay off their mortgages on time.
o   The more restrictions that are placed on financial institutions' providing home mortgages, the lower are the odds that a potential home buyer will be able to purchase a home.

MORTGAGE INCENTIVES

The more incentives there are for financial institutions to provide home mortgages, the more mortgage options financial institutions will provide to cater to different circumstances, and the odds that a potential home buyer is able to purchase a home are increased when more mortgage options are available. Therefore, by increasing incentives to financial institutions to provide home mortgages, the government can create circumstances that are more helpful for home buyers.

If the statements above are true, which of the following must be true?

○ The providers of mortgages can be of most help to potential home buyers by providing numerous financing options.
○ The higher are the odds that a potential home buyer can purchase a home, the more numerous are mortgage options provided to that potential home buyer.
○ If incentives to financial institutions to provide home mortgages are increased, the odds are increased that a potential home buyer will be able to purchase a home.
○ The more the government provides incentives to financial institutions to provide home mortgages, the greater are the odds that home buyers will pay off their mortgages on time.
○ The more restrictions that are placed on financial institutions' providing home mortgages, the lower are the odds that a potential home buyer will be able to purchase a home.

EXPLANATION

Reading the question: the prompt presents dubious facts in rapid succession. A natural and healthy impulse is to want to rip the flimsy argument to shreds. However, we don't argue with facts on these questions: what is stated as a fact is a fact. And the question stem is asking us what "must be true," *given the prompt*. So we should accept the prompt and see what can be inferred from it. We can skip using a filter altogether and go straight to applying the logical test to each answer choice: must it be true? Nothing else matters—including whether the answer choice seems plausible or important.

Logical proof: Testing the logic of each answer choice, we start by finding that (A) need not be true. We are told that mortgage options are helpful to customers, but not that they are most helpful. So (A) is out. Choice (B) is illogical. The converse of a true statement need not be true, and (B) is the converse of a statement in the prompt. Choice (C) looks correct. The prompt tells us, in logical terms, that X->Y->Z. Answer choice (C) says X->Z, which must be true if X->Y->Z. So (C) is in. Choice (D) looks similar to (C) at first, but it introduces a new concept of paying off mortgages on time, and we're not going to be able to establish anything about that concept that "must be true" from the information in the prompt. Choice (E) also contains an out-of-scope element, "restrictions," which we are told nothing about and hence can't draw conclusions about. The correct answer is (C).

The average text-format computer password is highly effective at stopping casual attempts by hackers to break into a critical, secured computer systems but can be hacked within a few minutes by a powerful computer permitted to make repeated remote login attempts. No critical, secured computer system can afford to be defended by a measure that will last as little time as a few minutes. Biometric authentication, on the other hand, has no vulnerability to remote repeated login attempts. Clearly, therefore, for critical, secured computer systems, the average text-format computer password can play no part in effectively stopping hacking attempts.

The argument is most vulnerable to the objection that it fails to

- ○ consider that there might be noncritical secured computer systems for which the average text-format computer password can be perfectly useful
- ○ identify any alternative method of stopping hackers that could be used instead of the method it rejects
- ○ distinguish among the various kinds of biometric authentication
- ○ consider the possibility of combining the two methods of stopping hackers that it mentions
- ○ consider that stronger-than-average text-format computer passwords take days to be cracked by repeated login attempts, making them effective enough for critical, secured computer systems

TEXT PASSWORDS

The average text-format computer password is highly effective at stopping casual attempts by hackers to break into a critical, secured computer systems but can be hacked within a few minutes by a powerful computer permitted to make repeated remote login attempts. No critical, secured computer system can afford to be defended by a measure that will last as little time as a few minutes. Biometric authentication, on the other hand, has no vulnerability to remote repeated login attempts. Clearly, therefore, for critical, secured computer systems, the average text-format computer password can play no part in effectively stopping hacking attempts.

The argument is most vulnerable to the objection that it fails to

○ consider that there might be noncritical secured computer systems for which the average text-format computer password can be perfectly useful
○ identify any alternative method of stopping hackers that could be used instead of the method it rejects
○ distinguish among the various kinds of biometric authentication
○ consider the possibility of combining the two methods of stopping hackers that it mentions
○ consider that stronger-than-average text-format computer passwords take days to be cracked by repeated login attempts, making them effective enough for critical, secured computer systems

EXPLANATION

Reading comprehension: our ears should prick up at the phrase "play no part." We can see by altering or omitting this phrase that represents a critical detail in the argument. Text passwords may be inferior in some ways, but that doesn't mean it won't help to use them in addition to some other measures; the argument fails to recognize that. We have a critical detail filter to apply to the answer choices, something like, "maybe the argument is wrong because it's worth using text passwords along with other measures."

Applying the filter: We compare the answer choices with our expectation. Choice (A) is immaterial, because the argument isn't discussing "noncritical" systems. Choice (B) contradicts the evidence we have been given, the argument *does* give an alternative to text passwords—it mentions biometrics. Choice (C) is irrelevant. Choice (D) delivers on our expectation: it says, in other words, text passwords can "play a part." Choice (E) is irrelevant, because the argument and its conclusion are about average text-format passwords only, not stronger ones.

Logical proof: We can't apply the negation test exactly to an answer choice, given the way they are wording. But we can negate the idea being conveyed by imagining that the argument *did* consider using both methods. We can confirm that such an argument would be stronger; it would have better grounds to say that text passwords can "play no part." We have confirmed that we are discussing a point of failure in the argument. The correct answer is (D).

Inhabitants of the country Orctania suffer from a much lower incidence of cancer than the inhabitants of other countries, for reasons that are generally theorized to be environmental and behavioral—the pollution-free air, stress-free and drug-free living, healthy dietary practices, and active lifestyle. Nevertheless, people from other countries who take up residence in Orctania and attempt to follow the practices of the inhabitants still have a radically higher incidence of cancer than do native Octanians.

Which of the following does NOT help to explain the higher incidence rate of cancer in non-native Orctanians?

○ The causes of some forms of cancer that are prevalent in Orctania are genetic, not environmental or behavioral.
○ People from other countries who take up residence in Orctania may fail to succeed in following the practices of native Orctanians in important respects.
○ The non-native Orctanians who take up residence in Orctania tend to be motivated to do so by a desire to improve their health.
○ It has not been established which one of several possible factors, or combination of these factors, is truly responsible for the low incidence of cancer in native Orctanians.
○ Most non-natives move to Orctania too late in life to reap the environmental and behavioral health benefits of living there.

ORCTANIAN HEALTH

Inhabitants of the country Orctania suffer from a much lower incidence of cancer than the inhabitants of other countries, for reasons that are generally theorized to be environmental and behavioral—the pollution-free air, stress-free and drug-free living, healthy dietary practices, and active lifestyle. Nevertheless, people from other countries who take up residence in Orctania and attempt to follow the practices of the inhabitants still have a radically higher incidence of cancer than do native Octanians.

Which of the following does NOT help to explain the higher incidence rate of cancer in non-native Orctanians?

○ The causes of some forms of cancer that are prevalent in Orctania are genetic, not environmental or behavioral.
○ People from other countries who take up residence in Orctania may fail to succeed in following the practices of native Orctanians in important respects.
○ The non-native Orctanians who take up residence in Orctania tend to be motivated to do so by a desire to improve their health.
○ It has not been established which one of several possible factors, or combination of these factors, is truly responsible for the low incidence of cancer in native Orctanians.
○ Most non-natives move to Orctania too late in life to reap the environmental and behavioral health benefits of living there.

EXPLANATION

Reading the question: we can see that this question looks like a lot of work. First, it has given us a difficult-seeming puzzle: this country is has a low cancer rate, for non-genetic reasons, but people who move there have a higher cancer rate. Secondly, we have a "NOT" question. Questions with "NOT," like those with "EXCEPT," tend to be labor intensive, since it's relatively slow to go through four good explanations and one bad one. The key technique here is to use a very basic filter. **In "NOT" and "EXCEPT" questions— and all questions that are involved—you're often basic served by a basic filter.**

Applying the filter: carefully asking this simple question, we can judge that (D) is the least explanatory of the cancer rate and is therefore the answer. In (D), even if the exact "factor" hasn't been determined, it doesn't matter, because the people who move to Orctania "attempt to follow the practices of the inhabitants." So, we don't know whether it's being pollution-free and stress-free *and* drug free and so on, but the people are doing *all* of them, so (D) doesn't help to clear up the mystery. Everything else is a good explanation. Choices (B) and (E) both point out that moving to the country does not automatically equate with enjoying the benefits of the environment or with adopting the behaviors. (C) points out that the population moving to the country might be doing so because they are unusually cancer-prone to begin with, which would explain why they would have a higher rate of cancer even after reaping benefits. Choice (A) points out the possibility that some forms of cancer aren't helped by living in Orctania—those kinds depend only on genes, and, critically, it's possible that the people who move to the country have genes more prone to those forms of cancer, somewhat like the case of (C).

Logical proof: finally, we can use a test of (D) that is similar to the negation test: say that it *has* been established which factor was responsible. That's not automatically an explanation, because, for all we know, the people who move to Orctania are perfectly recreating/copying that factor. Since the situation is unchanged given (D) or its negation, (D) is unimportant to the situation. The correct answer is (D).

For our nation to maintain a position of economic strength relative to other countries, it requires both accelerated personal investment levels and the unobstructed growth of production capacity, the factor which is known as A by economists and which increases grows largely spontaneously through society's development of technology. However, since technology development can be driven through economic support to individual entrepreneurs, ensuring these two key economic outcomes will require balancing these two kinds of financial incentives from the government to the individual.

If the statements in the passage above are true, for our nation to maintain a position of economic strength relative to other countries, it must

- ○ balance financial incentives to individuals, both to invest and to develop technology through entrepreneurship
- ○ balance two kinds of financial incentives: investment, on the personal level, and production capacity, on the level of the economy
- ○ drive accelerate personal investment while allowing production capacity to rise spontaneously
- ○ devote those financial incentives extended on the personal level to entrepreneurship
- ○ ensure that production growth remains unobstructed while balancing the two kinds of financial incentives driving personal investment

PRESERVING STRENGTH

For our nation to maintain a position of economic strength relative to other countries, it requires both accelerated personal investment levels and the unobstructed growth of production capacity, the factor which is known as *A* by economists and which increases grows largely spontaneously through society's development of technology. However, since technology development can be driven through economic support to individual entrepreneurs, ensuring these two key economic outcomes will require balancing these two kinds of financial incentives from the government to the individual.

If the statements in the passage above are true, for our nation to maintain a position of economic strength relative to other countries, it must

- ○ balance financial incentives to individuals, both to invest and to develop technology through entrepreneurship
- ○ balance two kinds of financial incentives: investment, on the personal level, and production capacity, on the level of the economy
- ○ drive accelerate personal investment while allowing production capacity to rise spontaneously
- ○ devote those financial incentives extended on the personal level to entrepreneurship
- ○ ensure that production growth remains unobstructed while balancing the two kinds of financial incentives driving personal investment

EXPLANATION

Reading the prompt: it's relatively easy to get confused near the end of the prompt in this question. The last sentence mentions "two key economic outcomes" and "two kinds of financial incentives"—what do these refer to? **One technique is to use the answer choices simply to understand a difficult prompt.** Struggling test-takers do this all the time: they jump to the answer choices long before they're ready, because they don't know what else to do. We won't do that, but when we are having trouble understanding the prompt, we can use the answer choices...and *then*, we go back up and we'll still attempt to create a filter heading back down again to evaluate the answer choices.

Creating a filter: glancing at (A) and (B), we get the idea that "the two kinds of financial incentives" mentioned in the last sentence are 1) to invest and 2) to be an entrepreneur. That makes sense, because those two things are somewhat opposite and hence could be "balanced," as the prompt says. Having cleared that up makes it easier to see that the "two key economic outcomes" are accelerated personal investment levels and the growth of production capacity. Now we are able to form a filter, a brief summary of the last sentence: "the country has to encourage both investment and entrepreneurship in a balanced way."

Applying the filter: on first pass with this summary filter, (A) is in, (B) is out, (C) is out, (D) is out, and (E) is out. All of them except (A) have a miswording of the basic answer, which is to balance the two personal actions, investing and entrepreneur-ing. For example, (E) sounds good until the end, where it says both incentives drive personal investment. The correct answer is (A).

Nationside, an insurance company, is considering issuing a new policy to insure automobile drivers who are elderly and have a record of car accidents. If premiums for the new policy are inappropriately high for a potential customer, that customer will not opt for the new policy. Therefore, Nationside is concerned that the income from the policies would not be sufficient to pay for the claims that would be made.

Which of the following strategies would be most likely to maximize Nationside's profits from the new policy?

o   Marketing the new policy to older drivers with a history of automobile accidents of any type
o   Marketing the new policy to older drivers with a history of minor automobile accidents only
o   Marketing the new policy to younger drivers with no history of automobile accidents
o   Marketing the new policy to younger drivers with some history of automobile accidents
o   Marketing the new policy to older drivers who were rejected by other companies for similar policies

ELDERLY POLICY

Nationside, an insurance company, is considering issuing a new policy to insure automobile drivers who are elderly and have a record of car accidents. If premiums for the new policy are inappropriately high for a potential customer, that customer will not opt for the new policy. Therefore, Nationside is concerned that the income from the policies would not be sufficient to pay for the claims that would be made.

Which of the following strategies would be most likely to maximize Nationside's profits from the new policy?

- Marketing the new policy to older drivers with a history of automobile accidents of any type
- Marketing the new policy to older drivers with a history of minor automobile accidents only
- Marketing the new policy to younger drivers with no history of automobile accidents
- Marketing the new policy to younger drivers with some history of automobile accidents
- Marketing the new policy to older drivers who were rejected by other companies for similar policies

EXPLANATION

Reading the question: this prompt presents a fairly weak argument; the many vulnerabilities are potentially distracting. But we are asked something rather specific: which strategy will maximize profits in the new policy. It looks like we might be able to largely ignore the conclusion of the argument and focus on a critical detail. It's a perfect example of why we should keep an eye on the question stem while digesting the prompt.

Creating a filter: the phrase "most likely" is a case of logical understatement in the argument. We can prove by stronger terms and look for what's *critical*. That's maximizing profits. Profits are revenues minus costs, so our strategy will maximize profits and/or minimize costs. A fact is that the drivers are elderly and accident-having. They sound expensive to insure, but we can't change that parameter. We can at least hope they have minimal accidents. Let's take that prediction as our filter to the answer choices.

Applying the filter: Our prediction exists in the form of answer choice (B). Choices (C) and (D) argue with the facts: this policy is for elderly drivers. Choice (A) describes an option that will cost more than (B), since Nationside will have to pay out more to cover accidents, so it's only better if we can jack up the revenues in (A) much higher than in (B). But the second sentence of the argument implies that we can't do that. So (A) is objectively inferior to (B) and is out. Choice (E) is similar to (A): if the drivers were rejected by other policies, it's probably because they are more expensive. Or, if that's outside knowledge that we're not supposed to bring to bear on this question, (E) is simply irrelevant. The correct answer is (B).

Elephants are one of few animal species with intelligence and a capacity for empathy similar to that of humans. They habitually bury their dead by placing sticks and leaves over a member of their herd that has died. They are not known to bury animals other than elephants, but in some cases they have mourned humans with which they had established a relationship, leading to the theory that elephants will bury other animals with which they have had a direct relationship, but only those animals. Surprisingly, however, elephants have been found to visit the burial locations of other elephants they never knew in life.

Which of the following, if true, most helps to explain the surprising finding?

○   The capacity of elephants to empathize extends to animals they did not personally know.
○   Elephants' rituals have the natural purpose of burying other elephants, but elephants will use them to bury other species.
○   Elephants have had regular direct relationships in life with animals that they have not been known to bury, such as birds.
○   Elephants who were previously members of a herd and known to that herd, especially males, may leave that herd and never return.
○   Elephants will bury and visit the graves of animals with which they can empathize, including animals they recognize as elephants and animals demonstrating a similar level of intelligence.

Elephant Burials

Elephants are one of few animal species with intelligence and a capacity for empathy similar to that of humans. They habitually bury their dead by placing sticks and leaves over a member of their herd that has died. They are not known to bury animals other than elephants, but in some cases they have mourned humans with which they had established a relationship, leading to the theory that elephants will bury other animals with which they have had a direct relationship, but only those animals. Surprisingly, however, elephants have been found to visit the burial locations of other elephants they never knew in life.

Which of the following, if true, most helps to explain the surprising finding?

○ The capacity of elephants to empathize extends to animals they did not personally know.
○ Elephants' rituals have the natural purpose of burying other elephants, but elephants will use them to bury other species.
○ Elephants have had regular direct relationships in life with animals that they have not been known to bury, such as birds.
○ Elephants who were previously members of a herd and known to that herd, especially males, may leave that herd and never return.
○ Elephants will bury and visit the graves of animals with which they can empathize, including animals they recognize as elephants and animals demonstrating a similar level of intelligence.

Explanation

Reading the question: This prompt starts off in a friendly manner but starts to get complicated near the end of the prompt. We can parse the prompt at the word "surprisingly." The surprise has two portions: before and after that word. The latter part is shorter, so we can start there. 2) Elephants visit the graves of stranger elephants. Why is that surprising? Because of everything before "surprisingly." Namely, because there is a theory that 1) they observe burials only of animals with which they've had a direct relationship—i.e., not stranger elephants. Point 1) involves burial of friends, while point 2) involves burial of strangers. A good explanation will connect to both points without contradicting them.

Applying the filter: Choice (A) touches on both 1) and 2), in that it may imply that strangers could be friends. However, Choice (A) introduces the idea of empathy without connecting it to *burial*. It's missing a critical phrase like, "and empathy is what motivates elephants to observe burial rituals." Another problem with (A) is that it doesn't explain why elephants bury some non-elephants, but not others. So (A) is out. Choices (B), (C), and (D) fail to touch on both points 1) and 2). Choice (B) essentially restates the mystery without adding any information. Choice (C) discusses animals that elephants do *not* bury, so it's not comparing points 1) and 2), which both involve burial. Choice (D) may be tempting, but it doesn't address the fact that elephants visited the graves elephants "they never knew in life," since (D) discusses elephants who were "previously members of a herd and known to that herd." It doesn't hit on any point of 2), stranger burials. Choice (E) connects to 1) and 2) and resolves the friend or stranger burial question. Namely, the true determinant of burial isn't friend or stranger; it's the ability to empathize, which can extend to known humans or unknown elephants. Comparing (E) with (A), we can see that it is much more explanatory. Unlike (A), (E) specifically connects empathy to the act of burial, and it also explains why elephants can empathize with some non-elephants but not others. The correct answer is (E).

Which of the following most logically completes the passage?

Archeologists believe a group of ancient tombs near the seaside town of Absuir, Egypt is home to the burial of the queen Cleopatra VII and her lover Mark Antony in the year 30 B.C. They base their judgment on the site's proximity to Alexandria and on the discovery of a partial mask showing a cleft chin reminiscent of Mark Antony, which, as is customary with burials of Egyptian rulers, would have been included with or near the mummified body at the time of the burial. Furthermore, _____.

○ miraculously, additional fragments of mask that were found scores of miles away in Cairo fit perfectly with the partial mask excavated at Abusir, together constituting a nearly perfect facial likeness of Mark Antony

○ Mark Antony is the only ruler in Egypt to have had the shape of cleft chin expressed on the partial mask, which always capture the facial features of the buried ruler accurately

○ a statue of two lovers in embrace, presumably the two rulers, was found near the partial mask and dated to the year 40 A.D.

○ it has been established beyond a doubt that Cleopatra and Mark Antony were not buried to the south of the country in the Valley of the Kings, which is by far the best-known set of tombs in Egypt

○ valuable coins inscribed with a faded woman's likeness that might be Cleopatra's were also discovered blanketing the partial mask

MARK'S MASK

Which of the following most logically completes the passage?

Archeologists believe a group of ancient tombs near the seaside town of Absuir, Egypt is home to the burial of the queen Cleopatra VII and her lover Mark Antony in the year 30 B.C. They base their judgment on the site's proximity to Alexandria and on the discovery of a partial mask showing a cleft chin reminiscent of Mark Antony, which, as is customary with burials of Egyptian rulers, would have been included with or near the mummified body at the time of the burial. Furthermore,

_____.

○ miraculously, additional fragments of mask that were found scores of miles away in Cairo fit perfectly with the partial mask excavated at Abusir, together constituting a nearly perfect facial likeness of Mark Antony

○ Mark Antony is the only ruler in Egypt to have had the shape of cleft chin expressed on the partial mask, which always capture the facial features of the buried ruler accurately

○ a statue of two lovers in embrace, presumably the two rulers, was found near the partial mask and dated to the year 40 A.D.

○ it has been established beyond a doubt that Cleopatra and Mark Antony were not buried to the south of the country in the Valley of the Kings, which is by far the best-known set of tombs in Egypt

○ valuable coins inscribed with a faded woman's likeness that might be Cleopatra's were also discovered blanketing the partial mask

EXPLANATION

Reading the question: We have a passage to complete logically. As with all logical continuation questions, it will be especially important to predict the correct answer. We see the word "furthermore" before the blank. That could introduce either additional evidence or an additional conclusion, but upon inspection, we see that it's introducing further evidence because it comes after the sentence, "They base their judgment on..." Meanwhile, the conclusion is the first sentence. So the blank will include either a new piece of evidence that Mark Antony was buried in this location, or a refinement or additional detail about the piece of information we already have—the partial mask. Most people would prefer the former possibility, but we would actually prefer the latter, what you could call "a mask evidence strengthener." We look for a mask evidence strengthener in the answer choices.

Applying the filter: Choice (A) is a mask evidence weakener, because it undermines the idea that we've nailed the mask to one location. So (A) doesn't pass the filter. Choice (B) is a mask evidence strengthener, so (B) passes the filter. (C) is a new piece of information and it's dated incorrectly anyway, so (C) is out. (D) is better than (C); it's not a mask strengthener, but rather a new piece of information. (E) is similar to (D); a new piece of evidence, not a mask strengthener. We're left at this point with (B), (D), and (E).

While Choices (D) and (E) lend strength to the argument, choice (B) is the most logical continuation of the passage. Choice (B) strengthens the main connection of the argument, which is between the mask and the rulers' burial location. And (B) is even so specific to say that masks "always capture the facial features of the buried ruler accurately," touching on a matter of supreme importance to the argument. Choice (D) is somewhat redundant, because the prompt has already indicated that a northern location is more likely, due to its proximity to Alexandria. Choice (E), unlike (B), doesn't strengthen the quality of the evidence that is the mask, and instead "piles on" new evidence of unclear merit: "faded coins." The correct answer is (B).

While our nation's law enforcement can search our bodily persons in public if they have just cause, they can search our homes only if they have a signed warrant. Therefore, our nation's law enforcement should be able to search our electronic communications only if they have a signed warrant.

The conclusion above would be more reasonably drawn if which of the following were inserted into the argument as an additional premise?

- ○ Our electronic communications are at least as private as our homes.
- ○ A search of a bodily person in public is more likely to discover something worthwhile to law enforcement than a search of electronic communications.
- ○ Hasty search of electronic communications, like that of homes, violates basic human rights.
- ○ In the experience of our nation's law enforcement, electronic communications are even more trustworthy sources of information than homes.
- ○ In terms of the criteria used to justify a search by law enforcement, electronic communications are more nearly comparable to homes than to bodily persons.

RIGHT TO SEARCH

While our nation's law enforcement can search our bodily persons in public if they have just cause, they can search our homes only if they have a signed warrant. Therefore, our nation's law enforcement should be able to search our electronic communications only if they have a signed warrant.

The conclusion above would be more reasonably drawn if which of the following were inserted into the argument as an additional premise?

○ Our electronic communications are at least as private as our homes.
○ A search of a bodily person in public is more likely to discover something worthwhile to law enforcement than a search of electronic communications.
○ Hasty search of electronic communications, like that of homes, violates basic human rights.
○ In the experience of our nation's law enforcement, electronic communications are even more trustworthy sources of information than homes.
○ In terms of the criteria used to justify a search by law enforcement, electronic communications are more nearly comparable to homes than to bodily persons.

EXPLANATION

In our approach, we can see that this argument is perfect for term matching. You might immediately sense the mismatch of terms, or you might have recognized the argument as one of those pseudo-syllogistic arguments, which are ripe for term matching.

Evidence Term	Matches?	Conclusion Term
Nation's law enforcement	=	Nation's law enforcement
Just cause	=	-
Signed warrant	=	Signed warrant
Homes (not bodily persons)	≠	Electronic communications

Note that, even though we have list the conclusion on the right side in these term-matching tables, you may find it easier to identify the conclusion first and fill in those terms first, since the conclusion is identifiable by its opinion-charged language.

In this case, the prompt mentions "electronic communications" for the first time in the conclusion. The fact that the term doesn't show up in the evidence statements hints at a missing logical bridge—in this case, it must be between "electronic communications" and "homes." If those two things are equivalent in all ways relevant to the argument, then the conclusion is logically drawn.

Applying the filter: (A), (D), and (E) all show some promise. Choices (A) and (D) both generate new problems by introducing out-of-scope concepts, unmatched terms: "private" and "trustworthy." (E) is incredibly exact in equating "electronic communications" and "homes" for the purposes of the argument.

Logical proof: we can use the negation test. If (E) were false, then electronic communications would *not* be more nearly comparable to homes than to bodily persons. They could be more comparable to bodily persons, and then they would be searchable without a warrant, and the argument would fall apart. Hence the non-negated (E) is indeed a premise of the argument. The correct answer is (E).

In harsh economic times, there is a shift in business from mainstream retail stores to discount retail stores as consumers aim to reduce their total monthly spending. For local discount stores, when unemployment rises or effective wages decline due to inflation or another cause, sales go up. By contrast, however, during periods of extreme economic hardship, business at discount stores stops improving and may even suffer.

Which of the following, if true, does most to explain the contrast described above?

○ During extreme economic hardship, businesses that are located near discount stores and which also cater to lower spending levels also suffer.
○ The lower overall levels of consumer spending are, the more discount stores will benefit.
○ When discount stores flourish, they may be able to hire additional staff and raise effective wages.
○ During extreme economic hardship, consumers may continue to reduce total spending even after they have shifted their purchases to the most economic outlets available.
○ Except during periods of extreme economic hardship, discount stores tend to thrive more in economies benefitting from a direct economic stimulus, which increases spending cash.

DISCOUNT HARDSHIP

In harsh economic times, there is a shift in business from mainstream retail stores to discount retail stores as consumers aim to reduce their total monthly spending. For local discount stores, when unemployment rises or effective wages decline due to inflation or another cause, sales go up. By contrast, however, during periods of extreme economic hardship, business at discount stores stops improving and may even suffer.

Which of the following, if true, does most to explain the contrast described above?

○   During extreme economic hardship, businesses that are located near discount stores and which also cater to lower spending levels also suffer.
○   The lower overall levels of consumer spending are, the more discount stores will benefit.
○   When discount stores flourish, they may be able to hire additional staff and raise effective wages.
○   During extreme economic hardship, consumers may continue to reduce total spending even after they have shifted their purchases to the most economic outlets available.
○   Except during periods of extreme economic hardship, discount stores tend to thrive more in economies benefitting from a direct economic stimulus, which increases spending cash.

EXPLANATION

   Reading the question: we notice that this is an "explain" question. There's not an argument here, but rather two facts separating by the phrase "by contrast." we try to sum up the contrast. It's that discount retail: 1) can do well in times of hardship, but 2) can also suffer in times of hardship. An explanation will contradict nothing so far and it will connect to both points, the dual success/failure.

   Applying the filter: Choice (A) doesn't address the dual success/failure aspect. Nor does (B). Choice (C) sounds promising; when discount stores are doing well, the costs of wages goes up; could that be enough to push their business down? But we look back at the prompt, and it says in the second part that "business at discount stores stops improving and may even suffer." It seems to be talking about the revenue side, not the cost side, especially given what precedes, and (C) doesn't explain that. Choice (D) works: consumers spend more at discount stores under some hardship, but less under severe hardship. Choice (E) discusses only one side of the contrast. The correct answer is (D).

Which of the following most logically completes the passage?

A tropical thorn forest was cleared and converted by humans into soybean fields. The loss of the original habitat poses a fatal threat to the area's population of cuis, which are wild guinea pigs. Ecologists originally estimated that the cuis in the area would vanish within four years. Two years year, the population of cuis is already cut in half, but it is unlikely that they will completely vanish from the region within the next two years, since _____.

- ○ the soybean farmers in the area intend to plant two crops of soybeans this year rather than the usual single crop
- ○ the original plans to clear additional nearby thorn forest have not been expanded in scope, as had been considered
- ○ the last cuis to remain alive are likely to be the most resilient
- ○ viscachas, a form of burrowing rodent also indigenous to thorn forests, have vanished from the area more slowly than expected
- ○ the local population of the maned wolf, a major predator of the cuis, has declined faster than predicted from the loss of habitat

Which of the following most logically completes the passage?

A tropical thorn forest was cleared and converted by humans into soybean fields. The loss of the original habitat poses a fatal threat to the area's population of cuis, which are wild guinea pigs. Ecologists originally estimated that the cuis in the area would vanish within four years. Two years year, the population of cuis is already cut in half, but it is unlikely that they will completely vanish from the region within the next two years, since _____.

○ the soybean farmers in the area intend to plant two crops of soybeans this year rather than the usual single crop
○ the original plans to clear additional nearby thorn forest have not been expanded in scope, as had been considered
○ the last cuis to remain alive are likely to be the most resilient
○ viscachas, a form of burrowing rodent also indigenous to thorn forests, have vanished from the area more slowly than expected
○ the local population of the maned wolf, a major predator of the cuis, has declined faster than predicted from the loss of habitat

EXPLANATION

Reading the question: since we have a logical continuation question, we will insist on predicting what goes in the blank, at least approximately, before turning to the answer choices.

Creating a filter: the cuis are endangered; half have vanished in the last two years, but the other half won't quite vanish in the next two year, because...something. Maybe the situation has slightly improved. We'll call our prediction "slightly improved situation" and turn to the answer choices.

Applying the filter: choices (B) and (E) both give us slightly improved situations. At first they seem equally good. Then we notice (B) uses the phrase "as had been considered." So (B) isn't an improved situation; it's a not-worsening situation. (E) is a better logical continuation, because the maned wolf has declined faster than predicted. None of the other answer choices involve an amendment to the prediction to explain why the cuis will hang on a little longer than expected. The correct answer is (E).

In the phenomenon known as blindsight, some people who have been diagnosed as completely blind through damage to their visual cortex retain the ability to make judgments and take actions that appear to require or demonstrate the use of sight, despite the fact that they consciously see nothing. Such an individual, if prompted, might catch a ball thrown to him, walk around obstacles without having been told obstacles are present, or guess with unusual accuracy whether an array of dots is moving or stationary. Individuals with blindsight are usually not surprised by these events and attribute them to coincidence.

Which of the following questions indicates the most serious weakness in the explanation described above?

- Why don't people who are blind since birth exhibit similar abilities through coincidence?
- Why are they not surprised by these events?
- Why do such individuals tend refuse to accept the suggestion that the events are not coincidence?
- If it feels like total blindness, but it is not functionally total blindness, is it still coincidence?
- If it's coincidental, then why does it happen repeatedly?

In the phenomenon known as blindsight, some people who have been diagnosed as completely blind through damage to their visual cortex retain the ability to make judgments and take actions that appear to require or demonstrate the use of sight, despite the fact that they consciously see nothing. Such an individual, if prompted, might catch a ball thrown to him, walk around obstacles without having been told obstacles are present, or guess with unusual accuracy whether an array of dots is moving or stationary. Individuals with blindsight are usually not surprised by these events and attribute them to coincidence.

Which of the following questions indicates the most serious weakness in the explanation described above?

○   Why don't people who are blind since birth exhibit similar abilities through coincidence?
○   Why are they not surprised by these events?
○   Why do such individuals tend refuse to accept the suggestion that the events are not coincidence?
○   If it feels like total blindness, but it is not functionally total blindness, is it still coincidence?
○   If it's coincidental, then why does it happen repeatedly?

Explanation

Reading the question: when we read this question, it may be difficult to avoid reading the answer choices, the questions, without having made a prediction first. But this impulse can be counterproductive, because **the less helpful the answer choices are, the more you'll need an exact filter, such as a prediction, to evaluate them.**

Creating a filter: the stem says, What's the most serious weakness in the explanation described above? We try to get more specific about what exactly the explanation is. It's the view of the individuals with blindsight. There are two things stated: they are not surprised, and they attribute their unusual abilities to coincidence. We're not sure whether both parts are the explanation or just the coincidence part. It must be the coincidence part: that's an opinion, whereas the lack of surprise is more a feeling. So, the right answer will undermine the idea that this is really happening by *coincidence*. That's our filter, the critical detail.

Applying the filter: Which answer choices undermine coincidence? Choice (A) does; it attacks the coincidence theory. (B) and (C) focus on the attitudes of the people with blindsight, not the coincidence explanation, so we will knock them out. (D) is trying to redefine what coincidence is, and it appears to take as granted that the individuals are not functionally totally blind, but they believe that they are. So (D) is out. Choice (E) does not attack the coincidence explanation. Coincidental events do happen repeatedly; some repetition, in and of itself, is not odd. It's rather that these coincidences happen so much more often than with people who are originally blind. That rules out (E) and leads us straight back to (A), which must be the correct answer. The correct answer is (A).

Last year, Company X reconfigured its direct sales team to include more experienced sales people. The company spent less time and money training the experienced sales staff than they had found necessary to do with the previous, less experienced staff and they obtained equal direct sales results to the previous year. The more experienced sales staff, however, received higher financial compensation, and what Company X saved on training costs was less than the additional expenditure of financial compensation. Company X concluded that the reconfiguration strategy would not increase profits in the future.

Which of the following would it be most useful to know in order to evaluate the argument?

- Whether there is a method of sales training that would be generally more effective and less expensive
- Whether the more experienced sales staff worked fewer hours
- Whether the training provided by Company X is more expensive than other companies' sales training
- Whether the company could spend less on training the more experienced staff in the future it would have to spend on less experienced staff, without sacrificing any direct sales
- Whether the less experienced sales staff had more passion for their work

VETERAN SALES STAFF

Last year, Company X reconfigured its direct sales team to include more experienced sales people. The company spent less time and money training the experienced sales staff than they had found necessary to do with the previous, less experienced staff and they obtained equal direct sales results to the previous year. The more experienced sales staff, however, received higher financial compensation, and what Company X saved on training costs was less than the additional expenditure of financial compensation. Company X concluded that the reconfiguration strategy would not increase profits in the future.

Which of the following would it be most useful to know in order to evaluate the argument?

- ○ Whether there is a method of sales training that would be generally more effective and less expensive
- ○ Whether the more experienced sales staff worked fewer hours
- ○ Whether the training provided by Company X is more expensive than other companies' sales training
- ○ Whether the company could spend less on training the more experienced staff in the future it would have to spend on less experienced staff, without sacrificing any direct sales
- ○ Whether the less experienced sales staff had more passion for their work

EXPLANATION

Reading the question: we have an argument, a prediction about the future based on how things have gone after this switch to more experienced salespeople. The question stem asks for what "would be most useful to know"; we will prove by stronger terms and find an assumption central to the argument. Nothing is more useful to know in evaluating an argument than whether its key assumption is correct. A couple of assumptions do come to mind: maybe more experience salespeople will improve their performance faster than the less experienced staff would have. Maybe they will turn over less often. Maybe, though they are more expensive now, their salaries will rise less slowly. So we're expecting an assumption that involves "more experienced improving faster," in terms of performance, or salary, or something else.

Applying the filter: Only (D) matches our filter. Choice (A) does not differentiate between more and less experienced salespeople, so it's immaterial to the prediction the argument is making. (B) and (E) don't address why things might be any better in the future than they have been this past year under the more experienced team. Choice (C) is an irrelevant comparison.

Logical proof: the word "whether" is a clue that we can establish logical proof through analysis by cases. We can consider two extremes. If (D) is true, the company could, for example, simply not train the new salespeople at all when hiring experienced salespeople; if turnover is large, that could save a lot of money and improve the outcome. And if (D) is *not* true, it's a further reason to agree with the prediction in the argument. The correct answer is (D).

Management: Our position relative to our main competitor, which is located in the country of Patrio, has improved this year. The Patrian government has placed steep tariffs on imported steel, forcing our competitor to buy steel from sources inside the country at a much higher price. We can conclude that their costs have increased greatly this year, to levels much higher than ours, and they will be forced to deplete their cash reserves, leaving them with less cash in reserve than we will to spend on marketing next year.

Which of the following conclusions is best supported by these comments about the management about its company and its competitor in Patrio?

○   Prior to this year, the competitor in Patrio had cash reserves no greater than those of the management's company.
○   The management's company and its competitor in Patrio have no other major competitors.
○   The management's company and its competitor in Patrio primarily market steel.
○   Prior to this year, the competitor in Patrio was in a position superior to the management's company.
○   This year, the revenues obtained by the competitor in Patrio declined considerably.

WEAKENED COMPETITOR

Management: Our position relative to our main competitor, which is located in the country of Patrio, has improved this year. The Patrian government has placed steep tariffs on imported steel, forcing our competitor to buy steel from sources inside the country at a much higher price. We can conclude that their costs have increased greatly this year, to levels much higher than ours, and they will be forced to deplete their cash reserves, leaving them with less cash in reserve than we will to spend on marketing next year.

Which of the following conclusions is best supported by these comments about the management about its company and its competitor in Patrio?

- ○ Prior to this year, the competitor in Patrio had cash reserves no greater than those of the management's company.
- ○ The management's company and its competitor in Patrio have no other major competitors.
- ○ The management's company and its competitor in Patrio primarily market steel.
- ○ Prior to this year, the competitor in Patrio was in a position superior to the management's company.
- ○ This year, the revenues obtained by the competitor in Patrio declined considerably.

EXPLANATION

Reading the question: the phrase "best supported by" is an example of test maker's understated language, as discussed in New Exercise system. So we have a filter; we can prove by stronger terms, looking for a correct answer that is not just *supported* by the prompt, but logically *required* by it. We can't be certain that there will be such an answer choice, but if there is, it will be certainly correct.

Applying the filter: We'll go out of order. Choice (B) need not be true based on the argument; the existence of other competitors is completely unrelated. Choice (B) is out. (C) is probably false; steel appears to be an input to their businesses, not a good, but we don't really have definitive information to defend (C). Choice (C) is out. Choice (D) need not be true. The relative position of the company speaking has improved, but they don't say from what position. Choice (E) need not be true. We know that steel costs go up, but we don't even know what the source of revenue for the competitor is, so we don't know that they even changed, much less declined considerably.

Logical proof: We are left with (A). Might this be logically required by the argument? We can attempt the negation test. If the competitor had a *massive* cash reserve, it might still have more cash than the speaker's company after taking a hit this year. So, if the conclusion is true, there is an upper limit on the cash that the other company has on hand. And, since we don't know how much it's depleted by, for the argument to be correct no matter what, the competitor's reserves must be no higher than ours in the prior year, as stated by (A). Answer choice (A), indeed, is well supported by the prompt. The correct answer is (A).

The council of Shelbyville, which wants to avoid overly depleting the surrounding forest through exports of lumber, is considering subsidizing the import of certain kinds of wood to offset partly the deforestation. Such a step could actually put the forest in more severe danger, since insects often get into wood and can be introduced as a highly destructive force into habitats where they are non-native. Moreover, in the vast majority of cases in which a lumber-exporting city has become a lumber-importing city, the forest surrounding that city has been wiped out a couple years after the switch.

The answer to which of the following would be most useful for evaluating the argument above?

- Have lobbyists representing the lumber industry in other cities successfully campaigned against subsidizing imports?
- Would it be feasible for a town that depends on lumber exports to import a significant fraction of the wood it uses?
- Did the other cities that switched to lumber importing do so because they had deforested the areas within reach of the city?
- What proportion of lumber jobs in Shelbyville would be lost from subsidies of lumber imports?
- Are the other cities that made the switch to imported lumber in similar climates?

STOPPING DEFORESTATION

The council of Shelbyville, which wants to avoid overly depleting the surrounding forest through exports of lumber, is considering subsidizing the import of certain kinds of wood to offset partly the deforestation. Such a step could actually put the forest in more severe danger, since insects often get into wood and can be introduced as a highly destructive force into habitats where they are non-native. Moreover, in the vast majority of cases in which a lumber-exporting city has become a lumber-importing city, the forest surrounding that city has been wiped out a couple years after the switch.

The answer to which of the following would be most useful for evaluating the argument above?

○ Have lobbyists representing the lumber industry in other cities successfully campaigned against subsidizing imports?
○ Would it be feasible for a town that depends on lumber exports to import a significant fraction of the wood it uses?
○ Did the other cities that switched to lumber importing do so because they had deforested the areas within reach of the city?
○ What proportion of lumber jobs in Shelbyville would be lost from subsidies of lumber imports?
○ Are the other cities that made the switch to imported lumber in similar climates?

EXPLANATION

Reading the question: the argument is not exactly airtight; it can probably be attacked in a number of ways. Arguments on Critical Reasoning questions tend to be flawed, since the questions tend to ask us to identify flaws. But any argument, even a good one, is prone to attack, and more difficult Critical Reasoning questions will tend to feature better-constructed arguments.

Creating a filter: The question stem has the classic understated testmaker's language. We can prove by stronger terms and interpret the phrase "what's most useful for evaluating" as what's *critical* for evaluating. And we have another shortcut, since there's a causal argument here. It's in the last sentence, which roughly asserts that switching from exporting to importing lumber causes a city's forest to go away (presumably because they introduced insects). Our expectation is that there might be "another cause" of the export-import switch, but regardless, we'll look for something on which the argument depends.

Applying the filter: Do any answer choices deal with "cause of export-import switch"? (C) does and (E) might. Choice (C), now that we look closer, is one of our specific expectations; it's a causality flip; switching to imports didn't cause deforestation; rather, deforestation led cities to import lumber. That makes a tremendous amount of sense and, if true, would deal a major blow to the argument, because the truth about other cities would have no connection to the insects.

Logical proof: We apply the negation test. If (C) is negated, cities *didn't* make the switch to import because they were deforested. That possibility would strengthen the argument by removing a major problem. If we have time, we could confirm that the other answer choices are not material to the argument by considering them in negated form. The correct answer is (C).

Download the free CR Strategy Sheets at GMATFree.com/CR-Strategy-Sheets

The founders of a new company believe they have developed a new standard of DVD that will display movies at far higher fidelity than any other existing standard. While they recognize that the benefits of the new technology may not be sufficient to induce the entire market to adopt the new player and disc formats, they predict that format will be worth the cost of adoption in commercial venues that show movies on large screens, where the improvement in quality would be quite noticeable.

Which of the following, if true, would most weaken the conclusion drawn above?

- The brand reputation of the current technology for movie filming is so strong that it is unlikely to be displaced in the near future for home viewing.
- Sound quality is important to commercial venues that show movies on large screens, and the sound quality of movies on the new technology would not be improved.
- The cost of the new system is high and would take even a major commercial venue several months to offset with improved business.
- Commercial venues can adopt the new technology easily only if the movies they want to show are available on the new disc format.
- Patrons of commercial venues that show movies on large screens may not appreciate the quality of the new format until they see it in person.

NEW DVD STANDARD

The founders of a new company believe they have developed a new standard of DVD that will display movies at far higher fidelity than any other existing standard. While they recognize that the benefits of the new technology may not be sufficient to induce the entire market to adopt the new player and disc formats, they predict that format will be worth the cost of adoption in commercial venues that show movies on large screens, where the improvement in quality would be quite noticeable.

Which of the following, if true, would most weaken the conclusion drawn above?

o   The brand reputation of the current technology for movie filming is so strong that it is unlikely to be displaced in the near future for home viewing.
o   Sound quality is important to commercial venues that show movies on large screens, and the sound quality of movies on the new technology would not be improved.
o   The cost of the new system is high and would take even a major commercial venue several months to offset with improved business.
o   Commercial venues can adopt the new technology easily only if the movies they want to show are available on the new disc format.
o   Patrons of commercial venues that show movies on large screens may not appreciate the quality of the new format until they see it in person.

EXPLANATION

Reading the question: we get a plan, and we have to choose what will most weaken the idea that the plan will work.

Creating a filter: the correct answer is likely not just to undermine the conclusion, but the logic of the argument. That involves quality, the new player and format, and large screens. The argument says that the new player and format are worth it because of the quality benefit on the large screens. The best weakener of this argument as a whole is likely to weaken that specific connection. We look for such a format-quality-screen weakener in the answer choices.

Applying the filter: (A) doesn't mention anything we're looking for. (B) doesn't, because "quality" is about sound quality. So (A) and (B) are out. (C) doesn't pertain to the connection we're interested in. Moreover, we're not expected to believe that there is a low cost to installation, but rather that the installation will be worth the cost, and maybe recouping in several months is not so bad. (D) is better; if movies aren't available in the new format, then improved visual quality might not merit switching to the new format. (D) is objectively superior because it alone undermines the logical connection in the argument between improved visual quality and being worth the switch. It does it somewhat indirectly, but since it hampers the conditions under which the switch can be adopted. (E) is not necessarily a problem for the argument. The correct answer is (D).

A minority but influential investor in Quell has recently claimed that **the company's stock is undervalued,** citing as evidence the announced plan of Quell's CEO, who is the majority shareholder, to sell the company within a short period of time. According to the minority investor, the CEO is permitting or even encouraging an undervalued stock price so that he may get the company sold and liquidate his stake in the company. By accusing the CEO of having personal motives allow the stock price to become distorted, however, the minority investor is **guilty of the precise accusation that he himself is making.** This investor is known for using his influence to attempt to sway public opinion and meddle in otherwise well-calibrated deals in order to drive up share prices for his personal financial benefit.

In the argument given, the two boldfaced portions play which of the following roles?

- ○ The first states the position that the argument as a whole opposes; the second provides reasoning to undermine the support for the position being opposed.
- ○ The first states the position that the argument as a whole opposes; the second is reasoning that has been used to support the position being opposed.
- ○ The first states the position that the argument as a whole opposes; the second states the conclusion of the argument as a whole.
- ○ The first is reasoning that has been used to support a position that the argument as a whole opposes; the second provides information to undermine the force of that reasoning.
- ○ The first is reasoning that has been used to support a position that the argument as a whole opposes; the second states the conclusion of the argument as a whole.

VOCAL SHAREHOLDERS

A minority but influential investor in Quell has recently claimed that **the company's stock is undervalued,** citing as evidence the announced plan of Quell's CEO, who is the majority shareholder, to sell the company within a short period of time. According to the minority investor, the CEO is permitting or even encouraging an undervalued stock price so that he may get the company sold and liquidate his stake in the company. By accusing the CEO of having personal motives allow the stock price to become distorted, however, the minority investor is **guilty of the precise accusation that he himself is making.** This investor is known for using his influence to attempt to sway public opinion and meddle in otherwise well-calibrated deals in order to drive up share prices for his personal financial benefit.

In the argument given, the two boldfaced portions play which of the following roles?

- The first states the position that the argument as a whole opposes; the second provides reasoning to undermine the support for the position being opposed.
- The first states the position that the argument as a whole opposes; the second is reasoning that has been used to support the position being opposed.
- The first states the position that the argument as a whole opposes; the second states the conclusion of the argument as a whole.
- The first is reasoning that has been used to support a position that the argument as a whole opposes; the second provides information to undermine the force of that reasoning.
- The first is reasoning that has been used to support a position that the argument as a whole opposes; the second states the conclusion of the argument as a whole.

EXPLANATION

Reading the question: the boldfaced text immediately gives away how this question will work. We don't need to analyze the argument; we need only identify the logical role of each sentence.

Sentence	Starts With.../Includes...	Function
1st	**"the company's stock is undervalued"**	Opinion (bold), evidence
2nd	"According to the minority investor"	Elaboration
3rd	"the minority investor is **guilty**"	Contrary opinion
4th	"known for using his influence"	Evidence for 2nd opinion

Creating a filter: The first bold portion gives an opinion, and the second one gives a contrary opinion. The author of the argument believes the second opinion. That's our filter.

Applying the filter: we look for these results in the answer choices. Judging the answer choices just up to the semicolons, we keep (A) through (C) and we toss out (D) and (E); the first statement is a position, not reasoning. Looking at the latter half for choices (A) through (C), we target (C), the only one that identifies the second boldfaced portion as an opinion. To confirm this, we reconfirm that the last sentence of the paragraph is not an opinion. The phrase "this investor is known" highlights that sentence as mutually agreed upon and hence a fact. The correct answer is (C).

Some companies that consume large quantities of oil keep their own oil reserves for years in which average oil prices are exceptionally high. Thus, at times when oil prices are quite high, they can partially deplete their reserves, using oil that they bought earlier at lower prices, with the intention of buying oil to add back to their reserves when average oil prices are lower. Nevertheless, last year, when average oil prices were astronomically high throughout the year for geopolitical reasons, not all of these companies partially depleted their reserves.

Which of the following, if true, best explains why not all of these companies partially depleted their reserves?

○ Oil prices were also high the previous two years, so these companies expected oil prices to continue to be high.

○ Also for geopolitical reasons, many of these companies had lower-than-average demand for their services last year and required less oil for their operations.

○ Some of these companies, which have some ability to influence the opinion of other oil buyers, expected oil prices to drop in following years.

○ Although oil prices were astronomical on average, some of these companies were able to buy the oil they needed at lower, acceptable prices.

○ The practice of partially depleting reserves did occur on average, but without all companies individually partially depleting their reserves.

RESERVE USAGE

Some companies that consume large quantities of oil keep their own oil reserves for years in which average oil prices are exceptionally high. Thus, at times when oil prices are quite high, they can partially deplete their reserves, using oil that they bought earlier at lower prices, with the intention of buying oil to add back to their reserves when average oil prices are lower. Nevertheless, last year, when average oil prices were astronomically high throughout the year for geopolitical reasons, not all of these companies partially depleted their reserves.

Which of the following, if true, best explains why not all of these companies partially depleted their reserves?

- o Oil prices were also high the previous two years, so these companies expected oil prices to continue to be high.
- o Also for geopolitical reasons, many of these companies had lower-than-average demand for their services last year and required less oil for their operations.
- o Some of these companies, which have some ability to influence the opinion of other oil buyers, expected oil prices to drop in following years.
- o Although oil prices were astronomical on average, some of these companies were able to buy the oil they needed at lower, acceptable prices.
- o The practice of partially depleting reserves did occur on average, but without all companies individually partially depleting their reserves.

EXPLANATION

Reading the question: the prompt is a bit hefty, so we go to the question stem. This is an "explain" question. So there will be two things in seeming contradiction. We look for the transition from thing 1) to thing 2): the word "nevertheless." Thing 2) is shorter, so we start there. The mystery is that companies did not deplete their reserves even when prices were high. Why is that so crazy? Thing 1) will tell us: it's because companies keep their reserves for this purpose, so they can overall buy at lower prices. We will paraphrase the mystery as: "didn't use when high." The correct answer will resolve the mystery and be compatible with all of the facts in the prompt.

Applying the filter: (A) sounds reasonable to us at first as an explanation. But the prompt leads us to understand that companies would still want to deplete their reserves even if prices will be high in the future. If they thought prices would be higher next year, that would be a good reason to wait, but (A) doesn't say that. (A) is out. (B) doesn't explain "didn't use when high"; even if they need less oil than usual, they would still save by not having to buy when price are high. (B) is out. (C) doesn't explain "didn't use when high"; it gives a *further* reason for them to use now, so as not to buy now and save the buying for when prices are better. (C) is out. (D) is a good explanation for "didn't use when high"; companies generally *did* use when high, on average, but not all companies had to. It's a surprise solution but consistent with the data in the prompt. (D) is in. (E) is quite similar to (D) and quite close, but it's not as good an explanation.

Logical proof: we can analyze by cases to see that (D) is superior to (E). Namely, (E) could still be true even if prices were high for all companies involved; in such a case, (E) would limit the mystery, but it wouldn't explain the mystery. The correct answer is (D).

In the face of consumer demands, many agricultural companies in this country have stopped growing genetically modified strains of some of their crops and resumed growing unmodified strains of those crops. Clearly less genetically modified produce is being farmed in this country as a result of this switch than would have been farmed if those companies had continued to produce the genetically modified variants.

Which of the following, if true, most strengthens the argument above?

- Many of the farms that have switched at least partly to the unmodified crops have increased their output.
- By meeting consumer demands, companies will sell the unmodified version of a particular crop more successfully than they will sell the genetically modified version of that crop.
- More farming cost is incurred by farming the unmodified version of a particular crop than by farming the genetically modified version.
- The companies that have switched to unmodified versions of some crops have not altered how much farmland they use to grow each type of crop.
- The production of the new amount of unmodified produce did not require as inputs any more modified produce than the new amount of unmodified produce had replaced.

DECLINE OF GMOS

In the face of consumer demands, many agricultural companies in this country have stopped growing genetically modified strains of some of their crops and resumed growing unmodified strains of those crops. Clearly less genetically modified produce is being farmed in this country as a result of this switch than would have been farmed if those companies had continued to produce the genetically modified variants.

Which of the following, if true, most strengthens the argument above?

○ Many of the farms that have switched at least partly to the unmodified crops have increased their output.
○ By meeting consumer demands, companies will sell the unmodified version of a particular crop more successfully than they will sell the genetically modified version of that crop.
○ More farming cost is incurred by farming the unmodified version of a particular crop than by farming the genetically modified version.
○ The companies that have switched to unmodified versions of some crops have not altered how much farmland they use to grow each type of crop.
○ The production of the new amount of unmodified produce did not require as inputs any more modified produce than the new amount of unmodified produce had replaced.

EXPLANATION

Reading the question: we have to strengthen this argument, and as usual, the easiest way to strengthen will be first to weaken.

Creating a filter: Some companies have switched from genetically modified crops to non-modified. And, as a result, the argument goes, less genetically modified produce is being farmed than would otherwise be the cause. We can start with a basic relevance filter, and, hopefully, clean up with the negation test.

Applying the filter: What answer choices are connected to less genetically modified production? Choice (A) does not; it seems to focus on whether we are producing more unmodified than modified, but that's not the argument. Choice (B) concerns sale, not production, and has no implications for production, so (B) is out. Similarly, (C) concerns cost, not production, and is out. Similarly, (D) concerns farmland, not production, and is out. Choice (E) at least discusses production.

Logical proof: to confirm choice (E), we use the negation test. What if the new levels of unmodified produce required *massive* inputs of modified produce? For example, if unmodified produce was generated with modified seed or modified fertilizer? In that case, the argument would be damaged. The negated (E) critically damages the argument, so the un-negated (E) is a true strengthener. The correct answer is (E).

The country of Paisi has generally relied on growing soybeans as an export. Recently, the ministry of agriculture has implemented a system to reduce dependence on this single crop by encouraging farmers to grow other legumes. Paisi currently grows more non-soy legumes each year than it consumes, and exports of soybeans are in decline, due to competition from suppliers in other nations. If these trends continue, Paisi's ability to export other legumes is likely to grow in the near future.

Which of the following would it be most useful to establish in evaluating the argument?

○   When, if ever, will the growth of non-soy legumes in Paisi surpass production of soybeans?
○   Is Paisi among the countries that export soybeans most?
○   What proportion of Paisi's agricultural exports consists of crops other than legumes?
○   Is the quantity of non-soybean legumes consumed in other countries each year increasing?
○   Have any existing soybean plots in Paisi already been converted to growing other legumes?

BEAN EXPORTS

The country of Paisi has generally relied on growing soybeans as an export. Recently, the ministry of agriculture has implemented a system to reduce dependence on this single crop by encouraging farmers to grow other legumes. Paisi currently grows more non-soy legumes each year than it consumes, and exports of soybeans are in decline, due to competition from suppliers in other nations. If these trends continue, Paisi's ability to export other legumes is likely to grow in the near future.

Which of the following would it be most useful to establish in evaluating the argument?

- ○ When, if ever, will the growth of non-soy legumes in Paisi surpass production of soybeans?
- ○ Is Paisi among the countries that export soybeans most?
- ○ What proportion of Paisi's agricultural exports consists of crops other than legumes?
- ○ Is the quantity of non-soybean legumes consumed in other countries each year increasing?
- ○ Have any existing soybean plots in Paisi already been converted to growing other legumes?

EXPLANATION

Reading the question: The question stem asks for an assumption. The conclusion is the last sentence. The critical piece of evidence is the preceding sentence; the prior sentences are primarily intro. Paisi has extra legumes to sell; that seems like a good reason why they could export them. Secondarily, the fact that soybeans are in decline is given as a reason. That connection is weaker: is the competition in non-legumes as strong as it is in soybeans? If it is, the argument has a big problem. We'll look for that.

Applying the filter: None of the answer choices address whether the competition in non-legumes as strong as it is in soybeans, but (D) is similar.

Logical proof: We try negating (D): say the quantity of non-soy legumes in other countries was decreasing. Say the amount imported by them was zero! That would destroy the argument. Hence, (D) pertains to a critical assumption and is the correct answer. The correct answer is (D).

Which of the following most logically completes the argument?

Loans extended from banks to individuals can allow individuals to take well-measured financial risks or pay off existing debts that carry higher interest rates. However, more aggressive banks extend freely to individuals loans that are too large for those individuals to pay back foreseeably, causing other problems. Therefore, the creation of a new department to monitor and restrict banks would benefit public well-being, since _____.

- ○ the new department would aim to restrict only aggressive lending
- ○ aggressive banks cause individuals to establish less overall debt than credit card companies do
- ○ other banks, while not aggressive, may still ultimately extend more total dollars in loans to individuals than aggressive banks
- ○ the loans of aggressive banks to borrowers other than individuals, such as businesses, can also cause problems
- ○ other measures to curb aggressive banks might have the inadvertent effect of preventing deserving individuals from getting the loans they need

AGGRESSIVE LOANS

Which of the following most logically completes the argument?

Loans extended from banks to individuals can allow individuals to take well-measured financial risks or pay off existing debts that carry higher interest rates. However, more aggressive banks extend freely to individuals loans that are too large for those individuals to pay back foreseeably, causing other problems. Therefore, the creation of a new department to monitor and restrict banks would benefit public well-being, since _____.

- ○ the new department would aim to restrict only aggressive lending
- ○ aggressive banks cause individuals to establish less overall debt than credit card companies do
- ○ other banks, while not aggressive, may still ultimately extend more total dollars in loans to individuals than aggressive banks
- ○ the loans of aggressive banks to borrowers other than individuals, such as businesses, can also cause problems
- ○ other measures to curb aggressive banks might have the inadvertent effect of preventing deserving individuals from getting the loans they need

EXPLANATION

Reading the question: we see that we have logical completion exercise. If more than one answer choice seems like a logical continuation, there will be clues in the sentence that make one logical continuation more logical, objectively superior to the other ones.

Creating a filter: the blank is part of the conclusion of the argument, marked by the word "therefore," but it comes after the word "since." It's a piece of evidence mentioned within the conclusion. Most logically, it will not introduce a random new piece of evidence, but will rearticulate the evidence that has been given above. Specifically, it will do so in the context of the conclusion sentence—in terms of the recommendation for the new department. So what belongs in the bank is something about how this new department is a great idea because right now the some loans are great, but others are harmful, and the situation is uncontrolled. So we expect something in the blank like "needs control."

Applying the filter: which answer choices are in line with that prediction? Too many, we find. We need to be more specific. What needs controlling? The bad banks, specifically. (A) matches that. (A) is in. (B) seems to match that, but then introduces credit cards out of nowhere, so (B) is out. (C) does not focus on the bad banks and is out. (D) focuses on bad banks, but a different practice they have other than what we are talking about, so it's out. (E) is fairly logical, especially after (B) through (D). But (E) really gives a reason why establishing a new department is a better way of curbing bad banks than other ways. That's not material to the conclusion, which is that establishing the new department "would benefit public well-being." (E) skips the point by saying that the new department would be avoid side problems without talking about why it would be good for its aim. The correct answer is (A).

Since publicly traded companies opt to shield some negative information about their company from the market, negative information tends to be shared progressively less and in wider communication channels of a company's organization. The public is, therefore, has less negative information about a publicly traded company than do the company's employees of the most private circles, such as the CEO.

The conclusion drawn above is based on the assumption that

- o positive information flows freely through the communication channels of a publicly traded company
- o employees of a publicly traded company never leak private information about that company to the market
- o CEOs and other members of the most private circles of a publicly traded company are willing to distort the perceived truth about the company in order to defend the company's share price
- o the public obtains negative information about a public company only from sources within that company
- o the public wants all relevant information about a publicly traded company, positive and negative

Inside Information

Since publicly traded companies opt to shield some negative information about their company from the market, negative information tends to be shared progressively less and in wider communication channels of a company's organization. The public is, therefore, has less negative information about a publicly traded company than do the company's employees of the most private circles, such as the CEO.

The conclusion drawn above is based on the assumption that

- ○ positive information flows freely through the communication channels of a publicly traded company
- ○ employees of a publicly traded company never leak private information about that company to the market
- ○ CEOs and other members of the most private circles of a publicly traded company are willing to distort the perceived truth about the company in order to defend the company's share price
- ○ the public obtains negative information about a public company only from sources within that company
- ○ the public wants all relevant information about a publicly traded company, positive and negative

Explanation

In our initial approach, a prediction of the answer may not spring to mind. Here we can make use of the fact that, **on questions asking for an assumption, the answer choices can always be evaluated with the negation test or analysis by cases.** If we apply the test correctly, we won't need a filter.

Logical proof: If (A) is negated, the conclusion is truer, if anything. So (A) is out. We'll negate (B); even if employees leak information sometimes, if it's shared progressively less as it propagates outward, the argument is still true, because the leak was either on the outside and there was less info to leak, or it leaked near the center but got muffled on the way to the outside. So (B) is out. We negate (C); if CEOs were unwilling to distort information, that wouldn't hurt the argument, because the information could still be "shielded"; (C) is not very relevant. (C) is out. We like (D), we skip forward and swiftly call (E) irrelevant. Back to (D), our favorite. We'll negate it: if the public obtains information from outside the company—maybe lots of information or superior information, even—then the public doesn't necessary have less negative information. (D) is evidently a critical assumption. The correct answer is (D).

Because they can craft objects of a new design without having extrusion fittings custom-designed for that purpose, **3D printers have an application in building prototypes of new models of objects long before those new models are on production lines,** and it was on this basis that they first captured the interest of the market. However, suitability for prototyping does not limit 3D printers to prototyping, and in fact their capability to craft items without specialized fittings for each design can allow them, in essence, to be the production line. **3D printers have this natural application to mass-production in part because they can produce items at a cost competitive with that of production lines.**

In the argument given, the two portions in boldface play which of the following roles?

○ The first and the second each describe evidence that has been used to challenge the position that the argument seeks to establish.
○ The first is evidence that forms the basis for an objection to the position that the argument seeks to establish; the second is that position.
○ The first is evidence that forms the basis for an objection to the position that the argument seeks to establish; the second is a consideration that is introduced to counter the force of that evidence.
○ The first and the second each provide evidence in support of the position that the argument seeks to establish.
○ The first provides evidence in support of the position that the argument seeks to establish; the second is that position.

Because they can craft objects of a new design without having extrusion fittings custom-designed for that purpose, **3D printers have an application in building prototypes of new models of objects long before those new models are on production lines,** and it was on this basis that they first captured the interest of the market. However, suitability for prototyping does not limit 3D printers to prototyping, and in fact their capability to craft items without specialized fittings for each design can allow them, in essence, to be the production line. **3D printers have this natural application to mass-production in part because they can produce items at a cost competitive with that of production lines.**

In the argument given, the two portions in boldface play which of the following roles?

○   The first and the second each describe evidence that has been used to challenge the position that the argument seeks to establish.
○   The first is evidence that forms the basis for an objection to the position that the argument seeks to establish; the second is that position.
○   The first is evidence that forms the basis for an objection to the position that the argument seeks to establish; the second is a consideration that is introduced to counter the force of that evidence.
○   The first and the second each provide evidence in support of the position that the argument seeks to establish.
○   The first provides evidence in support of the position that the argument seeks to establish; the second is that position.

EXPLANATION

Reading the question: we see boldfaced sentences, so we're certain that the question will involve identifying the logical roles of the sentences. We confirm this by checking out the question stem. Then we will go through the argument and identify the logical role of each sentence, not bothering to analyze the argument further.

Sentence	Starts With.../Includes...	Function
1st	**"3D printers have an application"**	Evidence, evidence
2nd	"However, suitability for prototyping"	Partial contradiction
3rd	**"3D printers have this natural application"**	Support to the partial contradiction

Creating a filter: the word "however" signals a shift in perspective. Both boldfaced portions are supporting statements; the first supports the first opinion (which is implicit), and the second supports the second opinion, which contradicts the first to some degree. We have our answer prediction.

Applying the filter: (A), (D), and (E) all express the statements as on the same side of the argument, so they are all out. We're left with (B) and (C). We can see (B) is wrong because of its latter portion; the second boldfaced statement does not express a position, but rather an explanation supporting the second position. So (C) must be the answer. We can confirm this. The "position that the argument seeks to establish" is that 3D printers can function as a production line. Indeed, the first statement is the basis for the first opinion, the objection to the idea that the 3D printers can be the production line. And the second, though we might not have phrased it in this way, is a consideration that is introduced to counter of the force of that evidence—namely, they can be mass-production even though they are good at prototyping. The correct answer is (C).

While is true that effects of disease have been overlooked in its history, the ancient kingdom of People X began to collapse because of the violence, not the new diseases, brought by explorers. This much is evident from the fact that the kingdom first fell in the south, in the region under attack by explorers, and only later in the northern part of the kingdom.

Which of the following, if true, would most strengthen the argument above?

○ There was a pause in violence after the explorers' attack on the south and before the attack on the north, and during this period, the condition of the kingdom did not appreciably worsen.

○ The northern portion of the kingdom was not substantially weakened until after the explorers attacked that region.

○ The north of the kingdom was well armed and well fortified, whereas the south was vulnerable to attack.

○ The south and the north of the kingdom were equally susceptible to the new diseases introduced into the region.

○ Armed conflict took more lives of People X than did disease.

CRUMBLING KINGDOM

While is true that effects of disease have been overlooked in its history, the ancient kingdom of People X began to collapse because of the violence, not the new diseases, brought by explorers. This much is evident from the fact that the kingdom first fell in the south, in the region under attack by explorers, and only later in the northern part of the kingdom.

Which of the following, if true, would most strengthen the argument above?

- There was a pause in violence after the explorers' attack on the south and before the attack on the north, and during this period, the condition of the kingdom did not appreciably worsen.
- The northern portion of the kingdom was not substantially weakened until after the explorers attacked that region.
- The north of the kingdom was well armed and well fortified, whereas the south was vulnerable to attack.
- The south and the north of the kingdom were equally susceptible to the new diseases introduced into the region.
- Armed conflict took more lives of People X than did disease.

EXPLANATION

Reading the question: we read about the ancient kingdom of People X. The conclusion here is that violence, not disease, brought them down. The evidence concerns the order in which the parts of the country collapsed. To strengthen this argument, we'll want to strengthen the logical connection between the geographical evidence and the attribution of violence over disease. For example, maybe disease also struck first in the part that fell first to violence? That would undermine the connection. We look for something relevant to this geography-attribution question.

Applying the filter: choice (D) is pretty close to the specific prediction we had in mind. The other answer choices are tempting. Choices (C) and (E) both give comparisons that are not material to whether violence or disease initiated the problems. We focus on that phrase in the prompt—*began* the attack. Choices (A) and (B) are talking about beginning the attack, so they are both out.

Logical proof: we can analyze choice (D) by extreme cases. If the regions of the country were equally susceptible to disease, then it would be less likely that one part would fall first, as was the case. That would, indeed, strengthen the explanation that violence caused the downfall in the south. Consider the contrary: if, say, the south was much more susceptible to the diseases, then the south could have fallen first, due to disease, not violence, and the presence of violence would be a coincidence. So (D) strengthens the argument. The correct answer is (D).

The year after a company whose success depends on product innovation has a profitable year, it invests more cash in its research and development department to attempt to generate innovations that can ensure future success. Therefore, companies whose success depends on product innovation should generate more innovations during the years following profitable years of business than during years following unprofitable years of business.

Which of the following, if true about a company whose success depends on product innovation during the year after a profitable year, casts the most serious doubt on the conclusion drawn above?

- ○ Its employees ask for higher wages than they do at other times.
- ○ Its management participates more in research and development and makes process alterations.
- ○ Its research and development team members propose more project ideas that the company does not have time to act on than usual.
- ○ Its management increases monetary team rewards for successful innovation.
- ○ Its innovations increase in quantity, but have a higher rate of failure when applied to the market.

R&D Investment

The year after a company whose success depends on product innovation has a profitable year, it invests more cash in its research and development department to attempt to generate innovations that can ensure future success. Therefore, companies whose success depends on product innovation should generate more innovations during the years following profitable years of business than during years following unprofitable years of business.

Which of the following, if true about a company whose success depends on product innovation during the year after a profitable year, casts the most serious doubt on the conclusion drawn above?

- ○ Its employees ask for higher wages than they do at other times.
- ○ Its management participates more in research and development and makes process alterations.
- ○ Its research and development team members propose more project ideas that the company does not have time to act on than usual.
- ○ Its management increases monetary team rewards for successful innovation.
- ○ Its innovations increase in quantity, but have a higher rate of failure when applied to the market.

Explanation

Reading the question: The first sentence is a fact and the second provides an opinion. We have another pseudo-syllogistic argument, so we can parse it by term matching:

Evidence Term	Matches?	Conclusion Term
Companies whose success depends on product innovation	=	Companies whose success depends on product innovation
Year after profitable year	=	Year after profitable year
Invest more in R&D	≠	Should generate more innovations

The kinds of companies and the timing of the actions in question both match up well. The mismatch is in the last row, especially between the verbs "invest" and "generate." Even if it's a fact that they invest in R&D the year after a good year, does that mean that they should *generate* more innovations the year after a good year? Maybe not; maybe the results are not so accurately timed, and/or occur after a delay. That's our weakener.

Applying the filter: our filter does not show up exactly as expected. But we're looking for yes on the investing and no on the generating, a failure to generate. Choices (A), (C), and (E) all sound negative, but don't necessarily impede the company's ability to generate the innovations. We're left with (B) and (D). (D), if anything, might help generating innovations. Choices (B) could be helpful or harmful, but it's the only one left. And if the "processes" have been "altered," they could be worse. The correct answer is (B).

In early civilizations, the development of the first calendar system often coincided with the advancement of mathematics and astronomy. Granted, the practice of studying celestial bodies also gave rise to astrology and religion, which often had the effect of slowing the progress of the former two areas. Nevertheless, it's by no means impossible that these partly contradictory human pursuits had a common cause, or at least a common contributing cause. **Therefore, in all likelihood, the advancement of agrarian science, which motivated the development of measuring seasons and time, led to improved understanding of mathematics and astronomy in early civilizations.**

In the argument given, the two boldfaced portions play which of the following roles?

- ○ The first is a claim that the argument disputes; the second is a conclusion that has been based on that claim.
- ○ The first is a claim that has been used to support a conclusion that the argument accepts; the second is that conclusion.
- ○ The first is evidence that has been used to support a conclusion for which the argument provides further evidence; the second is the main conclusion of the argument.
- ○ The first is a finding whose implications are at issue in the argument; the second is a claim presented in order to argue against deriving certain implications from that finding.
- ○ The first is a finding whose accuracy is evaluated in the argument; the second is evidence presented to establish that the finding is accurate.

In early civilizations, the development of the first calendar system often coincided with the advancement of mathematics and astronomy. Granted, the practice of studying celestial bodies also gave rise to astrology and religion, which often had the effect of slowing the progress of the former two areas. Nevertheless, it's by no means impossible that these partly contradictory human pursuits had a common cause, or at least a common contributing cause. **Therefore, in all likelihood, the advancement of agrarian science, which motivated the development of measuring seasons and time, led to improved understanding of mathematics and astronomy in early civilizations.**

In the argument given, the two boldfaced portions play which of the following roles?

o   The first is a claim that the argument disputes; the second is a conclusion that has been based on that claim.
o   The first is a claim that has been used to support a conclusion that the argument accepts; the second is that conclusion.
o   The first is evidence that has been used to support a conclusion for which the argument provides further evidence; the second is the main conclusion of the argument.
o   The first is a finding whose implications are at issue in the argument; the second is a claim presented in order to argue against deriving certain implications from that finding.
o   The first is a finding whose accuracy is evaluated in the argument; the second is evidence presented to establish that the finding is accurate.

EXPLANATION

Reading the question: we see boldfaced text, so we know (and can confirm) that the question will require us only to identify the logical role of the various parts of the prompt.

Sentence	Starts With.../Includes...	Function
1st	**"In early civilizations"**	Fact
2nd	"Granted"	Fact, somewhat contradictory
3rd	"Nevertheless"	Fact, somewhat reconciling
4th	**"Therefore"**	Opinion

Creating a filter: The first three sentences present facts. The final sentence is the opinion, introduced by "therefore." So we have "boldface 1 equals fact and 2 boldface equals opinion."

Applying the filter: Choices (A) and (B) are out, because they call 1 a claim. (E) is out because it calls the second statement evidence. We're left with (C) and (D). According to (C), the first statement supports the conclusion. Is that true? No; (D) is correct. The first statement talks about attributing math development to the development of a calendar, but the final opinion attributes math to agrarian science. The correct answer is (D).

Last year, Energy Corp's oil sales increased suddenly in the region of lower Ossamia. The Chief Financial Officer of the company explained this increase as the result of industrialization in the developing Ossamian nation of Kokua. He predicts that, consequently, trade made possible by industrialization will grow between Kokua and its Ossamian neighbors this year, leading to further increases in Energy Corp sales in the region.

Each of the following, if true, provides some support for the CFO's prediction described above EXCEPT:

○ Although non-Ossamian countries have a military and trade presence in Ossamia, their oil sales last year in the region were not significantly above normal levels.
○ Mines accessing Kokua's rich natural resources were put into operation for the first time last year.
○ Each of the Ossamian countries currently have few restrictions in place on the business that can be done with its neighboring countries.
○ One of Energy Corp's primary competitors had a tanker accident early last year that caused environmental damage in Ossamia and damaged the company's standing in the area.
○ One of Ossamia's neighbors, a developing nation, has a growing population with a reasonable amount of disposable wealth.

OIL PROJECTION

Last year, Energy Corp's oil sales increased suddenly in the region of lower Ossamia. The Chief Financial Officer of the company explained this increase as the result of industrialization in the developing Ossamian nation of Kokua. He predicts that, consequently, trade made possible by industrialization will grow between Kokua and its Ossamian neighbors this year, leading to further increases in Energy Corp sales in the region.

Each of the following, if true, provides some support for the CFO's prediction described above EXCEPT:

○   Although non-Ossamian countries have a military and trade presence in Ossamia, their oil sales last year in the region were not significantly above normal levels.
○   Mines accessing Kokua's rich natural resources were put into operation for the first time last year.
○   Each of the Ossamian countries currently have few restrictions in place on the business that can be done with its neighboring countries.
○   One of Energy Corp's primary competitors had a tanker accident early last year that caused environmental damage in Ossamia and damaged the company's standing in the area.
○   One of Ossamia's neighbors, a developing nation, has a growing population with a reasonable amount of disposable wealth.

EXPLANATION

Reading the question: we review the prompt, which contains a causal argument and also a prediction. The easiest thing to do will be to strengthen and/or weaken the prediction using the most common error of causation, introducing a new, real, cause. The question is whether X really causes Y, where X is industrialization in the country and Y is an increase in oil sales.

Applying the filter: (A) doesn't even concern the relevant countries, so it's not a strengthener and may be the correct answer. Choice (B) sounds like industrialization, which would make it a mild strengthener as the cause of oil sales, and hence not the answer. Choice (C) is a mild strengthener—few restrictions will allow oil sales to grow freely. Choice (D) is a strengthener, because it will help establish that Energy Corp and not its competitors will be able to reap benefits. Choice (E) is a mild strengthener, because it suggests there is a buyer of the oil. The correct answer is (A).

A study this year found that, among citizens of Patria whose tax reports were selected at random for an audit, 21% had prepared their taxes with the assistance of a tax accountant. However, among those whose audits uncovered indications of potential tax fraud, only 3% had prepared their taxes with the assistance of a tax accountant. Clearly, citizens of Patria who prepare their taxes without the assistance of a tax accountant are more likely to commit tax fraud.

The conclusion drawn above depends on which of the following assumptions?

- ○ Citizens who commit tax fraud with the assistance of a tax accountant are less likely to caught by an audit.
- ○ Citizens whose records have indications of potential tax fraud are more likely to commit tax fraud than those whose records do not.
- ○ Tax accountants will ensure that their clients file taxes that are not fraudulent.
- ○ Some citizens who choose to prepare their taxes without the assistance of a account do so in order to conceal tax fraud.
- ○ Citizens who prepare their taxes with the assistance of an accountant do so in order to avoid accidentally committing tax fraud.

LIKELY TAX FRAUD

A study this year found that, among citizens of Patria whose tax reports were selected at random for an audit, 21% had prepared their taxes with the assistance of a tax accountant. However, among those whose audits uncovered indications of potential tax fraud, only 3% had prepared their taxes with the assistance of a tax accountant. Clearly, citizens of Patria who prepare their taxes without the assistance of a tax accountant are more likely to commit tax fraud.

The conclusion drawn above depends on which of the following assumptions?

○ Citizens who commit tax fraud with the assistance of a tax accountant are less likely to caught by an audit.
○ Citizens whose records have indications of potential tax fraud are more likely to commit tax fraud than those whose records do not.
○ Tax accountants will ensure that their clients file taxes that are not fraudulent.
○ Some citizens who choose to prepare their taxes without the assistance of a account do so in order to conceal tax fraud.
○ Citizens who prepare their taxes with the assistance of an accountant do so in order to avoid accidentally committing tax fraud.

EXPLANATION

Reading the question: we're given an argument to pick apart. Term matching is a good candidate for any argument, but especially pseudo-syllogistic arguments such as this one, so we can create our filter by looking for a mismatch of terms:

Evidence Term	Matches?	Conclusion Term
In study	≈	In general
Citizens of Patria whose tax reports were selected at random for an audit	≈	Citizens of Patria
Preparing taxes with/without accountant	=	Preparing taxes with/without accountant
Indications of potential tax fraud	≠	More likely to commit tax fraud

Creating a filter: the first two rows highlight the same basic point, which is that, if the study has been conducted in a way such that it is not representative of the population of Patria as a whole, then the audit would be questionable. However, we've been told that the citizens selected for the audit were selected "at random," so they are most likely representative of the population. The most basic mismatch is the final one: the term in the conclusion "more likely to commit tax fraud" matches up imprecisely with the concept in the evidence "indications of potential tax fraud." For example, maybe it's typical to demonstrate indications of tax fraud and not commit fraud; maybe the indications are poor predictors overall of whether these people are actually *committing* the tax fraud more. There's our filter.

Applying the filter: we look for an answer choice that expresses this connection and find (B).

Logical proof: we can use the negation test to see whether (B) is critical to the argument. What if citizens whose records have indications of potential tax fraud are *not at all* more likely to commit tax fraud? Indeed, then the argument collapses, the higher incidence of these indications then would not constitute evidence of a higher rate of tax fraud in any group. The correct answer is (B).

A new café intends to open and offer to its patrons unusual beverages served in an unusual atmosphere. Prior to beginning construction on its location, it had already secured funding based on the quality of its beverages, which it served to potential investors. But when it conducted intensive tests to gauge the interest of potential customers, it tested not whether they liked the beverages, but whether they liked descriptions of the café's atmosphere.

Which of the following, if true, best accounts for the new café's approach to conducting tests with potential customers?

○ Investors are unlikely to invest substantial amounts of capital in a café whose own managers are skeptical about the commercial prospects of the beverages they are selling.
○ The potential customers are not likely to be able to envision how initial designs of the café and later designs of the atmosphere might differ.
○ If a new café succeeds, the commercial benefits will accrue largely to the investors, not to the patrons, of the café.
○ After opening its first location, the café will easily be able to make adjustments to the unusual beverages, but it will not be able to make adjustments to the location's unusual atmosphere.
○ Potential customers are unlikely to be able to predict which of the beverages at the café will be the most popular.

UNUSUAL CAFÉ

A new café intends to open and offer to its patrons unusual beverages served in an unusual atmosphere. Prior to beginning construction on its location, it had already secured funding based on the quality of its beverages, which it served to potential investors. But when it conducted intensive tests to gauge the interest of potential customers, it tested not whether they liked the beverages, but whether they liked descriptions of the café's atmosphere.

Which of the following, if true, best accounts for the new café's approach to conducting tests with potential customers?

○   Investors are unlikely to invest substantial amounts of capital in a café whose own managers are skeptical about the commercial prospects of the beverages they are selling.
○   The potential customers are not likely to be able to envision how initial designs of the café and later designs of the atmosphere might differ.
○   If a new café succeeds, the commercial benefits will accrue largely to the investors, not to the patrons, of the café.
○   After opening its first location, the café will easily be able to make adjustments to the unusual beverages, but it will not be able to make adjustments to the location's unusual atmosphere.
○   Potential customers are unlikely to be able to predict which of the beverages at the café will be the most popular.

EXPLANATION

Reading the question: in our initial approach, we might look first at the question stem. It specifically asks about the café's approach to testing with potential customers. The central issue is why they tested not the beverages but they *did* test the atmosphere. Evidently 1) the beverage does not need testing. And 2) the atmosphere needs testing. An explanation will touch on both points. And, definitely, the atmosphere needs testing more than the beverages do. That would be the ideal; a comparison of atmosphere and beverages establishing that atmosphere in more in need of testing. We can use that as our filter.

Applying the filter: Choice (A) doesn't involve a comparison of beverage and atmosphere, so we hold it in contempt. Choice (A) is out. Choice (B) is awkwardly phrased, comparing a café with its atmosphere, but it doesn't compare directly or indirectly with the beverages. Choice (B) is out. (C) is quite immaterial to the comparison; out. (D) is brilliant because it actually compares the beverages and the atmosphere. (D) is in. (E) does not involve a comparison. (E) is also nonsensical because customers don't have to make this prediction; the café owners are doing the "gauging," per the prompt. The correct answer is (D).

Analyst: In our nation's television news programs, the number of stories aired about armed conflicts in Africa was much lower last year than it had been previously. Many armed conflicts have been fully or partly resolved with ceasefire agreements, and others have lessened in intensity due to the fatigue of the combating forces, so it is probably that the low number of articles is due to a decline in armed conflict in Africa.

Which of the following, if true, most seriously undermines the analyst's argument?

○   Every story about armed conflict in Africa that was submitted to air last year was aired.
○   The time it takes to research, write, and air a journalistic report of an armed conflict has declined over the last several years.
○   The number of total stories aired on television news programs in the nation was the same last year as in previous years.
○   A single armed conflict can easily lead to newsworthy developments justifying a large number of stories aired on television.
○   Just prior to last year, several major news shows revised certain prohibitions against airing stories about armed conflict in Africa.

Analyst: In our nation's television news programs, the number of stories aired about armed conflicts in Africa was much lower last year than it had been previously. Many armed conflicts have been fully or partly resolved with ceasefire agreements, and others have lessened in intensity due to the fatigue of the combating forces, so it is probably that the low number of articles is due to a decline in armed conflict in Africa.

Which of the following, if true, most seriously undermines the analyst's argument?

○ Every story about armed conflict in Africa that was submitted to air last year was aired.
○ The time it takes to research, write, and air a journalistic report of an armed conflict has declined over the last several years.
○ The number of total stories aired on television news programs in the nation was the same last year as in previous years.
○ A single armed conflict can easily lead to newsworthy developments justifying a large number of stories aired on television.
○ Just prior to last year, several major news shows revised certain prohibitions against airing stories about armed conflict in Africa.

EXPLANATION

Reading the question: we can be pleased to see that we have what is essentially a causal argument: news coverage of Africa is down because armed conflicts have declined. Since we have a causal argument, we know that we can create a filter using the concept of "another cause."

Creating a filter: we can imagine another cause to explain the lower number of articles. For example, maybe something closer to our nation's hearts has been going on since then and it has seized the stage and that's the real reason coverage of Africa is down. We paraphrase what we're looking for as "alternate cause of decreased coverage."

Applying the filter: Choices (A) through (C) strengthen the argument, as much as anything. (D) allows the causal relationship suggested to stand; it doesn't even bar the possibility that the news stations are out of articles. Choice (E) gives us what we're looking for: an alternative explanation.

Logical proof: we can use the negation test on choice (E). Negating (E), we can suppose, what if news shows had *not* changed any policies about showing these stories? In that case, policies at the news stations would not be an explanation for the decreased coverage. And then it would appear more likely that the cause attributed by the argument was correct. The negated (E) is a strengthener of the argument, so non-negated (E) is a weakener of the argument. The correct answer is (E).

Cattle rancher: The new government regulations requiring the testing of all cattle crossing state borders would cost cattle ranchers $1 billion annually. These regulations would damage the nation's economy.

Health regulator: Some of the $1 billion spent or lost by ranchers will be revenue for other businesses. Profits will be gained as well as lost.

The health regulator responds to the cattle rancher by

○ demonstrating that the rancher's conclusion is based on evidence that is not relevant to the issue at hand
○ challenging the plausibility of the evidence that serves as the basis for the rancher's argument
○ suggesting that the rancher's argument overlooks a mitigating consequence
○ reinforcing the rancher's conclusion by supplying a complementary interpretation of the evidence the rancher cites
○ agreeing with the main conclusion of the rancher's argument but construing that conclusion as grounds for optimism rather than for pessimism

CATTLE COST

Cattle rancher: The new government regulations requiring the testing of all cattle crossing state borders would cost cattle ranchers $1 billion annually. These regulations would damage the nation's economy.

Health regulator: Some of the $1 billion spent or lost by ranchers will be revenue for other businesses. Profits will be gained as well as lost.

The health regulator responds to the cattle rancher by

- demonstrating that the rancher's conclusion is based on evidence that is not relevant to the issue at hand
- challenging the plausibility of the evidence that serves as the basis for the rancher's argument
- suggesting that the rancher's argument overlooks a mitigating consequence
- reinforcing the rancher's conclusion by supplying a complementary interpretation of the evidence the rancher cites
- agreeing with the main conclusion of the rancher's argument but construing that conclusion as grounds for optimism rather than for pessimism

EXPLANATION

Reading the question: we get our task from the question stem. How does the health regulator respond to the cattle rancher? We note the answer choices: we're asked for the logical form of what the regulator is saying, not his actual point.

Creating a filter: The cattle rancher's point can be summed up with the words, "1 billion dollars." The regulator doesn't argue with 1 billion dollars; he redefines it; it's not all loss. We will paraphrase this as "redefine" and go to the answer choices looking for something like this.

Applying the filter: Scanning the beginning of the choices, we can eliminate based on some verbs. The regulator's not agreeing with the rancher, so (D) and (E) are out. He's not subtracting evidence from the situation, so (A) and (B) are out. He's adding information to the situation, through his redefinition. The correct answer is (C).

Which of the following most logically completes the argument?

This claim that homo habilis, homo rudolfensis and homo erectus, the three species previously identified as existing worldwide in the era of approximately 2 million years ago, might represent a single species, is considered tentative, since it is based on a single analysis in the journal *Science* of a single fossil specimen known as "skull 5." One evolutionary biologist predicts that a wealth of new articles will support this case in the coming year, but even if that prediction proves correct, the new articles will lend no support to the claim that the three species are in fact one, since _____.

- ○ only fossils can lend support to this claim, not articles about fossils
- ○ subsequent articles will expand upon and improve the argument presented in the original article in *Science*
- ○ the new articles will most likely construct new arguments based on fossils previously discovered and attributed to the three species
- ○ the new articles, like the original article, will most likely draw their conclusion from a single fossil record, "skull 5"
- ○ no articles prior to the original article in *Science* give any credibility to the claim that the three species might in fact be a single species

SKULL 5

Which of the following most logically completes the argument?

This claim that homo habilis, homo rudolfensis and homo erectus, the three species previously identified as existing worldwide in the era of approximately 2 million years ago, might represent a single species, is considered tentative, since it is based on a single analysis in the journal *Science* of a single fossil specimen known as "skull 5." One evolutionary biologist predicts that a wealth of new articles will support this case in the coming year, but even if that prediction proves correct, the new articles will lend no support to the claim that the three species are in fact one, since _____.

○ only fossils can lend support to this claim, not articles about fossils
○ subsequent articles will expand upon and improve the argument presented in the original article in *Science*
○ the new articles will most likely construct new arguments based on fossils previously discovered and attributed to the three species
○ the new articles, like the original article, will most likely draw their conclusion from a single fossil record, "skull 5"
○ no articles prior to the original article in *Science* give any credibility to the claim that the three species might in fact be a single species

EXPLANATION

Reading the question: we have a logical argument to complete. Although we intend to digest the argument, we will gloss over the technical terms at first. We have three species and then some opinion language at the phrases "might represent a single species" and "is considered tentative." First opinion: what we'll call the single-species theory. Second opinion: that of the biologist, the opinion that a wealth of articles is on the way in support of the single-species theory. Third opinion: that of the author of this paragraph, namely, that the wealth of articles will "lend no support" to the single-species theory. He's not exactly saying the theory is wrong; he's saying something closer to the fact that the wealth of articles will not be so valuable.

Creating a filter: given the third opinion, our crude prediction for the blank is something like, "the articles will be worthless." Maybe the single species theory is in vogue and insubstantial articles will be written about it.

Applying the filter: Choice (A) contradicts the prompt, since, if the claim about Skull 5 couldn't be supported by articles at all, then the status of the claim in question would be worse than "tentative." Choice (B) says the articles will *improve* the theory, so it's out. Choice (C), similarly, implies that the articles might be useful, so (C) is out. Choice (D) might match our prediction; these articles doesn't sound so useful. Choice (E) discusses *earlier* articles and is irrelevant. Everything is out except for (D). Choice (D) is not the most powerful argument imaginable, but it's logical: the new articles will not add credibility because they will be based on the same critical piece of evidence, Skull 5. Choice (D) would be better yet if it specified that the new articles would not analyze the skull in a substantially new way or otherwise advance the analysis of the skull, but that detail is not required. The correct answer is (D).

Disease X has afflicted cattle and cut into ranchers' profits. A genetic cause of the disease has been identified, as well as a gene therapy that can completely eradicate the cause of the disease in cattle. By applying this gene therapy to their cattle and eradicating the genetic susceptibility to the disease, ranchers will be able to carry on business in the future without incidence of Disease X in their cattle.

Which of the following is an assumption on which the argument depends?

○   The gene therapy will not cause any defects in cattle.
○   All cases of Disease X are equally severe.
○   There are no treatments of Disease X that are more effective than the gene therapy in question.
○   There are no diseases other than Disease X that currently threaten the cattle.
○   There are no precursors to or triggers of Disease X, genetic or otherwise, other than the one targeted by the new gene therapy.

CAUSE OF DISEASE X

Disease X has afflicted cattle and cut into ranchers' profits. A genetic cause of the disease has been identified, as well as a gene therapy that can completely eradicate the cause of the disease in cattle. By applying this gene therapy to their cattle and eradicating the genetic susceptibility to the disease, ranchers will be able to carry on business in the future without incidence of Disease X in their cattle.

Which of the following is an assumption on which the argument depends?

- ○ The gene therapy will not cause any defects in cattle.
- ○ All cases of Disease X are equally severe.
- ○ There are no treatments of Disease X that are more effective than the gene therapy in question.
- ○ There are no diseases other than Disease X that currently threaten the cattle.
- ○ There are no precursors to or triggers of Disease X, genetic or otherwise, other than the one targeted by the new gene therapy.

EXPLANATION

Reading the question: we learn about the deadly Disease X. Since we have a brief argument, we can use term matching here: what terms are left poorly matched between evidence and conclusion?

Evidence Term	Matches?	Conclusion Term
Disease X	=	Disease X
Ranchers	=	Ranchers
Gene therapy	=	Gene therapy
Completely eradicate the cause of the disease	≠	Will be able to carry on business in the future without incidence of the disease

Creating a filter: the last row gives us a mismatch. In the evidence, we have the phrase "completely eradicate the cause of the disease," and in the conclusion we have "will be able to carry on business in the future without incidence." This is the shaky logical connection. Maybe the therapy will have to be applied to each new generation of cattle? We look for something along the lines—it doesn't attack the therapy so much as the connection between therapy and no incidence in the future.

Applying the filter: (A) and (B) do not concern the connection between therapy and intended outcome. Neither do (C) and (D). Choice (E) is suggesting that there is some other cause of Disease X. In such a case, the therapy could work perfectly, but the intended outcome might not manifest. This might seem to contradict the prompt, at first; doesn't the prompt say that the therapy eradicates the cause? On closer inspection, we can see that the prompt says, "*A* [single] genetic cause of the disease has been identified..." The prompt leaves open the possibility that there is another cause of the disease, beyond the genetic one that has been identified and which is addressed by the therapy. The correct answer is (E).

Nanotechnology may pose risks in the coming decades as we find it increasingly commonplace to introduce small robots into our bodies. But the fact that these robots might be invisible to the naked eye doesn't mean we are helpless against them. After all, since the initial development of germ theory, we have designed and continuously improved upon ways to protect ourselves from a variety of germs.

In the passage, the author develops the argument by

- ○ forming the hypothesis that best explains several apparently conflicting pieces of evidence
- ○ reinterpreting evidence that had been used to support an earlier theory
- ○ using an analogy with a known phenomenon to draw a conclusion about an unknown phenomenon
- ○ speculating about how characteristics of small robots in the future might develop from characteristics of germs
- ○ pointing out differences between natural and human-made microscopic threats

SMALL ROBOTS

Nanotechnology may pose risks in the coming decades as we find it increasingly commonplace to introduce small robots into our bodies. But the fact that these robots might be invisible to the naked eye doesn't mean we are helpless against them. After all, since the initial development of germ theory, we have designed and continuously improved upon ways to protect ourselves from a variety of germs.

In the passage, the author develops the argument by

○ forming the hypothesis that best explains several apparently conflicting pieces of evidence
○ reinterpreting evidence that had been used to support an earlier theory
○ using an analogy with a known phenomenon to draw a conclusion about an unknown phenomenon
○ speculating about how characteristics of small robots in the future might develop from characteristics of germs
○ pointing out differences between natural and human-made microscopic threats

EXPLANATION

Reading the question: the stem of this question is unusual, since it asks how "the author develops the argument." It's worth a glance at the answer choices to determine their format. The answer choices are somewhat generalized descriptions of how the author has formed his argument. We can create a filter by starting with the opinion in the prompt.

Creating a filter: The conclusion of the argument doesn't really appear until the second sentence, with the opinion, "doesn't mean we are helpless against them." The "development" of the argument is simply the final sentence. This is a comparison with germ theory. We'd call it either a comparison or an example and will look for "comparison or example" in the answer choices.

Applying the filter: Looking at the first couple words of each answer choice, we're left with (C). Indeed, an analogy is a comparison. The "known" phenomenon is germ theory and the "unknown" phenomenon is nanotech. We confirm that the author is not doing the other things. The correct answer is (C).

The percentage of global tourists who visit Kokua has increased by five percentage points over the past three years. Since tourism contributes an estimated 7% of Kokua's gross domestic product, this increase is likely to have a positive impact on the economy of Kokua.

Which of the following, if true, most strengthens the argument given?

○ People who visit international destinations travel a much greater distance to their destination, on average, currently than such people did three years ago.
○ People are more likely to visit Kokua's neighbor countries for pleasure now than they were three years ago.
○ The number of people who travel internationally for pleasure has increased slightly over the past three years.
○ The percentage of people who choose to revisit an international tourist destination within a year of a given prior visit has increased dramatically in the last two years.
○ Kokua is the leading international tourist destination in its region.

TOURISTIC IMPACT

The percentage of global tourists who visit Kokua has increased by five percentage points over the past three years. Since tourism contributes an estimated 7% of Kokua's gross domestic product, this increase is likely to have a positive impact on the economy of Kokua.

Which of the following, if true, most strengthens the argument given?

o   People who visit international destinations travel a much greater distance to their destination, on average, currently than such people did three years ago.
o   People are more likely to visit Kokua's neighbor countries for pleasure now than they were three years ago.
o   The number of people who travel internationally for pleasure has increased slightly over the past three years.
o   The percentage of people who choose to revisit an international tourist destination within a year of a given prior visit has increased dramatically in the last two years.
o   Kokua is the leading international tourist destination in its region.

EXPLANATION

Reading the question: The question asks us to strengthen, so we will first attack. There are a number of points we can attack, but reasoning involving percentages tends to be erroneous, so we will focus there. We can filter for "*not* confusing numbers and percentages" as a strengthener.

Applying the filter: choices (A), (B), and (E) all fail to clarify the distinction between absolute number and percentage, so they fail to pass our filter. Choices (C) and (D) are close to the filter.

Logical proof: we can evaluate choice (C) by the negation test. What if the number of international travelers had *not* increased over the past three years? What if it had *plummeted*? That is in fact not accounted for by the prompt, and it would crush the argument. The percentage of the pie who visit Kokua is larger, but the pie is much smaller, so the actual number of visitors to Kokua could have greatly decreased. By ruling out that possibility, the non-negated (C) fixes a major flaw in the argument and is therefore a strengthener. Choice (D), which we liked at first, is still vulnerable to (C), as is the argument as a whole. The correct answer is (C).

Domestic agriculture is struggling because agriculture from overseas is available at lower prices. Since improved agrarian technology would enable domestic farmers to produce agriculture at more competitive costs, to improve the competitiveness of domestic agriculture, the government plans to subsidize domestic farmers, because as it pays subsidies directly to these domestic farmers, the farmers will have the funds they need to invest in technology.

Which of the following, if true, raises the most serious doubt regarding the effectiveness of the government's plan to improve the competitiveness of domestic agriculture?

- ○ The cost benefits of investing in agrarian technology could take several years to manifest.
- ○ Overseas farmers might have some competitive advantage over domestic farmers other than price competitiveness.
- ○ Domestic producers of agriculture have some incentive not use the subsidies to invest in agrarian technology.
- ○ The technological enhancement will be valid only for two years, after which competitors in other countries would have outpaced the capabilities of domestic agriculture.
- ○ The subsidies paid to domestic farmers will come out of national tax funds that would be better spent in other ways.

SUBSIDIZED FARMERS

Domestic agriculture is struggling because agriculture from overseas is available at lower prices. Since improved agrarian technology would enable domestic farmers to produce agriculture at more competitive costs, to improve the competitiveness of domestic agriculture, the government plans to subsidize domestic farmers, because as it pays subsidies directly to these domestic farmers, the farmers will have the funds they need to invest in technology.

Which of the following, if true, raises the most serious doubt regarding the effectiveness of the government's plan to improve the competitiveness of domestic agriculture?

- ○ The cost benefits of investing in agrarian technology could take several years to manifest.
- ○ Overseas farmers might have some competitive advantage over domestic farmers other than price competitiveness.
- ○ Domestic producers of agriculture have some incentive not use the subsidies to invest in agrarian technology.
- ○ The technological enhancement will be valid only for two years, after which competitors in other countries would have outpaced the capabilities of domestic agriculture.
- ○ The subsidies paid to domestic farmers will come out of national tax funds that would be better spent in other ways.

EXPLANATION

Reading the question: the prompt gives a plan, and the question stem asks us to cast doubt on the plan. We care about whether or not domestic agriculture improves in competitiveness. So we can use that as a basic filter and ask of each answer choice, "does or could domestic agriculture still improve in competitiveness?"

Applying the filter: choice (A) is irrelevant, because the domestic agriculture could still improve in competitiveness; the plan doesn't have a deadline. Choice (B) tells us that competitors might still have an advantage. But even then, the domestic agriculture may be in a better relative position that it was before; the gap has narrowed; it has improved. So (B) is out. Choice (C) looks promising; if domestic farmers pocket the money, domestic agriculture does *not* become more competitive. So choice (C) stays in. (D) is hardly great news, but the domestic agriculture could still improve in competitiveness. So (D) is out. We eliminate (E), also, since (E) raises considerations immaterial to whether the plan will work. We're left with (C).

Logical proof: we can apply the negation test to (C). If we negate (C), domestic producers of agriculture have *lots* of incentive to use the subsidies to invest in agrarian technology. In that case, the expectation that domestic agriculture would improve in competitiveness is strengthened. The fact that the negated (C) is a strengthener confirms that non-negated (C) is a weakener. The correct answer is (C).

Given that, recently, **the founders of startup company Zeddifreddo have confirmed that they are in the late stages of discussion of an acquisition offer from another company,** other potential acquirers of the company, who had suspected that Zeddifreddo's business performance was mostly hype and not a product of sound financials, have taken interest in making their own acquisition offers. They figure that, if Zeddifreddo's current potential acquirer has reached late stages of an acquisition discussion without having withdrawn its bid, that the acquirer must have had a chance to audit Zeddifreddo's financial position and has found it to be sound. Such reasoning might be hasty, however, since **potential acquirers of a startup have been known to overlook that company's financial soundness and favor the acquisition on other grounds, however ill-advised such a position may be.**

In the argument given, the two boldfaced portions play which of the following roles?

- The first describes evidence that has been taken as supporting a conclusion; the second gives a reason for questioning that support.
- The first describes evidence that has been taken as supporting a conclusion; the second states a contrary conclusion that is the main conclusion of the argument.
- The first provides evidence in support of the main conclusion of the argument; the second states that conclusion.
- The first describes the circumstance that the argument as a whole seeks to explain; the second gives the explanation that the argument seeks to establish.
- The first describes the circumstance that the argument as a whole seeks to explain; the second provides evidence in support of the explanation that the argument seeks to establish.

ZEDDIFREDDO'S ACQUISITION

Given that, recently, **the founders of startup company Zeddifreddo have confirmed that they are in the late stages of discussion of an acquisition offer from another company,** other potential acquirers of the company, who had suspected that Zeddifreddo's business performance was mostly hype and not a product of sound financials, have taken interest in making their own acquisition offers. They figure that, if Zeddifreddo's current potential acquirer has reached late stages of an acquisition discussion without having withdrawn its bid, that the acquirer must have had a chance to audit Zeddifreddo's financial position and has found it to be sound. Such reasoning might be hasty, however, since **potential acquirers of a startup have been known to overlook that company's financial soundness and favor the acquisition on other grounds, however ill-advised such a position may be.**

In the argument given, the two boldfaced portions play which of the following roles?

○ The first describes evidence that has been taken as supporting a conclusion; the second gives a reason for questioning that support.
○ The first describes evidence that has been taken as supporting a conclusion; the second states a contrary conclusion that is the main conclusion of the argument.
○ The first provides evidence in support of the main conclusion of the argument; the second states that conclusion.
○ The first describes the circumstance that the argument as a whole seeks to explain; the second gives the explanation that the argument seeks to establish.
○ The first describes the circumstance that the argument as a whole seeks to explain; the second provides evidence in support of the explanation that the argument seeks to establish.

EXPLANATION

Reading the question: we're in boldfaced territory, so we confirm from the question that our task here is to identify the logical roles played by the various sentences in the prompt.

Sentence	Starts With.../Includes...	Function
1st	"Given that **the founders...have confirmed**"	Supports view of other potential acquirers
1st	"who had suspected that..."	View of other potential acquirers
2nd	"they figure that..."	Supports view of other potential acquirers
3rd	"Such reasoning might be hasty, however,"	Contrary view
3rd	"since **potential acquirers...have been known**"	Supports contrary view

Creating a filter: opinion-charged words help parse the prompt into two views. Boldfaced portion #1 supports opinion #1, and boldfaced #2 supports opinion #2, which is a contrary opinion.

Applying the filter: (B) and (C) call sentence #2 a conclusion, so they are out. Choice (D) is out; the argument as a whole is not seeking to explain the fact that Zeddifreddo is in the late states of the acquisition, but rather what the late stage says about its financials. (E) is out for the same reason. We go back to confirm (A). The first sentence has indeed been taken as support that the company has sound financials, and the second sentence gives a reason to question it. The correct answer is (A).

Car dealerships in the state of Fairview have prospered over the term of the current governor: sales are up by 10 percent relative to four years ago. Nevertheless, car manufacturers have found that the proportion of credit they have extended to dealerships that was paid off on time, despite rising over the first two years of this period, has fallen sharply in the latter two years of the governor's term.

Which of the following, if true, most helps to explain the change between the first two and the second two years of the governor's term in the proportion of credit paid off on time?

○   There are essentially constant sources of demand for cars, such as local and state police departments, and sales to these sources have neither increased nor declined especially during the latter two years of the term.
○   Between the first two and the second two years of the term, dealerships in Fairview saw some or many of their costs, such as real estate and marketing, decrease.
○   New, less successful, dealerships have recently opened business in an attempt to profit from the health of car sales.
○   Dealerships in Fairview have made strategic business decisions in the second two years of the governor's term that are likely to hurt business outcomes.
○   The total amount of credit extended to dealerships by manufacturers decreased between the first two years of the governor's term and the second two years.

Car Dealer Credit

Car dealerships in the state of Fairview have prospered over the term of the current governor: sales are up by 10 percent relative to four years ago. Nevertheless, car manufacturers have found that the proportion of credit they have extended to dealerships that was paid off on time, despite rising over the first two years of this period, has fallen sharply in the latter two years of the governor's term.

Which of the following, if true, most helps to explain the change between the first two and the second two years of the governor's term in the proportion of credit paid off on time?

○ There are essentially constant sources of demand for cars, such as local and state police departments, and sales to these sources have neither increased nor declined especially during the latter two years of the term.

○ Between the first two and the second two years of the term, dealerships in Fairview saw some or many of their costs, such as real estate and marketing, decrease.

○ New, less successful, dealerships have recently opened business in an attempt to profit from the health of car sales.

○ Dealerships in Fairview have made strategic business decisions in the second two years of the governor's term that are likely to hurt business outcomes.

○ The total amount of credit extended to dealerships by manufacturers decreased between the first two years of the governor's term and the second two years.

Explanation

Reading the question: we dig into the argument. This question doesn't have much to do with the governor; just a four-year period. Sales are up over the last four years, but credit paid off was higher for two years and then much lower for two years. We need to explain 1) the drop in credit paid off on time. Above all, the correct explanation will accommodate the fact 2) sales have been up. We can use that simple fact as a basic relevance filter.

Applying the filter: (A) doesn't address explicitly or implicitly the fact that sales are up, so it doesn't pass the filter. Choice (B) is an anti-explanation; if costs went down in the latter two years, it should have been *easier* to pay off credit. Choice (C) is an explanation. It connects to both 1) and 2). We might have imagined that the body of dealerships was unchanging the whole time, but the argument didn't actually say that. Choice (D) ends up saying nothing because it only hints at a possible future outcome, not something affecting the last two years. (E) at least discusses credit and involves a change between the first two years and the second two years. But most likely extending less credit would lead to getting more of it paid off on time, not less. It's also unclear from (E) whether the credit is due during these periods, because we care not so much about when it's extended as whether it's paid when due during one period and the next. So (E) is out. The correct answer is (C).

Studies indicate that potential buyers of an expensive product are more likely to go through with their purchase if they have first made a purchase of a related product, such as an inexpensive product sold by the same company in the same place. Psychologists attribute this behavior to commitment bias, in which people's present actions are influenced by a desire to act consistently with their past actions. A company that sells expensive products will increase sales of these items by first inducing customers to buy inexpensive, easy-to-sell items.

Which of the following, if true, most strongly supports the interpretation of the studies?

○ The effect noted in the studies applies to purchases made both in person and online.
○ Customers who have already declared their intent to purchase one item from such a company will not act on their intention by purchasing an inexpensive product in place of an expensive product.
○ Not all companies that sell expensive products have inexpensive, easy-to-sell items available to sell.
○ Commitment bias has been found to be equally strong for purchase made by cash and by credit card.
○ The perception that buying an expensive product is consistent with a past purchase of an inexpensive item is strengthened if both of those products prominently feature the same company branding.

BUYERS' COMMITMENT

Studies indicate that potential buyers of an expensive product are more likely to go through with their purchase if they have first made a purchase of a related product, such as an inexpensive product sold by the same company in the same place. Psychologists attribute this behavior to commitment bias, in which people's present actions are influenced by a desire to act consistently with their past actions. A company that sells expensive products will increase sales of these items by first inducing customers to buy inexpensive, easy-to-sell items.

Which of the following, if true, most strongly supports the interpretation of the studies?

o   The effect noted in the studies applies to purchases made both in person and online.
o   Customers who have already declared their intent to purchase one item from such a company will not act on their intention by purchasing an inexpensive product in place of an expensive product.
o   Not all companies that sell expensive products have inexpensive, easy-to-sell items available to sell.
o   Commitment bias has been found to be equally strong for purchase made by cash and by credit card.
o   The perception that buying an expensive product is consistent with a past purchase of an inexpensive item is strengthened if both of those products prominently feature the same company branding.

EXPLANATION

Reading the question: The argument seems reasonable, which make a question difficult. The question asks us to strengthen this argument, and to do that we're going to have to be tough and weaken it. Supposing that we can't come up with a filter, we can move straight to the answer choices and use the negation test.

Logical proof: Choice (A) doesn't strengthen the argument itself. If we negate (A)—it applies only to in person, for example—sales might still go up somewhat, and the argument could still be true. So (A) is out. (C) doesn't strengthen the argument—it points out a problem. So (C) is not the answer. (D) is similar to (A) and out on similar grounds. (E) is out, which we can confirm by denying it and finding it's not relevant to the argument. That leaves us with (B). Negating (B) gives us: "Customers who have already declared their intent to purchase one item from such a company *will* act on their intention by purchasing an inexpensive product in place of an expensive product." This statement would mean people who are already committed to buy something buy the little thing, not the big thing. If that's true, that's a huge problem. So establishing the opposite point of the negation, as (B) does, does strengthen the argument. The correct answer is (B).

Professor: in one method of international conflict resolution, a nation that perceives itself to have been wronged by another nation should demand that conditions be met by the wrongdoing nation before negotiations between both parties can begin. If all countries behaved according to this method, countries in conflict would never succeed in beginning negotiations.

The professor's argument relies on which of the following assumptions?

○ No country truly acts in accordance with this method of international conflict resolution.
○ In conflict resolution, no country should announce conditions for negotiations.
○ International conflicts should be settled by an objective international third party.
○ No country in conflict with another country will meet any of that country's demands in advance of beginning negotiations.
○ Countries place conditions on negotiation so that those negotiations might ultimately be successful.

BEGINNING NEGOTIATIONS

Professor: in one method of international conflict resolution, a nation that perceives itself to have been wronged by another nation should demand that conditions be met by the wrongdoing nation before negotiations between both parties can begin. If all countries behaved according to this method, countries in conflict would never succeed in beginning negotiations.

The professor's argument relies on which of the following assumptions?

○ No country truly acts in accordance with this method of international conflict resolution.
○ In conflict resolution, no country should announce conditions for negotiations.
○ International conflicts should be settled by an objective international third party.
○ No country in conflict with another country will meet any of that country's demands in advance of beginning negotiations.
○ Countries place conditions on negotiation so that those negotiations might ultimately be successful.

EXPLANATION

Reading the question: with a quasi-syllogistic argument, this prompt may succumb to term matching. The last sentence is the conclusion. What terms in there are not matched properly to the evidence?

Evidence Term	Matches?	Conclusion Term
Nations that perceive themselves to have been wronged	≈	Countries in conflict
Beginning negotiations	=	Beginning negotiations
Demand that conditions be met before negotiations	=	"This method"

"Beginning negotiations" is properly matched. "This method," while vague on its own, is well matched with a reference on the other side. But "countries at conflict" does not precisely match with "a nation that perceives itself to have been wronged." Those two things are not necessarily the same. For example, the argument appears to assume that all countries in conflict perceive themselves to have been wronged by another nation. We have our filter.

Applying the filter leaves us with (D), which is similar to our filter, as it involves nations being standoffish always.

Logical proof: we can use the negation test. What if countries generally *do* meet other countries' demands in advance of beginning negotiations? Well, then, the argument would be quite wrong—countries *would* generally meet each other's demands, and then they *would*, in fact, start negotiations. The argument breaks if (D) is false; therefore, the argument indeed assumes that (D) is true. The correct answer is (D).

Recycled plastic lumber is a building material made from plastic bottles and other plastic waste. Unlike traditional lumber, it won't rot or absorb water, and it is highly resistant to insect damage, so it is well-suited for marine and outdoor applications. Recycled plastic lumber is worth considering as an alternative to traditional lumber for most building projects, with the exception of interior residential projects.

Which of the following, if true, most helps to explain the exception noted above?

○ Residential homes built entirely with recycled plastic lumber are virtually immune to damage from flooding.
○ Increased rates of thermal expansion and contraction of plastic lumber can cause doorways constructed of this material to warp and either fail to close or fail to seal tightly.
○ Currently 25 percent of the trash that is in landfills is plastic that could be used to produce recycled plastic lumber.
○ Because of its resistance characteristics, recycled plastic lumber does not need to be treated with chemicals, allowing homeowners to live in an interior space with lower levels of chemicals.
○ Seldom painted, plastic lumber comes in different colors that can be chosen by the consumer.

RECYCLED PLASTIC LUMBER

Recycled plastic lumber is a building material made from plastic bottles and other plastic waste. Unlike traditional lumber, it won't rot or absorb water, and it is highly resistant to insect damage, so it is well-suited for marine and outdoor applications. Recycled plastic lumber is worth considering as an alternative to traditional lumber for most building projects, with the exception of interior residential projects.

Which of the following, if true, most helps to explain the exception noted above?

○ Residential homes built entirely with recycled plastic lumber are virtually immune to damage from flooding.
○ Increased rates of thermal expansion and contraction of plastic lumber can cause doorways constructed of this material to warp and either fail to close or fail to seal tightly.
○ Currently 25 percent of the trash that is in landfills is plastic that could be used to produce recycled plastic lumber.
○ Because of its resistance characteristics, recycled plastic lumber does not need to be treated with chemicals, allowing homeowners to live in an interior space with lower levels of chemicals.
○ Seldom painted, plastic lumber comes in different colors that can be chosen by the consumer.

EXPLANATION

Reading the question: We read the prompt, which is rich in fact and low in opinion. We have to explain an "exception." The exception, evidently, is "interior residential projects." The objectively best answer will have to do with the fact that this plastic lumber won't rot, won't absorb water, and is highly resistant to insect damage. We will look for explanations that are relevant directly or indirectly to this information.

Applying the filter: We don't see our expectation, but we can broaden and use a basic filter. The point is that we shouldn't use this houses. (A), (C), (D), and (E) all fail to hit that basic point, while (B) does. Basic relevance was sufficient, in this case. The correct answer is (B).

Columnist: The chief of police has claimed in a recent press conference that the decline in the number of pickpockets caught on the street indicates that his department that has partly eliminated this petty crime. He might as well argue that because there are higher levels of fog over L.A., there are fewer stars in the night sky. The gentlemen of our police department, in all likelihood, have caught fewer acts of petty crime lately simply because their vigilance is haphazard, at best.

The columnist's statements, if true, best support which of the following as a conclusion?

- ○ Catching acts of petty crime requires vigilance above all.
- ○ It is possible to estimate roughly how many petty crimes are committed in the area through methods of inference.
- ○ Crimes unobserved due to negligence and stars unobserved due to fog stand in roughly equal proportion over time.
- ○ Rather than believe the chief of police, the people of the town should demand greater vigilance of the police force.
- ○ Pickpockets continue to carry on their petty crimes.

DECLINE IN PICKPOCKETS

Columnist: The chief of police has claimed in a recent press conference that the decline in the number of pickpockets caught on the street indicates that his department that has partly eliminated this petty crime. He might as well argue that because there are higher levels of fog over L.A., there are fewer stars in the night sky. The gentlemen of our police department, in all likelihood, have caught fewer acts of petty crime lately simply because their vigilance is haphazard, at best.

The columnist's statements, if true, best support which of the following as a conclusion?

o   Catching acts of petty crime requires vigilance above all.
o   It is possible to estimate roughly how many petty crimes are committed in the area through methods of inference.
o   Crimes unobserved due to negligence and stars unobserved due to fog stand in roughly equal proportion over time.
o   Rather than believe the chief of police, the people of the town should demand greater vigilance of the police force.
o   Pickpockets continue to carry on their petty crimes.

EXPLANATION

Reading the question: we read the statements of the columnist, which turn out to be a brief rant. We don't have to criticize what the columnist said; rather, we have to draw a conclusion. We can prove by stronger terms; most likely, the correct answer choice will be not only a good conclusion, but a *required* conclusion. Such a choice may not be the most natural conclusion, but it will be the most objectively flawless one. That's our filter.

Applying the filter: (A) does not follow from the prompt, which gives a lack of vigilance as a failure mode here, but not necessarily how we catch petty crime *above all*. (B) is neither indicated nor required by the argument. Same with (C). (D) sounds natural, but it need not be true. The columnist's point might be, for example, that we can't trust the chief at all, and need to demand his replacement. That leaves us with (E).

Logical proof: we can see that (E) must be true. If the police have caught fewer acts only because they haven't been trying as hard, then there are at least as many acts as before. We apply the negation test. Suppose that pickpockets do *not* carry on their petty crimes. Suppose there were no more pickpockets at all In that case, the decline in pickpocket cases cannot be attributed to poor vigilance. The correct answer is (E).

Astrology is considered by many a false science, but it is in fact a true field of science, because it uses scientific methods, such as the analysis of cause and effect and careful documentation of observations over time by many individuals.

The conclusion above is properly drawn if which of the following is assumed?

- ○ If a field of study can conclusively answer the questions it raises, then it is a genuine science.
- ○ Since astrology uses scientific methods, it will produce credible results.
- ○ Any enterprise that does not use the analysis of cause and effect and careful documentation of observations over time by many individuals is not genuine science.
- ○ If a field of study employs scientific methods, that field of study is true field of science, regardless of what that field of study might concern or conclude.
- ○ Since astrology depends on the observation of stars, it depends on the analysis of cause and effect and careful documentation of observations over time by many individuals.

FALSE SCIENCE

Astrology is considered by many a false science, but it is in fact a true field of science, because it uses scientific methods, such as the analysis of cause and effect and careful documentation of observations over time by many individuals.

The conclusion above is properly drawn if which of the following is assumed?

○ If a field of study can conclusively answer the questions it raises, then it is a genuine science.
○ Since astrology uses scientific methods, it will produce credible results.
○ Any enterprise that does not use the analysis of cause and effect and careful documentation of observations over time by many individuals is not genuine science.
○ If a field of study employs scientific methods, that field of study is true field of science, regardless of what that field of study might concern or conclude.
○ Since astrology depends on the observation of stars, it depends on the analysis of cause and effect and careful documentation of observations over time by many individuals.

EXPLANATION

Reading the question: this is a brief, pseudo-syllogistic argument, so we will use term matching.

Evidence Term	Matches?	Conclusion Term
Astrology uses scientific methods	≠	Astrology is a true field of science

The conclusion comes at the beginning of this argument; "Astrology is a true field of science" is the opinion that draws on the other facts for support. The improperly matched term is "true field of science." The most critical assumption is roughly, "A field that uses scientific methods is a true field of science." That statement or a variant of it, such as its contrapositive, is what we're expecting as the answer.

Applying the filter: (C) and (D) both have the right terms involved. Choice (D) matches our prediction. Choice (C) is the logical inversion of what we're looking for, so it is not correct.

Logical proof: We can prove choice (D) with the negation test. Say that employing scientific methods did *not* make that field of study is true field of science. In that case, the argument falls apart. Since the negation of (D) destroys the argument, (D) itself is assumed by the argument. The correct answer is (D).

A number of college students were recruited by the psychology department to participate in a paid, unspecified experiment, which turned out to be a menial, monotonous counting exercise. Unbeknownst to the students, half of the participants were paid a meager rate for their participation, while half received a generous rate. After the counting exercise was complete, each student was asked questions on his or her perception of the counting exercise. Surprisingly, the participants who had been paid less reported higher levels of enjoyment in completing the exercise than the higher-paid participants did.

Which of the following hypotheses, if true, best accounts for the findings of the experiment?

○ In both groups, the portion of the brain activated by counting was disrupted by the exercise and distorted perceptions of financial quantities.

○ Those who counted faster in the experiment experienced more satisfaction than those who counted more slowly.

○ The participants who were paid less had more motivation, conscious or unconscious, to justify their participation in the menial exercise.

○ The energy expenditure of counting in the human mind was associated with the cognitive load of worrying about a quantity of money.

○ Counting is most capably performed by accountants, whose level of satisfaction is highest while they are at work.

Monotonous Counting Exercise

A number of college students were recruited by the psychology department to participate in a paid, unspecified experiment, which turned out to be a menial, monotonous counting exercise. Unbeknownst to the students, half of the participants were paid a meager rate for their participation, while half received a generous rate. After the counting exercise was complete, each student was asked questions on his or her perception of the counting exercise. Surprisingly, the participants who had been paid less reported higher levels of enjoyment in completing the exercise than the higher-paid participants did.

Which of the following hypotheses, if true, best accounts for the findings of the experiment?

- In both groups, the portion of the brain activated by counting was disrupted by the exercise and distorted perceptions of financial quantities.
- Those who counted faster in the experiment experienced more satisfaction than those who counted more slowly.
- The participants who were paid less had more motivation, conscious or unconscious, to justify their participation in the menial exercise.
- The energy expenditure of counting in the human mind was associated with the cognitive load of worrying about a quantity of money.
- Counting is most capably performed by accountants, whose level of satisfaction is highest while they are at work.

Explanation

Reading the question: we read about the menial, monotonous counting exercise and learn that the participants who were paid less liked it more. How could this be possible? A prediction doesn't spring to mind. The key is that the correct answer will need to link 1) getting paid less with 2) higher levels of enjoyment. And it must do so without fighting any of the facts on the table.

Applying the filter: what answer choices do this? Most answer choices fail to connect to the first of the two parts, lower pay. In fact, (C) is the only answer choice that connects to points 1) and 2). Does it explain this situation? Yes: it gives a reason for unpaid individuals to state higher levels of enjoyment—exactly what we were looking for. The correct answer is (C).

Fund manager: over the last five years, the various stock funds managed by our company increased on average by 7 percent more in value than the market as a whole annually. Furthermore, the performance of each particular stock fund has not varied much from one year to the next, and our few investment products other than stock funds have stayed even with the market. These results show the success of our company: each year, most of our investment products have increased in value more than the market.

The debater's argument is most vulnerable to criticism on which of these grounds?

○ It takes for granted that the stock funds are typical of the company with regard to the average increase in value per year.

○ It takes for granted that if a certain average annual increase in value was obtained by each investment product, then each stock fund increased each year by approximately the same amount.

○ It confuses a claim from which the argument's conclusion about the company would necessarily follow with a claim that would follow from the argument's conclusion only with a high degree of probability.

○ It overlooks the possibility that even if, on average, the stock funds increased by an average annual value, many stock funds may have increased less than the market as whole.

○ It overlooks the possibility that even if most investment products at the company have increased in value more than the market this year, any one investment product may, in some years, fail to increase in value at all.

STOCK FUND PERFORMANCE

Fund manager: over the last five years, the various stock funds managed by our company increased on average by 7 percent more in value than the market as a whole annually. Furthermore, the performance of each particular stock fund has not varied much from one year to the next, and our few investment products other than stock funds have stayed even with the market. These results show the success of our company: each year, most of our investment products have increased in value more than the market.

The debater's argument is most vulnerable to criticism on which of these grounds?

○ It takes for granted that the stock funds are typical of the company with regard to the average increase in value per year.

○ It takes for granted that if a certain average annual increase in value was obtained by each investment product, then each stock fund increased each year by approximately the same amount.

○ It confuses a claim from which the argument's conclusion about the company would necessarily follow with a claim that would follow from the argument's conclusion only with a high degree of probability.

○ It overlooks the possibility that even if, on average, the stock funds increased by an average annual value, many stock funds may have increased less than the market as whole.

○ It overlooks the possibility that even if most investment products at the company have increased in value more than the market this year, any one investment product may, in some years, fail to increase in value at all.

EXPLANATION

Reading the question: the fund manager's argument has many error-prone features. It draws conclusions from a group of things, it deals in percentages, and it makes comparisons. We will use term matching to hunt for an error, starting with the conclusion.

Evidence Term	Matches?	Conclusion Term
Various stock funds managed by our company; each particular; investment products other than stock funds	≠	Most of our investment products
[various]	≠	Have increased in value more than the market

Creating a filter: each half of the conclusion is connected in multiple dubious ways to the evidence. The right answer will probably involve a bad bridge from the evidence to one or to the other. For example, the evidence is saying stock funds have beat the market "on average." But that is not the same as saying that "most of our investment products" have beat the market. Most could, in fact, be failures, with one anomalous market saving the average. The second sentence doesn't help this problem. So we'll paraphrase this error as "average <> most" and use that as our filter.

Applying the filter: (D) matches our filter precisely. Choice (A) is not really an error, given the second sentence of the prompt. (B), similarly, describes something the argument doesn't do. (C) is similar to (D)— but who knows what the probability really is? It's not necessarily high. (E) is similar to (D)—but pointing out that "any one" product might have done poorly doesn't actually undermine the argument much, because it still allows for "most of our investment products" to beat the market. The correct answer is (D).

This year, our company has moved its call center service team from within the country to an offshore location. Some members of our organization have questioned whether **we are providing equal customer service, per dollar of cost, as we did before.** We most certainly are, as is indicated by our satisfaction surveys administered at random to people who call the company help line.

In the argument given, the two boldfaced portions play which of the following roles?

○ The first identifies the content of the conclusion of the argument; the second provides support for that conclusion.
○ The first provides support for the conclusion of the argument; the second identifies the content of that conclusion.
○ The first states the conclusion of the argument; the second calls that conclusion into question.
○ The first provides support for the conclusion of the argument; the second calls that conclusion into question.
○ Each provides support for the conclusion of the argument.

This year, our company has moved its call center service team from within the country to an offshore location. Some members of our organization have questioned whether **we are providing equal customer service, per dollar of cost, as we did before.** We most certainly are, as is indicated by our satisfaction surveys administered at random to people who call the company help line.

In the argument given, the two boldfaced portions play which of the following roles?

o   The first identifies the content of the conclusion of the argument; the second provides support for that conclusion.
o   The first provides support for the conclusion of the argument; the second identifies the content of that conclusion.
o   The first states the conclusion of the argument; the second calls that conclusion into question.
o   The first provides support for the conclusion of the argument; the second calls that conclusion into question.
o   Each provides support for the conclusion of the argument.

EXPLANATION

Reading the question: since this is a boldfaced question, our task is to identify the role of each sentence in the argument given.

Sentence	Starts With.../Includes...	Function
1st	**"This year, our company has moved"**	Fact
2nd	"questioned whether **we are providing**"	Question raised (with implicit opinion)
3rd	"We most certainly are, as is..."	Opinion + evidence answering question

The first sentence gives a fact, in bold. The second gives a question that has been raised, with an implied opinion. That question is in bold. The third gives a direct opinion, contrary to the implied opinion, with a piece of evidence attached on the end.

Applying the filter: according to the answer choices, the first bold part either "lends support" or "states the conclusion." But the content of the conclusion is not the first statement—it's the second one. We are providing equal customer service, per dollar of cost, as we did before. That's what the author believes. So choices (A) and (C) are out. We look for an answer choice that attributes the second boldfaced sentence correctly. Only (B) makes that attribution correctly. The correct answer is (B).

Wappo, a company that manufactures turbine blades for hydroelectric dams, has designed a new model of blade with a superior hydrodynamic form that will save energy and hence cost in implementation. Wappo is willing to sell these blades to a particular hydroelectric dam at no initial cost. The only payment will be the difference between, first, a percentage of the dam's improved profits, as measured by the percentage improvement of the hydroelectric dam efficiency times the value of energy sold by the plant over an 18-month period, and, second, the additional cost of installation and maintenance of the new turbines. On installation, the dam will make an estimated payment, which will be adjusted after eighteen months to equal the proper amount.

Which of the following, if it occurred, would constitute a disadvantage for Wappo of the plan described above?

- ○ Another manufacturer's introduction to the market of a similarly efficient turbine blade
- ○ The dam's need for a large number of turbine blades
- ○ Energy efficiency of the dam's current turbines somewhat below the industry average
- ○ Levels of demand for hydroelectric power that were stagnant but above predicted levels
- ○ Uncharacteristic weather conditions decreasing the amount of energy that can be harvested through hydroelectric means at the dam's location

TURBINE PRICING MODEL

Wappo, a company that manufactures turbine blades for hydroelectric dams, has designed a new model of blade with a superior hydrodynamic form that will save energy and hence cost in implementation. Wappo is willing to sell these blades to a particular hydroelectric dam at no initial cost. The only payment will be the difference between, first, a percentage of the dam's improved profits, as measured by the percentage improvement of the hydroelectric dam efficiency times the value of energy sold by the plant over an 18-month period, and, second, the additional cost of installation and maintenance of the new turbines. On installation, the dam will make an estimated payment, which will be adjusted after eighteen months to equal the proper amount.

Which of the following, if it occurred, would constitute a disadvantage for Wappo of the plan described above?

○ Another manufacturer's introduction to the market of a similarly efficient turbine blade
○ The dam's need for a large number of turbine blades
○ Energy efficiency of the dam's current turbines somewhat below the industry average
○ Levels of demand for hydroelectric power that were stagnant but above predicted levels
○ Uncharacteristic weather conditions decreasing the amount of energy that can be harvested through hydroelectric means at the dam's location

EXPLANATION

Reading the question: first, we grasp the fact that there is a unique payment structure dependent on two variables. Then, we try to understand what the variables are. And we note the fact there's an estimated payment. A "disadvantage" for Wappo in this rather creative payment scheme would come if it somehow got paid very little. It does the installation at no cost and things don't go according to plan. Obviously, if the product is poor that would be a problem. Slightly more subtly, Wappo isn't getting a payment past 18 months, is it? Other than new turbines. So things would go very badly if the dam didn't sell much for 18 months, then sold a lot and loved Wappo, but didn't install any more. We've got a sort of prediction to use as our filter.

Applying the filter: choices (A) and (B) don't impact the variables that are inputs to Wappo's pay. And choice (C) will increase Wappo's payout. (D) is basically our prediction, but it gets twisted at the end with "above predicted levels." If demand is at or above predicted levels, Wappo revenue should be at or above predicted levels. Choice (E) is in the spirit of our prediction, because unusual weather conditions are impairing revenue. And "uncharacteristic" indicates the opposite of what we have in (D); in (E), the weather predictions have not been planned for.

Logical proof: we can confirm (E) with the negation test. What if weather conditions *dramatically increased* the amount of energy that could be harvested? That would dramatically *increase* the "value of energy sold by the plant over an 18-month period" and create an advantage to the plan. Just as the negated (E) is an advantage, the non-negated (E) is a disadvantage. The correct answer is (E).

Which of the following most logically completes the argument?

Pasteurization greatly reduces the number of potentially disease-causing microbes in milk. However, it destroys enzymes that contribute to immunity and also digestive enzymes, such as lactase, that aid the body in assimilating milk's nutrients. Some parties, pointing out that for some milk drinkers, such as infants, the benefits of drinking unpasteurized milk are outweighed by the risks, conclude too hastily that unpasteurized milk is too dangerous, overlooking the fact that _____.

- ○ strict regulations imposed on dairies over the last decades have greatly reduced the risks of drinking unpasteurized milk
- ○ the universal popularity of pasteurized milk is due largely to the unavailability of alternatives and political lobbying by the dairy industry
- ○ for other drinkers of milk, the benefits may outweigh the risks
- ○ there are alternative methods of pasteurization, such as ultra-high temperature pasteurization, which may be even more effective
- ○ legislation has banned the retail sale of raw milk in most states and only allows it to be purchased directly at certified farms

Unpasteurized Milk

Which of the following most logically completes the argument?

Pasteurization greatly reduces the number of potentially disease-causing microbes in milk. However, it destroys enzymes that contribute to immunity and also digestive enzymes, such as lactase, that aid the body in assimilating milk's nutrients. Some parties, pointing out that for some milk drinkers, such as infants, the benefits of drinking unpasteurized milk are outweighed by the risks, conclude too hastily that unpasteurized milk is too dangerous, overlooking the fact that _____.

- ○ strict regulations imposed on dairies over the last decades have greatly reduced the risks of drinking unpasteurized milk
- ○ the universal popularity of pasteurized milk is due largely to the unavailability of alternatives and political lobbying by the dairy industry
- ○ for other drinkers of milk, the benefits may outweigh the risks
- ○ there are alternative methods of pasteurization, such as ultra-high temperature pasteurization, which may be even more effective
- ○ legislation has banned the retail sale of raw milk in most states and only allows it to be purchased directly at certified farms

Explanation

Reading the question: we will logically complete the argument, knowing that clues in the prompt will render one choice objectively more logical than the others. Given a blank, we will always guess what goes in that blank before looking at the choices. The prompt switches points of view midway. Where we end up is that the thing in the blank needs to be a reason that UNpasteurized is milk is NOT too dangerous—even though it's too dangerous for babies. So it's going to be something like, "it's perfectly safe for most people, just keep it away from the babies." That's our filter.

Applying the filter: the closest answer choice is (C). Other answer choices are pro-unpasteurized milk, namely (A). But (C) is better than (A) because it specifically draws the distinction that has been set up about babies. As we were predicting, "just keep it away from the babies." (C) expresses that logical continuation with the phrase "for other drinkers of milk." The correct answer is (C).

Consuming gluten, a protein composite found in foods processed from wheat and related grains, causes allergic reactions in some adults. Medical records indicate that the percentage of adults in our country who have seen a doctor for gluten allergies has increased significantly in the last four years. Either our adults have been exposed to more glutens, or they have developed a greater sensitivity to them.

Which of the following is an assumption on which the argument depends?

- The number of doctors specializing in nutrition in our country has not decreased over the past four years.
- Adults who are allergic to gluten are no more likely than other adults to have allergies to other food ingredients.
- Adults who have allergic reactions to gluten are not more likely to be see a doctor for treatment now than they were four years ago.
- In our country, either more gluten has been introduced into foods artificially, or adults have eaten more food naturally containing gluten.
- The percentage of the population in our country of adult age has not changed relative to four years ago.

GLUTEN INCREASE

Consuming gluten, a protein composite found in foods processed from wheat and related grains, causes allergic reactions in some adults. Medical records indicate that the percentage of adults in our country who have seen a doctor for gluten allergies has increased significantly in the last four years. Either our adults have been exposed to more glutens, or they have developed a greater sensitivity to them.

Which of the following is an assumption on which the argument depends?

○ The number of doctors specializing in nutrition in our country has not decreased over the past four years.
○ Adults who are allergic to gluten are no more likely than other adults to have allergies to other food ingredients.
○ Adults who have allergic reactions to gluten are not more likely to be see a doctor for treatment now than they were four years ago.
○ In our country, either more gluten has been introduced into foods artificially, or adults have eaten more food naturally containing gluten.
○ The percentage of the population in our country of adult age has not changed relative to four years ago.

EXPLANATION

Reading the question: we read the prompt and find a somewhat hasty argument. The first two statements are facts, while the last one is an opinion and is the conclusion. One weakness here is that the author has allowed for only two possibilities. There might be another possibility. And that makes us notice: we have a causal argument! So we will look for a different cause in the answer choices—for the increased percentage of adults who have seen a doctor for gluten allergies. Specifically, given the format of the answer choices, which one rules out a new cause for increased visits? That's our filter.

Applying the filter: (A), (B), and (E) all rule something out, but the things they rule out wouldn't cause more gluten visits. Choice (C) rules out something that *would* cause more gluten visits, so it looks correct.

Logical proof: Negating (C) proves it: if people with the allergy are more likely to go in, that could be a different reason than given in the conclusion and the argument would be weakened or broken. Meanwhile, choice (D) does not pass the negation test; it merely states a possibility. The correct answer is (C).

One method of predicting the future value of a particular company's stock is to attempt to correlate the pattern of its recent performance with the past performance of other companies, even companies in different industries, whose subsequent stock performance is known. This technique, known as "technical analysis," provides a readily available basis for predicting the future value of a company's stock without special knowledge of that company or company's industry.

Which of the following, if true, would most strengthen the grounds on which to believe predictions made about the future stock price of a particular company according to technical analysis, as described above?

- For a prediction about a company's stock price to be useful, it must be more accurate or accurate more in advance than the predictions of the rest of the potential buyers and sellers of that company's stock.
- Getting "inside" information about a particular company about what will influence that company's future stock price is difficult and often illegal.
- Stock analysts cover a range of companies or even single industries, so they can focus their attention more effectively by using predictive methods that will be applicable across industries and companies.
- There is a wealth of historical stock performance data which can be analyzed and compared to a particular stock's recent performance.
- At any given time, the near-term performance of a particular company's stock depends not on industry-specific factors but on trends of buyers' and sellers' behavior that can be inferred from the near past.

STOCK PREDICTIONS

One method of predicting the future value of a particular company's stock is to attempt to correlate the pattern of its recent performance with the past performance of other companies, even companies in different industries, whose subsequent stock performance is known. This technique, known as "technical analysis," provides a readily available basis for predicting the future value of a company's stock without special knowledge of that company or company's industry.

Which of the following, if true, would most strengthen the grounds on which to believe predictions made about the future stock price of a particular company according to technical analysis, as described above?

○ For a prediction about a company's stock price to be useful, it must be more accurate or accurate more in advance than the predictions of the rest of the potential buyers and sellers of that company's stock.

○ Getting "inside" information about a particular company about what will influence that company's future stock price is difficult and often illegal.

○ Stock analysts cover a range of companies or even single industries, so they can focus their attention more effectively by using predictive methods that will be applicable across industries and companies.

○ There is a wealth of historical stock performance data which can be analyzed and compared to a particular stock's recent performance.

○ At any given time, the near-term performance of a particular company's stock depends not on industry-specific factors but on trends of buyers' and sellers' behavior that can be inferred from the near past.

EXPLANATION

Reading the question: the prompt doesn't present much argument but the question stem itself contains an opinion. It asks, what gives us grounds to trust technical analysis? There's not much for us to grab onto. The first sentence discusses "past performance of companies in other industries." And the last sentence goes farther somewhat and points out that we lack knowledge of the company's industry. So, technical analysis is good if 1) industry knowledge doesn't matter and 2) performance of companies in other industries is useful. It's kind of an "anti-industry method," to put it crudely; not investing based on industry knowledge. We look for so called "anti-industry" answer choices as our filter.

Applying the filter: (A) and (B) are neutral on the industry question. (C) is pro-industry, so it's the opposite of our filter – it's a weakener – so (C) is out. (D) seems required; how can we use this method without data? But it's industry-neutral, so it doesn't pass the filter. Moreover, a "wealth of data" may not be required, as long as we have sufficient data. Maybe just one good match for a particular stock is all that's needed, or something less than a complete "wealth." Choice (E) is anti-industry, so it passes the filter.

Logical proof: if we negate (E), that means we need industry knowledge and technical analysis will *not* work. The correct answer is (E).

For a country to obtain the benefits of direct investment by foreign multinationals in its industries, unrestricted incentives to foreign multinationals and a high degree of support to local businesses are both necessary. While the government of Kokua is prepared to offer incentives to foreign multinationals, the population of the country would most likely demand that the national legislature place restrictions on these incentives by the next voting term.

The claims above, if true, most strongly support which of the following conclusions?

○   If Kokua offers unrestricted incentives to foreign multinationals, public discord will make it impossible to provide a high degree of support to local businesses.
○   As long as support to local businesses in Kokua is generous, direct investment by foreign multinationals is likely to succeed.
○   Incentives to foreign multinationals are sufficient to generate direct investment by those multinationals, if those incentives are unrestricted.
○   Direct investment by foreign multinationals in Kokua is likely to fail in the long term.
○   Overwhelming popular support is required for successful direct investment by foreign multinationals in Kokua.

FOREIGN DIRECT INVESTMENT

For a country to obtain the benefits of direct investment by foreign multinationals in its industries, unrestricted incentives to foreign multinationals and a high degree of support to local businesses are both necessary. While the government of Kokua is prepared to offer incentives to foreign multinationals, the population of the country would most likely demand that the national legislature place restrictions on these incentives by the next voting term.

The claims above, if true, most strongly support which of the following conclusions?

○ If Kokua offers unrestricted incentives to foreign multinationals, public discord will make it impossible to provide a high degree of support to local businesses.
○ As long as support to local businesses in Kokua is generous, direct investment by foreign multinationals is likely to succeed.
○ Incentives to foreign multinationals are sufficient to generate direct investment by those multinationals, if those incentives are unrestricted.
○ Direct investment by foreign multinationals in Kokua is likely to fail in the long term.
○ Overwhelming popular support is required for successful direct investment by foreign multinationals in Kokua.

EXPLANATION

Reading the question: we glance at the prompt but skip down and check out the question stem. The understated language "most strongly support" tips us off that we can answer this question by proving in stronger terms. We will determine which answer choice *must be true*, given the prompt.

Logical proof: Choice (A) need not be true – we just have grounds to know it *must* be true – so it's out. Choice (B) sounds false, because we know there is the problem with the unrestricted incentives. (C) is wrong: the prompt makes clear that there are two key things we need, not just one. (C) is out. (D) has some potential: it's at least pointing out that there are problems with getting the investment done. We're down to (D) and (E). One must be true, given the prompt; the other need not be true. In (E), "overwhelming" is a very strong term that decreases the quality of the answer. After all, we don't really need overwhelming popular support—only enough for the incentives to be unrestricted and for support to local businesses to be in place. So (E) is out. Meanwhile, the prompt states as a fact that if Kokua offers incentives, the people will make demands messing it up. According to the prompt, it hasn't already happened, but it's a fact that it's *likely* to happen. On those grounds, it must be true that failure is likely. The correct answer is (D).

Company A provides a business software for which companies pay an annual subscription fee, which includes help support provided by Company A's team of account managers. To reduce the cost of providing help support to half of last year's cost, Company A has redesigned its product offering to include two variants. To achieve this, Company A plans this year to move enough of its clients into a cheaper subscription that includes no access to help support to reduce the number of account managers to half of last year's number.

Which of the following is required for the redesigned product offering to achieve its aim?

- ○ The majority of clients who are willing to switch to the cheaper subscription will move to that product.
- ○ Moving customers to the new product will be achieved at a net cost of zero.
- ○ No more than half of new subscribers to Company A's products this year should subscribe to the option that includes customer service.
- ○ Customer service this year will cost no more per account manager than it did last year.
- ○ The total number of client accounts this year should be no more than fifty percent greater than last year's number.

CHEAPER SUBSCRIPTION PRODUCT

Company A provides a business software for which companies pay an annual subscription fee, which includes help support provided by Company A's team of account managers. To reduce the cost of providing help support to half of last year's cost, Company A has redesigned its product offering to include two variants. To achieve this, Company A plans this year to move enough of its clients into a cheaper subscription that includes no access to help support to reduce the number of account managers to half of last year's number.

Which of the following is required for the redesigned product offering to achieve its aim?

- ○ The majority of clients who are willing to switch to the cheaper subscription will move to that product.
- ○ Moving customers to the new product will be achieved at a net cost of zero.
- ○ No more than half of new subscribers to Company A's products this year should subscribe to the option that includes customer service.
- ○ Customer service this year will cost no more per account manager than it did last year.
- ○ The total number of client accounts this year should be no more than fifty percent greater than last year's number.

EXPLANATION

Reading the question: the prompt presents a plan, which is to create a new cheaper product and move customers into it. The "aim" referred to by the question stem is to reduce cost. Actually, it's more specific: it's to reduce the cost of providing help support to half of last year's cost. The stem already uses logically strong terms, for once: the word "required." So we can move straight to the answer choices and use the negation test.

Logical proof: If (A) were false, might the plan achieve its aim? It still might; for example, maybe all customers are willing to switch, so only half need to be migrated. (A) is out. We negate (B). The plan isn't impacted, because we are trying simply to reduce help support cost, as the plan's aim; total costs are out of scope of this plan. We negate (C). More than half of new customers go for the service option. We had 100 clients, say, and we moved 50 to the non-service option to establish 50-50. But now 20 new clients come in and go for service, and we are at 70-50. But does that mean the unit cost is now 70 relative to 100 last year? Not necessarily; we don't know that each subscriber requires the same level of service. The negation does not decisively break the plan, so the non-negated statement is not required for the plan. In this regard, (E) is equivalent to (C). But we *have* been told about these account managers. They provide the customer service, and that last, odd-sounding phrase of the argument becomes important. The account managers are reduced to half; the cost is to be reduced to half; so (D) must be true. If, for example, the average account manager compensation went up, the cost would be higher than half and the plan would fail. The correct answer is (D).

Book reviewer: the author of this book confirms that it was inspired by the plot of *Anthony Adverse,* the 1933 book by Hervey Allen, but maintains that the style of writing is unique. Orpheo, the author's main character, is an orphan, like the lead character of the earlier novel, but Orpheo's dialogue is of a style that would never been heard in the 1930s.

The considerations given best serve as part of an argument that

○   modern readers would find it hard to tolerate certain characteristics of a historically accurate remake of a novel from the 1930s
○   the character Orpheo is essentially similar to the lead character of *Anthony Adverse*
○   the style of writing fiction has not changed much between the 1933 and the time of the book inspired by *Anthony Adverse,* if these two works are any evidence
○   the similarities between the plot events concerning Orpheo and those concerning the lead character of *Anthony Adverse* do not diminish the stylistic differences between the two books describing those characters
○   Hervey Allen must have known and influenced the author of the later book

HERVEY ALLEN

Book reviewer: the author of this book confirms that it was inspired by the plot of *Anthony Adverse,* the 1933 book by Hervey Allen, but maintains that the style of writing is unique. Orpheo, the author's main character, is an orphan, like the lead character of the earlier novel, but Orpheo's dialogue is of a style that would never been heard in the 1930s.

The considerations given best serve as part of an argument that

- modern readers would find it hard to tolerate certain characteristics of a historically accurate remake of a novel from the 1930s
- the character Orpheo is essentially similar to the lead character of *Anthony Adverse*
- the style of writing fiction has not changed much between the 1933 and the time of the book inspired by *Anthony Adverse,* if these two works are any evidence
- the similarities between the plot events concerning Orpheo and those concerning the lead character of *Anthony Adverse* do not diminish the stylistic differences between the two books describing those characters
- Hervey Allen must have known and influenced the author of the later book

EXPLANATION

Reading the question: The question stem is of a less common type. It's like a logical continuation, a fill-in-the-blank. As with a logical continuation question, we'll focus on making a prediction of the answer.

Creating a filter: We're talking about a book inspired by the older book. The argument is that there are some similarities, but some key differences. The logical continuation or logical overall point appears to be that the similarities don't comprise everything that is important. There are important differences. The new book is different in important ways. We might even go on and say that the new book is still original, creative, or a great book. We'll look for something like "new book is different / creative / great" in the answer choices.

Applying the filter: all the answer choices miss that fundamental positive point about the new book, with the exception of (D). Choice (D) says "the similarities... do not diminish the stylistic differences." That's right; the point is that there are similarities, but the new book is different in important ways. The correct answer is (D).

The cost of producing cell phones in Country A is 12 percent less than the cost of producing cell phones in Country C. Even after transportation fees are added, it is still cheaper for a company to import cell phones from Country A to Country C than to produce cell phones in Country C.

The statements above, if true, best support which of the following assertions?

- ○ Labor costs in Country A are 12 percent below those in Country C.
- ○ Importing cell phones from Country A to Country C will eliminate 12 percent of the manufacturing jobs in Country C.
- ○ The transportation fee on a cell phone imported from Country A to Country C is less than 12 percent of the cost of manufacturing the cell phone in Country C.
- ○ The fee for transporting a cell phone from Country A to Country C is more than 12 percent of the cost of manufacturing the cell phone in Country A.
- ○ It takes 12 percent less time to manufacture a cell phone in Country A than it does in Country C.

CELL PHONE MANUFACTURE

The cost of producing cell phones in Country A is 12 percent less than the cost of producing cell phones in Country C. Even after transportation fees are added, it is still cheaper for a company to import cell phones from Country A to Country C than to produce cell phones in Country C.

The statements above, if true, best support which of the following assertions?

o Labor costs in Country A are 12 percent below those in Country C.
o Importing cell phones from Country A to Country C will eliminate 12 percent of the manufacturing jobs in Country C.
o The transportation fee on a cell phone imported from Country A to Country C is less than 12 percent of the cost of manufacturing the cell phone in Country C.
o The fee for transporting a cell phone from Country A to Country C is more than 12 percent of the cost of manufacturing the cell phone in Country A.
o It takes 12 percent less time to manufacture a cell phone in Country A than it does in Country C.

EXPLANATION

Reading the question: we will try evaluating this brief argument by matching terms.

Evidence Term	Matches?	Conclusion Term
Lower production costs and higher transportation costs	≠	Cheaper to import
Country A, C	=	Country A, C
Cell phones	=	Cell phones

The key word in the conclusion is "cheaper," and we notice it doesn't appear at all in the evidence. So the logical connection to attack is the connection between lower production costs, higher transportation costs, and "cheaper to import." ("Import" also is only in the conclusion.) We'll use that expectation as our filter.

Applying the filter: (C) and (D) have the right terms. (A), (B), and (E) all introduce new terms—labor, jobs, time—and introducing a new term usually generates a problem. (C) and (D) are similar, but switch the positions of the countries. We are talking about producing in Country A and shipping to Country C. That situation is described by answer choice (C).

Logical proof: We can prove (C) with the negation test. If the transportation fee is equal to or greater than the money saved in production, then how could it be cheaper to produce in Country A? It couldn't be. Therefore choice (C) is the correct answer. The correct answer is (C).

A luxury car dealership in Shelbyville is expected to close due to competition from an Alexa dealership, which also sells luxury cars. Nevertheless, the demand for cars in Shelbyville will be sufficient for a new dealership to succeed as a new business. After all, in previous years, the Dealeo discount car dealership in Shelbyville has driven several other dealerships out of business, but in every case there has been sufficient demand for a new dealership to enter the city and be successful for a time.

Which of the following, if true, most seriously weakens the argument?

- All of Dealeo's competitors eventually go out of business.
- The demand for luxury cars in Shelbyville has decreased over time.
- Shelbyville has a higher-than-average number of car dealerships.
- Over the course of the next five years, it is expected that Shelbyville's population will grow at a unprecedented rate.
- Some dealerships in Shelbyville sell cars that are not available at either the Alexa dealership.

SHELBYVILLE'S NEW DEALERSHIP

A luxury car dealership in Shelbyville is expected to close due to competition from an Alexa dealership, which also sells luxury cars. Nevertheless, the demand for cars in Shelbyville will be sufficient for a new dealership to succeed as a new business. After all, in previous years, the Dealeo discount car dealership in Shelbyville has driven several other dealerships out of business, but in every case there has been sufficient demand for a new dealership to enter the city and be successful for a time.

Which of the following, if true, most seriously weakens the argument?

- ○ All of Dealeo's competitors eventually go out of business.
- ○ The demand for luxury cars in Shelbyville has decreased over time.
- ○ Shelbyville has a higher-than-average number of car dealerships.
- ○ Over the course of the next five years, it is expected that Shelbyville's population will grow at an unprecedented rate.
- ○ Some dealerships in Shelbyville sell cars that are not available at either the Alexa dealership.

EXPLANATION

Reading the question: we have three dealerships that are compared in a roundabout fashion. To establish which ideas are connected and which things are compared, we can use term matching:

Evidence Term	Matches?	Conclusion Term
In every other case, there has been sufficient demand for a new dealership to enter the city and be successful for a time	≠	[In this case,] The demand for cars in Shelbyville will be sufficient for a new dealership to succeed as a new business
Demand	=	Demand
The city	=	Shelbyville
Be successful for a time	≈	Succeed as a new business
A new dealership	?	A new dealership

There are a couple of points of technique that we can highlight here. First, if an argument does not easily break up into terms, you can make some progress by simply imagining (or jotting down, if necessary) entire clauses on both sides of the table. Second, the conjunctions "nevertheless" and "but" indicate that the clause that comes before each one is neither evidence nor conclusion; it's something the argument is disputing. Matching terms further, we see that the terms of the evidence and the conclusion match well. The question really boils down to whether this case is like "every other case." Do any answer choices suggest this case is different? We can use that as our basic relevance filter.

Applying the filter: (B) and (D) are closest to our expectation. Choice (A) is immaterial to the "successful for a time" condition and is out. We also knock out (C) as there is no contrast in time or in dealerships. Choice (D) would strengthen the argument, not weaken it. We're down to (B) and (E). Both of them require us to get specific about luxury vs. discount. Fact #1 of the argument is that a luxury dealer knocked out a luxury dealer. We don't know whether there is demand for more than one luxury dealer. Answer choice (B) indicates that demand for luxury cars is down, so it weakens the idea that there is room for another one after Alexa. (B) looks good. Choice (E) could either weaken or strengthen the argument. It would suggest that there is plenty of demand other than luxury, which would strengthen the argument. Or it could suggest that non-luxury demand is already covered. But (B) objectively weakens the argument and therefore is the correct answer. The correct answer is (B).

A restaurant owner plans to replace the restaurant's tables and chairs, which are currently of a generic design, with sturdier models from a manufacturer in Maine. The newer tables and chairs are more expensive, but they are extremely durable, so the owner expects to have to replace them far less frequently, saving money in the long term.

Which of the following must be studied in order to evaluate the argument presented above?

○   The amount of money the owner has already spent on the current set of tables and chairs
○   The degree to which the new tables and chairs fit the ambience of the restaurant
○   The degree to which the price and availability of the new designs and those of the old designs are equally dependable in the long run
○   The degree to which tables and chairs of the newer design are more carefully manufactured than those of the old design
○   The number of customers visiting the restaurant on a weekly basis

RESTAURANT TABLES AND CHAIRS

A restaurant owner plans to replace the restaurant's tables and chairs, which are currently of a generic design, with sturdier models from a manufacturer in Maine. The newer tables and chairs are more expensive, but they are extremely durable, so the owner expects to have to replace them far less frequently, saving money in the long term.

Which of the following must be studied in order to evaluate the argument presented above?

- ○ The amount of money the owner has already spent on the current set of tables and chairs
- ○ The degree to which the new tables and chairs fit the ambience of the restaurant
- ○ The degree to which the price and availability of the new designs and those of the old designs are equally dependable in the long run
- ○ The degree to which tables and chairs of the newer design are more carefully manufactured than those of the old design
- ○ The number of customers visiting the restaurant on a weekly basis

EXPLANATION

Reading the question: supposing we don't see a flaw, we can jump straight to a logical proof. The answer choices are not statements, so we can't negate them, but they can be evaluated by analysis by extreme cases to detect impact on the argument. **Answer choices that represent variable ranges or amounts are suited to analysis by cases.**

Logical proof: we look at (A). Extreme case: the owner has spent a lot of money on the current set. That doesn't impact the ability to save in the long run. We're more interested in how expensive they are relative to the cost of the new ones given how often the old ones need to be replaced and how often the new ones need to be replaced. *That*, in fact, might be the answer. With that expectation in mind, we eliminate everything except (C). Is (C) critical? Yes; we can complete the analysis by cases. If the new designs will go up in price and/or go out of production, the plan will fail. If they don't, the plan may succeed. The correct answer is (C).

State government manager: the fax machines in our state government offices can be eliminated without any loss of efficiency in how we do our work. We all have access to computers in our offices and we can make sure those computers are equipped with electronic faxing accounts. Meanwhile, by removing the fax machines, we will save costs and also avoid the hassle of maintaining and replacing or repairing fax machines.

Which of the following, if true, most strongly supports the claim that the proposal, if carried out, will have the announced effect?

- ○ Citizens who visit state government offices do not require the use of fax machines.
- ○ Maintaining the fax machines costs $100,000 annually.
- ○ The computers in the state government offices are old and frequently need repairs.
- ○ Officials in state government offices sometimes waste large amounts of time dealing with broken fax machines.
- ○ On any given day, a significant percentage of the fax machines in state government offices are out of service.

ELIMINATING FAX MACHINES

State government manager: the fax machines in our state government offices can be eliminated without any loss of efficiency in how we do our work. We all have access to computers in our offices and we can make sure those computers are equipped with electronic faxing accounts. Meanwhile, by removing the fax machines, we will save costs and also avoid the hassle of maintaining and replacing or repairing fax machines.

Which of the following, if true, most strongly supports the claim that the proposal, if carried out, will have the announced effect?

- ○ Citizens who visit state government offices do not require the use of fax machines.
- ○ Maintaining the fax machines costs $100,000 annually.
- ○ The computers in the state government offices are old and frequently need repairs.
- ○ Officials in state government offices sometimes waste large amounts of time dealing with broken fax machines.
- ○ On any given day, a significant percentage of the fax machines in state government offices are out of service.

EXPLANATION

Reading the question: our ears prick up at the strong language in the phrase "without any loss of efficiency." Quite possibly, the rest of the argument could be true (as we take it to be, as evidence) and there could be *some* loss of efficiency. That will be our prediction. More specifically, the question asks for a strengthener, we will look for an answer choice like, "We won't lose efficiency from the change."

Applying the filter: our filter involves imagining the future state, but choices (B), (D), and (E) are all relevant only to the state of affairs before the change. Choice (C) *weakens* the plan, by giving a reason to that the cost and/or efficiency may worsen. That leaves us only with (A).

Logical proof: we apply the negation test to (A). Say citizens who visit the offices *do* require the use of fax machines. Then removing the fax machines would result in a loss of efficiency. The correct answer is (A).

Taaffeite costs more per ounce than painite. But since plutonium costs more per ounce than platinum, it follows that taaffeite costs more per ounce than platinum.

Any of the following, if introduced into the argument as an additional premise, makes the argument above logically correct EXCEPT:

- Plutonium costs more per ounce than taaffeite.
- Taaffeite and plutonium cost the same per ounce.
- Painite and plutonium cost the same per ounce.
- Painite costs more per ounce than platinum.
- Painite costs more per ounce than plutonium.

TAAFFEITE, PAINITE & CO.

Taaffeite costs more per ounce than painite. But since plutonium costs more per ounce than platinum, it follows that taaffeite costs more per ounce than platinum.

Any of the following, if introduced into the argument as an additional premise, makes the argument above logically correct EXCEPT:

○ Plutonium costs more per ounce than taaffeite.
○ Taaffeite and plutonium cost the same per ounce.
○ Painite and plutonium cost the same per ounce.
○ Painite costs more per ounce than platinum.
○ Painite costs more per ounce than plutonium.

EXPLANATION

Reading the question: we have some fragments of logical reasoning here. Alternatively, we can view them as mathematical equations expressed in words. We will write them as equations with variables:

T > Pain; and

Plu > Pla;

therefore: T > Pla

The most obvious way to add the missing piece is to establish Pain > Plu, connecting the two statements. That's answer choice (E). But this is an EXCEPT question, so that means (E) is out, not in. We go through the others. (A) says that Plu > T. That doesn't immediately seem to work, so we skip it. How about (B)? (B) gives T = Plu. Then we can substitute. (B) works and so it's out. (C) gives Pain = Plu. Again we can substitute and obtain success, so (C) is out. (D) says Pain > Pla. T is greater than something that is greater than Pla. So (D) works. The correct answer is (A).

Since Bordland dropped all tariffs on our country's automobiles one year ago, the number of automobiles sold annually in Bordland has not changed. However, recent statistics show a drop in the number of automobile assemblers in Bordland. Meanwhile, the number of people employed by automobile assemblers in our country has long been significantly higher than in neighboring Bordland. Therefore, updated trade statistics will probably indicate that the number of automobiles Bordland imports annually from our country has increased.

Which of the following is an assumption on which the argument depends?

- Automobiles assembled in our country are preferred in Bordland to automobiles assembled in Bordland.
- The number of automobile assemblers in our country has increased by at least as much as the number of automobile assemblers in Borodia has decreased.
- The average number of hours it takes a Bordland automobile assembler to assemble an automobile has not decreased significantly during the last twelve months.
- The number of automobiles assembled annually in our country has increased.
- The difference between the hourly wage of automobile assemblers in our country and the hourly wage of automobile assemblers in Bordland is likely to decrease in the next few years.

AUTOMOBILES IN BORDLAND

Since Bordland dropped all tariffs on our country's automobiles one year ago, the number of automobiles sold annually in Bordland has not changed. However, recent statistics show a drop in the number of automobile assemblers in Bordland. Meanwhile, the number of people employed by automobile assemblers in our country has long been significantly higher than in neighboring Bordland. Therefore, updated trade statistics will probably indicate that the number of automobiles Bordland imports annually from our country has increased.

Which of the following is an assumption on which the argument depends?

o   Automobiles assembled in our country are preferred in Bordland to automobiles assembled in Bordland.
o   The number of automobile assemblers in our country has increased by at least as much as the number of automobile assemblers in Borodia has decreased.
o   The average number of hours it takes a Bordland automobile assembler to assemble an automobile has not decreased significantly during the last twelve months.
o   The number of automobiles assembled annually in our country has increased.
o   The difference between the hourly wage of automobile assemblers in our country and the hourly wage of automobile assemblers in Bordland is likely to decrease in the next few years.

EXPLANATION

Reading the question: We can focus on opinion, which surfaces with the word "therefore." The conclusion resembles a prediction: auto imports from our country into Bordland should have increased. The primary reason is that there are fewer assemblers in that country, while the number of autos sold is the same. The argument overlooks some possibilities: the auto sellers might have had spare inventory, or become more efficient. Or Bordland could be importing more from some other country and not ours. We can look for any of these possibilities as our filter.

Applying the filter: choice (C) matches our prediction. The other answer choices give irrelevant comparisons.

Logical proof: we can attempt to confirm (C) with the negation test. Suppose that the time to assemble an automobile *has* decreased significantly – for example, due to improved technology. That would explain how the production and hence volume of imports might have remained the same, even given lower staffing levels. The negated (C) would critically damage the argument, so the argument depends on the non-negated version of (C). The correct answer is (C).

A theory argues that racial differences can lead to differences in cranial size and, in turn, brain size. However, another study suggests that **humans who grow up farther from the equator are exposed to less ambient sunlight and therefore develop larger eyes, which in turn lead to larger visual cortices, increasing total brain size.** Since the populations of some races are concentrated closer to the equator and the populations of other races are concentrated farther from the equator, **data that appear to support the racial theory of brain size may fit the ambient-light theory of brain size equally well or even better.**

In the argument given, the two portions in boldface play which of the following roles?

- ○ The first is an objection that has been raised against a position defended in the argument; the second is that position.
- ○ The first is evidence that has been used to support an explanation that the argument challenges; the second is that explanation.
- ○ The first is evidence that has been used to support an explanation that the argument challenges; the second is a competing explanation that the argument favors.
- ○ The first is a claim, the accuracy of which is at issue in the argument; the second is an objection to that claim.
- ○ The first is a claim, the accuracy of which is at issue in the argument; the second is a conclusion about the likelihood of accuracy of that claim.

CRANIAL SIZE

A theory argues that racial differences can lead to differences in cranial size and, in turn, brain size. However, another study suggests that **humans who grow up farther from the equator are exposed to less ambient sunlight and therefore develop larger eyes, which in turn lead to larger visual cortices, increasing total brain size.** Since the populations of some races are concentrated closer to the equator and the populations of other races are concentrated farther from the equator, **data that appear to support the racial theory of brain size may fit the ambient-light theory of brain size equally well or even better.**

In the argument given, the two portions in boldface play which of the following roles?

○   The first is an objection that has been raised against a position defended in the argument; the second is that position.
○   The first is evidence that has been used to support an explanation that the argument challenges; the second is that explanation.
○   The first is evidence that has been used to support an explanation that the argument challenges; the second is a competing explanation that the argument favors.
○   The first is a claim, the accuracy of which is at issue in the argument; the second is an objection to that claim.
○   The first is a claim, the accuracy of which is at issue in the argument; the second is a conclusion about the likelihood of accuracy of that claim.

EXPLANATION

Reading the question: since we have boldfaced text, we don't need to analyze the argument. We will just identify the logical role of each sentence.

Sentence	Starts With.../Includes...	Function
1st	"A theory argues"	States a theory
2nd	"However, another study suggests that **humans**"	States another theory
3rd	"Since the populations"	Fact
3rd	**"data that appear to support the racial theory"**	Opinion about theories

Sentence 1 states a theory, and sentence 2 states another theory; the bold part is the content of the belief of the second theory. Then we have some un-bolded evidence, and then the conclusion, in bold, the first hint of the author's opinion, which is a comparison of the theories.

Applying the filter: Let's see which answer choices get the first statement right. The first statement isn't an objection or evidence. That leaves only (D) and (E). The author's position is that evidence for the racial theory could be construed as support for the ambient-light theory. The author favors the ambient-light theory, which is expressed in the first statement. So the two bolded statements are in harmony. That rules out (D), and also confirms that (B) and (C) are out. And the first statement definitely isn't an objection, so (A) is out. The correct answer is (E).

A technical proposal has been advanced for a transportation system in individuals travel through tubes in pressurized capsules on a cushion of air. One individual in a capsule, according to the proposal, will be able to travel up to ten times as faster as an automobile on a highway. Such a futuristic means of conveyance would surely be thrilling for individuals, but the cost of building the new transport tube between two major cities has been estimated at six billion dollars. Even if this doubtful cost figure is accurate, it represents a waste of money. The cost of maintaining the existing roads between the two cities in question is negligible compared to the cost of building the tube, and those six billion dollars can be dedicated to more vital public works projects.

Which of the following, if true, most severely weakens the argument presented above?

○ The transport tube can be built between only two cities initially, and then further decisions can be made based on the outcome of that project.
○ The cost of building the transport tube between cities after the first two connected will be less than the cost of building the original route.
○ The technology developed in the course of the new transportation system could be applied to most vital public works projects, reducing their costs to negligible levels.
○ Developing the new transport system between the two cities identified will allow the government to stop spending funds on maintaining the roads between those two cities.
○ For city dwellers who do not own cars, traveling by road rather than by the new transport system is not an option.

TRAVEL THROUGH TUBES

A technical proposal has been advanced for a transportation system in individuals travel through tubes in pressurized capsules on a cushion of air. One individual in a capsule, according to the proposal, will be able to travel up to ten times as faster as an automobile on a highway. Such a futuristic means of conveyance would surely be thrilling for individuals, but the cost of building the new transport tube between two major cities has been estimated at six billion dollars. Even if this doubtful cost figure is accurate, it represents a waste of money. The cost of maintaining the existing roads between the two cities in question is negligible compared to the cost of building the tube, and those six billion dollars can be dedicated to more vital public works projects.

Which of the following, if true, most severely weakens the argument presented above?

○ The transport tube can be built between only two cities initially, and then further decisions can be made based on the outcome of that project.
○ The cost of building the transport tube between cities after the first two connected will be less than the cost of building the original route.
○ The technology developed in the course of the new transportation system could be applied to most vital public works projects, reducing their costs to negligible levels.
○ Developing the new transport system between the two cities identified will allow the government to stop spending funds on maintaining the roads between those two cities.
○ For city dwellers who do not own cars, traveling by road rather than by the new transport system is not an option.

EXPLANATION

Reading the question: this argument contains a lot of introductory material and bluster. The important stuff starts with "it represents a waste of money," the conclusion. The key piece of evidence is the cost comparison: maintaining existing roads vs. building the tube. Even if that evidence is true, as we take it to be, there might be benefits to this tube idea that have not been considered within the argument. We'll take that observation and use "new benefit," a tube-positive idea, as our filter for an answer choice that weakens the argument.

Applying the filter: choice (A) is tube-negative, so it doesn't pass the filter. Choice (B) is tube-positive, but barely, and it's not a new benefit. (B) is out. (C) is a big new benefit: looks good. (D) is not much of a new benefit, since we are told the cost of maintaining the roads is negligible. (D) is out. (E) is better than the other wrong answers, but it doesn't clearly establish a benefit.

Logical proof: using the negation test, we can observe that if the new technology for the tube system had *no* application outside this project, then the tube project would be harder to justify. The negated (C) strengthens the argument, confirming that the non-negated (C) weakens the argument. The correct answer is (C).

The design of an ancient pyramid suggests that the population who built the structure had developed the solar calendar. The exterior walls of the partly ruined pyramid consist of four successive stairways, and if a platform at the top of the structure is imagined as a single step atop four stairways of 91 steps each, the total number of steps corresponds to the number of days in the year according to the solar calendar.

Which of the following, if true, most strongly supports the hypothesis?

○   The ancient pyramid was the only major architectural structure known to have been built by the population.
○   No evidence of a solar calendar in the area predates the time of the construction of the pyramid.
○   Diagrams of agricultural practices that have been dated to the same time as the pyramid also indicate knowledge of the solar calendar.
○   Pyramids are among the simplest and earliest major architectural achievements of human civilization.
○   Archeologists found a well-preserved model of the pyramid confirming that the structure in question had consisted of four, 91-step stairways and in fact had a final platform at the top.

Calendrical Pyramid

The design of an ancient pyramid suggests that the population who built the structure had developed the solar calendar. The exterior walls of the partly ruined pyramid consist of four successive stairways, and if a platform at the top of the structure is imagined as a single step atop four stairways of 91 steps each, the total number of steps corresponds to the number of days in the year according to the solar calendar.

Which of the following, if true, most strongly supports the hypothesis?

○ The ancient pyramid was the only major architectural structure known to have been built by the population.
○ No evidence of a solar calendar in the area predates the time of the construction of the pyramid.
○ Diagrams of agricultural practices that have been dated to the same time as the pyramid also indicate knowledge of the solar calendar.
○ Pyramids are among the simplest and earliest major architectural achievements of human civilization.
○ Archeologists found a well-preserved model of the pyramid confirming that the structure in question had consisted of four, 91-step stairways and in fact had a final platform at the top.

Explanation

Reading the question: The first sentence is the conclusion. The evidence is quirky. Supposedly, the pyramid structure reveals a calendar mentality because it has (91 x 4) + 1 = 365 steps. The ideal strengthener of the argument will strengthen the link between this wacky evidence and the conclusion. It might discuss how we have established in other cases that pyramids in this culture are always built to reflect science. It might describe how the stairs are further broken into 28-day or 30-day chunks by color, or how each of the four stairways appears to represent a different season. Regardless, optimally, it will be about the pyramid and the pyramid's connection as evidence. We have our filter.

Answer choice (A) is about the pyramid, but it doesn't connect well to the calendar. Choice (B) could be taken as a weakener, so we eliminate (B). (C) is a mild strengthener, but not an ideal one – it doesn't match our filter. Choice (D) is like (A) and is out. Choice (E) confirms that the pyramid has the 91 x 4 structure and that it has a final platform at the top. Was that in doubt? We look back at the prompt, which says, "If a platform at the top is *imagined*." Evidently, the pyramid is not intact. Whether or not it has the imagined shape will be critical thing #1 in whether its shape is an expression of anything. So (E) address a point that is critical to the argument.

Logical proof: We can use the negation test on (E). Say that they found a model that established that the structure had not consisted of the calendar-suggestive shape? Then the argument collapses. The correct answer is (E).

Solutional caves are formed in the earth when a soft rock, usually limestone, is eroded by rainwater that has mixed with soils and carbon dioxide to form carbonic acid. Troglotopia Cave and the surrounding earth contain low amounts of soft rock, so it is not a solutional cave.

For purposes of evaluating the argument it would be most useful to establish which of the following?

○ Whether soft rock is commonly eroded by any substance other than carbonic acid
○ Whether carbonic acid commonly erodes away most of the soft rock in a given area
○ Whether rainwater that mixed with soils and atmosphere ever forms an acid other than carbonic acid
○ Whether Troglotopia Cave is of a shape commonly seen in caves known to be solutional caves
○ Whether there are areas of soft rock where caves commonly fail to form even when exposed to carbonic acid

TROGLOTOPIA CAVE

Solutional caves are formed in the earth when a soft rock, usually limestone, is eroded by rainwater that has mixed with soils and carbon dioxide to form carbonic acid. Troglotopia Cave and the surrounding earth contain low amounts of soft rock, so it is not a solutional cave.

For purposes of evaluating the argument it would be most useful to establish which of the following?

○ Whether soft rock is commonly eroded by any substance other than carbonic acid
○ Whether carbonic acid commonly erodes away most of the soft rock in a given area
○ Whether rainwater that mixed with soils and atmosphere ever forms an acid other than carbonic acid
○ Whether Troglotopia Cave is of a shape commonly seen in caves known to be solutional caves
○ Whether there are areas of soft rock where caves commonly fail to form even when exposed to carbonic acid

EXPLANATION

Reading the question: We have a brief argument, so we can use term matching.

Evidence Term	Matches?	Conclusion Term
Solutional cave	=	Solutional cave
Formed when soft rock erodes	≠	Surrounded by amounts of soft rock

There is an assumed relationship between "formed from" and "surrounded by." In short, the argument says that Troglotopia Cave wasn't formed from soft rock because it's not surrounded by soft rock. We'll filter for answer choices that relate these two concepts.

Applying the filter: choice (B) matches our filter, because it basically asks whether the formation process means there will be no surrounding soft rock, so it connects "formed from" and "surrounded by."

Logical proof: as the "whether" words hint, we can logically prove that (B) is correct and the other answer choices are incorrect through analysis by extreme cases. In (B), if the cave formation *always* erode *all* surrounding soft rock, then the conclusion of the argument is incorrect. On the other hand, if the cave formation *never* erodes all surrounding soft rock, then the conclusion of the argument is correct. So we have found that the correctness of the argument depends on (B). We don't get a similar result for analysis by cases in the other answer choices. In the case of choice (D), for example, we can imagine that Troglotopia Cave has a shape that highly resembles other solutional caves or that it has a very different shape. The argument is unaffected by these considerations, because the argument does not draw on the shape of the cave as evidence. Most of the other answer choices have the wrong focus, which is on carbonic acid, which isn't central to the evidence or conclusion. The correct answer is (B).

A statistical review of word types and frequencies in all of the works of fiction in a library has found that the works of fiction published prior to 1970 use far fewer slang words, measured as a percentage of the book's total words, than the works of fiction published in 1970 or later. Evidently, whether or not they intended to do so, authors of works published prior to 1970 used less slang than authors of later books.

Which of the following, if true, most seriously weakens this argument?

- ○ The amount of slang used in non-fiction books in the statistical review is essentially constant across periods of history.
- ○ Works of fiction published in 1970 or later are often just as critically acclaimed as works of fiction published prior to 1970.
- ○ Prior to widespread means of information communication, slang words were less likely to be understood by the entirety of a widespread readership.
- ○ The less slang a published book uses, the more likely it is to remain stocked by a library over time.
- ○ Writers of manuscripts prior to 1970 used as much slang as those of later manuscripts, but due to more conservative attitudes of editors during the earlier period, the manuscripts written during the earlier period were less likely to be published.

A statistical review of word types and frequencies in all of the works of fiction in a library has found that the works of fiction published prior to 1970 use far fewer slang words, measured as a percentage of the book's total words, than the works of fiction published in 1970 or later. Evidently, whether or not they intended to do so, authors of works published prior to 1970 used less slang than authors of later books.

Which of the following, if true, most seriously weakens this argument?

○ The amount of slang used in non-fiction books in the statistical review is essentially constant across periods of history.
○ Works of fiction published in 1970 or later are often just as critically acclaimed as works of fiction published prior to 1970.
○ Prior to widespread means of information communication, slang words were less likely to be understood by the entirety of a widespread readership.
○ The less slang a published book uses, the more likely it is to remain stocked by a library over time.
○ Writers of manuscripts prior to 1970 used as much slang as those of later manuscripts, but due to more conservative attitudes of editors during the earlier period, the manuscripts written during the earlier period were less likely to be published.

Explanation

Reading the question: since we have an argument, we can do some term matching.

Evidence Term	Matches?	Conclusion Term
Books	≠	Authors
Slang	=	Slang

The conclusion is the last sentence: a comparison of authors and slang. The evidence doesn't discuss authors; it discusses books and slang. So an assumption appears to be a connection between books and authors. Is there some mismatch in how the books represent the authors? We'll use that expectation as our filter.

Applying the filter: we can see that the only answer choice that mentions both authors and books explicitly is (E). But choice (E) is flawed; if the books aren't published, they aren't material to the conclusion, which limits itself to authors of works published. Therefore, (E) is out. Starting back at the top of the answer choices: choices (A), (B), and (C) all introduce new concepts that fail to bridge "books" and "authors"; they are non-fiction books, critical acclaim, and likelihood of being understood. Typically, introducing new concepts only causes problems. Choice (D) talks about being "stocked by a library." This may sound irrelevant at first, but in fact, being stocked in this library is the way in which a book represents an author; the authors who don't have books stocked in the library are omitted from this study, potentially distorting it. In other words, if (D) is true, 21st century books may or may not have lots of slang, but older books in a library will only be the non-slang ones. Choice (D) would give an alternate explanation for the point of evidence in the argument, so it seriously weakens the argument. The correct answer is (D).

The Hubble telescope has the great advantage over land-based telescopes of taking images from outside of the planet's atmosphere, which greatly blurs images. Nevertheless, the Hubble has two major disadvantages relative to land-based telescopes: it is difficult to repair, and to maneuver it requires the use of fuel, which will ultimately run out. An advisor at the space agency has proposed equipping the International Space Station with small robotic spacecraft that can be launched from orbit to repair the Hubble at a much lower cost than a repair craft launched from earth would cost.

Which of the following, if true, is NOT a serious weakness of the space agency advisor's plan?

o While in flight, the robotic spacecraft are roughly as likely to break down and require repairs as the Hubble, and they are not capable of repairing each other.
o The robotic spacecraft will themselves need fuel and will require fuel to be sent from Earth at a total cost comparable to that of launching repair craft from Earth.
o The robotic spacecraft proposed by the advisor will incur significant design costs not incurred by a repair craft launched from earth, which already exists.
o To be effective, the proposed robotic spacecraft may require human maintenance on the International Space Station when all astronauts aboard are committed to other uses of their time.
o The robotic spacecraft will not have the capability to refuel the Hubble.

Repairing Hubble

The Hubble telescope has the great advantage over land-based telescopes of taking images from outside of the planet's atmosphere, which greatly blurs images. Nevertheless, the Hubble has two major disadvantages relative to land-based telescopes: it is difficult to repair, and to maneuver it requires the use of fuel, which will ultimately run out. An advisor at the space agency has proposed equipping the International Space Station with small robotic spacecraft that can be launched from orbit to repair the Hubble at a much lower cost than a repair craft launched from earth would cost.

Which of the following, if true, is NOT a serious weakness of the space agency advisor's plan?

○ While in flight, the robotic spacecraft are roughly as likely to break down and require repairs as the Hubble, and they are not capable of repairing each other.
○ The robotic spacecraft will themselves need fuel and will require fuel to be sent from Earth at a total cost comparable to that of launching repair craft from Earth.
○ The robotic spacecraft proposed by the advisor will incur significant design costs not incurred by a repair craft launched from earth, which already exists.
○ To be effective, the proposed robotic spacecraft may require human maintenance on the International Space Station when all astronauts aboard are committed to other uses of their time.
○ The robotic spacecraft will not have the capability to refuel the Hubble.

Explanation

Reading the question: we are presented with a plan to repair the Hubble. Specifically, our aim is to repair the Hubble at much lower cost than launching a repair craft from Earth. The all-caps NOT leaps out at us: four of these answer choices will give flaws in the plan. Since we have a NOT, we'll use a very basic relevance filter and see which answer choices which are related to the cost of repairing the Hubble.

Applying the filter: choice (A) presents a problem, because if the spacecraft break down they will fail to achieve their goal of repairing the Hubble. It's a valid weakness so it's not the answer and is out. (B) is definitely an issue, because part of the aim is lower cost and (B) invokes cost. So (B) *is* a problem and is not the answer and is out. Choice (C) is out on similar grounds. Choice (D) says we might not be able to launch the things at all, which is an even bigger problem. So (D) is not the answer and is out. (E) is not great news, but it's not the aim of this plan to refuel the Hubble, only to repair it. So it's not a weakness in the plan as proposed. The correct answer is (E).

The company Straffkey guarantees in its contracts with clients that for every ten computer programmers employed by Straffkey on a client project, Staffkey will employ at least one certified project manager. Since many of Straffkey's contracts are with the nation's government, its business increases during economic recessions, when the government spends more, and it has to hire more computer programmers at these times to complete its contracts. Therefore, while many jobs are threatened by economic recessions, the prospects of being hired as a project manager at Straffkey will not be lessened by the state of the economy as a whole.

Which of the following would be most important to determine in order to evaluate the argument?

o Whether Straffkey's competitors bid to complete Straffkey's targeted government contracts at lower cost, especially during economic recessions
o Whether the number of certified project managers applying for positions at Straffkey increases significantly during economic recessions
o The requirements for certification as a project manager for the purposes of hiring at Straffkey
o The changes in workforce size at Straffkey upon the completion of large contracts
o Whether in the past a Straffkey has always honored its contractual computer programmer-to-project manager ratio

Straffkey's Project Guarantee

The company Straffkey guarantees in its contracts with clients that for every ten computer programmers employed by Straffkey on a client project, Staffkey will employ at least one certified project manager. Since many of Straffkey's contracts are with the nation's government, its business increases during economic recessions, when the government spends more, and it has to hire more computer programmers at these times to complete its contracts. Therefore, while many jobs are threatened by economic recessions, the prospects of being hired as a project manager at Straffkey will not be lessened by the state of the economy as a whole.

Which of the following would be most important to determine in order to evaluate the argument?

o   Whether Straffkey's competitors bid to complete Straffkey's targeted government contracts at lower cost, especially during economic recessions
o   Whether the number of certified project managers applying for positions at Straffkey increases significantly during economic recessions
o   The requirements for certification as a project manager for the purposes of hiring at Straffkey
o   The changes in workforce size at Straffkey upon the completion of large contracts
o   Whether in the past a Straffkey has always honored its contractual computer programmer-to-project manager ratio

Explanation

Reading the question: in this prompt, the opinion comes near the end. We can match terms to see how well they are connected.

Evidence Term	Matches?	Conclusion Term
At least one certified PM per 10 programmers	≠	
Hires more programmers during recessions	≠	Prospects of being hired as PM never lessened

In the conclusion, the phrase "never lessened" looks most vulnerable. The language pertaining to time on the left is "during recessions," which is a lot shorter than "never" or "always." Could the prospects somehow be only temporary? For example, when the economy recovered, the government spent less, Straffkey had to get rid of programmers, and then also PMs. Then the conclusion would be false, because hiring would be lessened the state of the economy. We have a filter "hiring during recessions is temporary."

Applying the filter: (B) and (D) both match our filter. Choice (E) discusses only whether it has honored the contract in the past, whereas the conclusion concerns the future.

Logical proof: we can analyze (B) and (D) by cases. In (B), if Staffkey were mobbed with applicants during recessions, that mobbing could outweigh their increased demand for PM's, hurting the argument. And if, somehow, *fewer* people applied, that would strength the argument. So (B) looks quite good. We consider extreme cases for (D). Say after large contracts, tons of people get laid off. That doesn't quite impact the argument, because we have no information on whether Straffkey's contracts are always or even generally completed under specific economic conditions, which is the key condition of the argument. So (D) is out. The correct answer is (B).

An obscure novel from the thirteenth century has been attributed to Author X, although whether she was the sole author of the long work is often disputed. The year of completion has also been disputed but should be accepted as 1221, because in this year Author X wrote a diary entry about her joy at having completed the work. In this diary entry she also mentions a specific character who appears only in the last chapter of the book. While doubts may remain about certain aspects of the book's authorship, there is no doubt about its chronology.

Which of the following, if true, most strongly supports the argument above?

- In several diary entries in the year 1220, Author X mentioned that she was lonely working on the obscure novel but that it was almost complete.
- For record-keeping purposes, Author X had a court scribe copy her diary, so a second copy of her diary verifies the authenticity of her entry about the obscure novel in 1221.
- No writers other than Author X wrote interior portions now accepted as part of the obscure novel after Author X had finished her portion in 1221.
- Early in 1222, a political coup took place that would have made life so turbulent for Author X that it would have been virtually impossible for her to continue to edit and add to the obscure novel.
- The last chapter of the book was the last one Author X wrote.

AUTHOR X'S NOVEL

An obscure novel from the thirteenth century has been attributed to Author X, although whether she was the sole author of the long work is often disputed. The year of completion has also been disputed but should be accepted as 1221, because in this year Author X wrote a diary entry about her joy at having completed the work. In this diary entry she also mentions a specific character who appears only in the last chapter of the book. While doubts may remain about certain aspects of the book's authorship, there is no doubt about its chronology.

Which of the following, if true, most strongly supports the argument above?

- In several diary entries in the year 1220, Author X mentioned that she was lonely working on the obscure novel but that it was almost complete.
- For record-keeping purposes, Author X had a court scribe copy her diary, so a second copy of her diary verifies the authenticity of her entry about the obscure novel in 1221.
- No writers other than Author X wrote interior portions now accepted as part of the obscure novel after Author X had finished her portion in 1221.
- Early in 1222, a political coup took place that would have made life so turbulent for Author X that it would have been virtually impossible for her to continue to edit and add to the obscure novel.
- The last chapter of the book was the last one Author X wrote.

EXPLANATION

Reading the question: The conclusion is that the year of completion of this book was 1221. If no flaw is obvious, we jump to the answer choices and apply the negation test.

Logical proof: choice (A) a weak strengthener, but when we negate it, the argument could still hold. It's not unusually material to the argument whether or not Author X wrote such diary entries. Same with (B); it strengthens the argument, but is not required. Choice (C) is different; if we negate (C), the argument blows up. In such a case, there were writers other than Author X who later wrote interior portions of the book, after 1221, so the year of completion wasn't 1221. (C) is in. (D) is quite similar to (A) and (B). (E) strengthens as well, but the argument doesn't break if (E) is false. The correct answer is (C).

Women who are married sleep more soundly than women who have never married or lost a partner, according to research from an eight-year study. Furthermore, it is well established that sleeping less than six hours a night makes you 12% more likely to die prematurely than someone who sleeps up to eight hours. Therefore, getting married increases a woman's life expectancy.

Which of the following, if true, does NOT strengthen the argument above?

- ○ Populations with lower odds of premature death have higher life expectancies.
- ○ Getting married does not lead to oversleep.
- ○ Marriage may introduce lifespan-shortening factors into a woman's life, but these factors tend to be collectively of less consequence than the benefit of sounder sleep.
- ○ Not sleeping soundly is the key reason women who cannot sleep at least eight hours a night fail to do so.
- ○ The psychology of women who marry is, on average, more conducive to sound sleep than that of women who have never married or lost a partner.

MARRIED WOMEN'S SLEEP

Women who are married sleep more soundly than women who have never married or lost a partner, according to research from an eight-year study. Furthermore, it is well established that sleeping less than six hours a night makes you 12% more likely to die prematurely than someone who sleeps up to eight hours. Therefore, getting married increases a woman's life expectancy.

Which of the following, if true, does NOT strengthen the argument above?

○ Populations with lower odds of premature death have higher life expectancies.
○ Getting married does not lead to oversleep.
○ Marriage may introduce lifespan-shortening factors into a woman's life, but these factors tend to be collectively of less consequence than the benefit of sounder sleep.
○ Not sleeping soundly is the key reason women who cannot sleep at least eight hours a night fail to do so.
○ The psychology of women who marry is, on average, more conducive to sound sleep than that of women who have never married or lost a partner.

EXPLANATION

Reading the question: Usually, in a strengthen question, we will look for the greatest weakness and then a strengthener that patches that weakness, because there is no greater way to strengthen an argument. But here we have a NOT question, so the correct answer is likely to be a weakener or be irrelevant. We'll use a basic filter: what answer choice weakens the idea that getting married makes a woman sleep longer and hence live longer?

Applying the filter: (A) patches a weak connection between dying prematurely and having a longer life expectancy. So (A) is a strengthener and hence is NOT the answer. Choice (B) also strengthens the argument, because it removes a problem and the prompt mentions specifically sleeping "up to 8 hours." So (B) is out. Choice (C) also removes a problem, that of an unintended consequence. So (C) is out. Choice (D) patches a weak connection between soundness of sleep and amount of sleep, so it's a strengthener and is out. Choice (E) may sound irrelevant initially, but it weakens the argument. It's saying that getting married isn't the cause of sleeping better; the cause, rather, is being the type of person, psychologically, who's likely to get married. It weakens the causal argument by establishing a different cause than the one given. The correct answer is (E).

Geologists believe that one of the largest volcanic eruptions in human history occurred 74,000 years ago, the Toba supereruption. In one area, Middle Paleolithic tools of similar styles have been found and dated to closely before and after the Toba supereruption, indicating that the humans who lived after the supereruption were members of the population that had lived in that area prior to the eruption.

Which of the following, if true, most seriously weakens the argument?

○   Most tools used by the population prior to the supereruption were destroyed in the aftermath of the eruption.

○   Other evidence indicates that tools of similar styles had been used in the area long prior to the supereruption.

○   Some populations under the massive supereruption traveled long distances to attempt to find a better place to live.

○   After the supereruption, a new population might have found and adopted use of the tools that had originally belonged to a population that was destroyed by the supereruption.

○   Research has suggested that many animal species went extinct as a consequence of the supereruption.

Geologists believe that one of the largest volcanic eruptions in human history occurred 74,000 years ago, the Toba supereruption. In one area, Middle Paleolithic tools of similar styles have been found and dated to closely before and after the Toba supereruption, indicating that the humans who lived after the supereruption were members of the population that had lived in that area prior to the eruption.

Which of the following, if true, most seriously weakens the argument?

○   Most tools used by the population prior to the supereruption were destroyed in the aftermath of the eruption.
○   Other evidence indicates that tools of similar styles had been used in the area long prior to the supereruption.
○   Some populations under the massive supereruption traveled long distances to attempt to find a better place to live.
○   After the supereruption, a new population might have found and adopted use of the tools that had originally belonged to a population that was destroyed by the supereruption.
○   Research has suggested that many animal species went extinct as a consequence of the supereruption.

EXPLANATION

Reading the question: the final clause harbors the conclusion, which is that people after the Toba eruption were members of the same population as before. We sense a term mismatch:

Evidence Term	Matches?	Conclusion Term
Before/after Toba supereruption	=	Before/after Toba supereruption
Tools	≠	Humans; members of population

The evidence doesn't talk about populations; it talks about tools. The assumption is, crudely, "Same tools? Same population!" To weaken it, we expect an answer that says, "Same tools doesn't mean same population." That's our filter.

Applying the filter: choice (D) matches our prediction and is the only answer choice to discuss both tools and populations.

Logical proof: We can confirm (D) by the negation test. If it were impossible for another people to adopt and use the tools, that would greatly strengthen the argument that the people before and after the eruption were the same folks. The correct answer is (D).

White-labelling is the practice is providing a product to another company to be sold under that company's high-quality brand. Since white-labelling allows the designer of a product to obtain additional revenue from a given design at minimal cost, and it allows the seller of the white-labelled product to sell a product and obtain product without having had to design the product, white-labelling is usually advantageous for both parties.

Which of the following, if true, most seriously weakens the argument?

- When the designer of a white-labelled product improves the design, the seller may be able to benefit immediately by switching over to the new design.
- If consumers learn the details of a white-labelling arrangement, they may perceive the provider of the product as being of low quality.
- The products best suited to white-labelling are those that are related but not core to the seller's key product offering, if the seller specializes in one offering.
- The seller of a white-labelled product will have to make some investment in the product, such as designing a brand and a name for the product and dedicating inventory space to that product.
- The seller of a white-labelled product may not have sufficient knowledge to sell the product through its own sales channels as well as the designer of the product might be able to do.

White-labelling is the practice is providing a product to another company to be sold under that company's high-quality brand. Since white-labelling allows the designer of a product to obtain additional revenue from a given design at minimal cost, and it allows the seller of the white-labelled product to sell a product and obtain product without having had to design the product, white-labelling is usually advantageous for both parties.

Which of the following, if true, most seriously weakens the argument?

- When the designer of a white-labelled product improves the design, the seller may be able to benefit immediately by switching over to the new design.
- If consumers learn the details of a white-labelling arrangement, they may perceive the provider of the product as being of low quality.
- The products best suited to white-labelling are those that are related but not core to the seller's key product offering, if the seller specializes in one offering.
- The seller of a white-labelled product will have to make some investment in the product, such as designing a brand and a name for the product and dedicating inventory space to that product.
- The seller of a white-labelled product may not have sufficient knowledge to sell the product through its own sales channels as well as the designer of the product might be able to do.

EXPLANATION

Reading the question: The opinion is the last clause: "white-labelling is advantageous for both parties." We might notice that "advantageous" hasn't been mentioned earlier. **When a term appears for the first time in the conclusion of an argument, try term matching.**

Evidence Term	Matches?	Conclusion Term
White-labelling	=	White-labelling
Additional revenue for creator and design-free product for seller	≠	Advantageous for both parties

The strained connection is that the revenue and free product are necessarily advantageous. This would fail to be true, for example, if there is something else needed for advantageousness that is missing, or if there is some overriding disadvantage. That's our filter.

Applying the filter: (A) is a strengthener, so it's out. Choice (B) points out a disadvantage of the arrangement, so it's in. (C) provides a comparative elaboration that is immaterial to establishing advantage. Out. (D) provides a condition that must be met by one party to capture the advantage, but it doesn't deny that there is an advantage. Choice (D) is out. (E) is more promising: it points out an potential inability of the seller to grasp the advantage. But it doesn't go far enough because it ends up claiming that the seller only can't sell the thing as well as the creator. That could be true and the arrangement could still be tremendously beneficial for the seller. So (E) is out.

Logical proof: if (B) is true, we have an overlooked and potentially overriding problem. Moreover, it's a quality perception issue, and part of the argument was specifically that there is a good brand perception. We can try the negation test. If (B) is false, then we have eliminated a concern, strengthening the argument. We have a disadvantage that the argument failed to point out. The correct answer is (B).

It is the opinion of the student council that the school's strict proctoring guidelines, which sometimes create situations in which a student may have to take three final exams in quick succession, can be done away with. If, as most faculty appear to believe, **take-home exams, which are not proctored anyway, are the only exams on which students might actually dare cheat,** then by doing away with the proctoring requirements, **the school would allow students to schedule their own final exams without damaging the integrity of these exams.** The fact that there is a very small percentage of students who are liable to attempt to cheat on a final exam when they take it within the school's walls is really a separate issue.

In the argument above, the two portions in boldface play which of the following roles?

○ The first is an objection that has been raised against the position taken by the argument; the second is the position taken by the argument.

○ The first is the position taken by the argument; the second is the position that the argument calls into question.

○ The first is a judgment that has been offered in support of the position that the argument calls into question; the second is a circumstance on which that judgment is, in part, based.

○ The first is a judgment that has been offered in support of the position that the argument advances; the second is that position.

○ The first is a claim that the argument calls into question; the second is the position taken by the argument.

It is the opinion of the student council that the school's strict proctoring guidelines, which sometimes create situations in which a student may have to take three final exams in quick succession, can be done away with. If, as most faculty appear to believe, **take-home exams, which are not proctored anyway, are the only exams on which students might actually dare cheat,** then by doing away with the proctoring requirements, **the school would allow students to schedule their own final exams without damaging the integrity of these exams.** The fact that there is a very small percentage of students who are liable to attempt to cheat on a final exam when they take it within the school's walls is really a separate issue.

In the argument above, the two portions in boldface play which of the following roles?

○ The first is an objection that has been raised against the position taken by the argument; the second is the position taken by the argument.
○ The first is the position taken by the argument; the second is the position that the argument calls into question.
○ The first is a judgment that has been offered in support of the position that the argument calls into question; the second is a circumstance on which that judgment is, in part, based.
○ The first is a judgment that has been offered in support of the position that the argument advances; the second is that position.
○ The first is a claim that the argument calls into question; the second is the position taken by the argument.

EXPLANATION

Reading the question: the prompt is long, but since we have boldfaced language, we need only slice and dice the logical function of the statements.

Sentence	Starts With.../Includes...	Function
1st	"It is the opinion of the student council that"	Council's opinion
2nd	"If, as...faculty believe...**take-home exams**"	View of faculty
2nd	"then by doing away with..."	Proposed change
2nd	**"the school would allow students"**	Benefit of proposed change
3rd	"The fact that..."	Elaboration upon benefit

The first sentence gives the council's opinion. The second sentence has a few parts, which we can call 2a through 2c. In 2a, we have the view of faculty, 2b we do away with proctoring, and in 2c we have an effect, a benefit, of making the change proposed by the council. The final sentence gives additional elaboration. So in the first bold portion we have the view of the faculty, and in the second bold portion we have a beneficial effect of making the change proposed by the council. The second is a prediction drawn based on the first one. Although the opinions belong to different people, they are not contrary.

Applying our filter, we can start with the fact that the second boldface is an opinion. That rules out (B) and (C) based on their latter portions. Then we review based on the first boldface, a view that is used as evidence. The boldfaced statements are on the same "side" as each other and as the argument as a whole. That fact rules out (A), (B), (C), and (E). The correct answer is (D).

The design of an article of clothing generally cannot be patented, but functional aspects or devices attached to clothing or included as attributes of clothing can usually be patented. Therefore, the design of a website selling fashion accessories should not be patentable, but the programming of that website, it if is unique, should be patentable.

Which of the following statements, if true, would most strengthen the argument above?

○ Programming a website selling fashion accessories is at least as difficult as designing a functional device attached to clothing.
○ The programming of a website is more useful than its design.
○ The design of a website is as unique as the design of an article of clothing.
○ Whether something can be patented has nothing to do with how much money it can or will make the designer of that thing.
○ The programming of a website selling fashion accessories is more like the design of a functional aspect of an article of clothing than it is like the design of an article of clothing.

PATENTED CLOTHING

The design of an article of clothing generally cannot be patented, but functional aspects or devices attached to clothing or included as attributes of clothing can usually be patented. Therefore, the design of a website selling fashion accessories should not be patentable, but the programming of that website, it if is unique, should be patentable.

Which of the following statements, if true, would most strengthen the argument above?

o   Programming a website selling fashion accessories is at least as difficult as designing a functional device attached to clothing.
o   The programming of a website is more useful than its design.
o   The design of a website is as unique as the design of an article of clothing.
o   Whether something can be patented has nothing to do with how much money it can or will make the designer of that thing.
o   The programming of a website selling fashion accessories is more like the design of a functional aspect of an article of clothing than it is like the design of an article of clothing.

EXPLANATION

Reading the question: this prompt presents an argument—and it's pseudo-syllogistic—so we can analyze it through term matching.

Evidence Term	Matches?	Conclusion Term
Design of clothing cannot be patented	≠	Design of site should not be patentable
Functional clothing can be patented	≠	Programming of site should be patentable

Here we have a double comparison, which is much clearer now that we have omitted the distracting fact that the website is about fashion. There are two key connections or assumptions, one for each row. We can be pretty confident that the answer will give us one or both of these and will filter the answer choices on that basis.

Applying the filter, we focus on (E). We confirm by comparing the phrases with the prompt; it matches our second prediction. Choices (A) through (C) all introduce out-of-scope comparisons; each of those new terms, "difficult," "useful," "unique," essentially creates a problem, because in each case another statement is missing, such as "whether something is difficult is key to whether it should be patentable." Choice (D) is off, because it could easily be true or false, as the material points of the argument are the two comparisons made.

Logical proof: we can use the negation test. Suppose that the programming of the website were *nothing at all* like functional clothing design? If we accepted that statement as a fact, the argument would fall apart. The negation of (E) weakens, the argument, so (E) strengthens the argument. The correct answer is (E).

It is fitting that we ended with term matching, which we saw in our first Critical Reasoning question. GMAT questions do not require ornate methods. If you master the process of creating an expectation of the answer choices, applying that filter, and seeking logical proof, you will have mastered GMAT Critical Reasoning.

WHAT'S NEXT?

Welcome to the end of the book! If you've worked through all of the practice questions in these pages, you are now familiar with the Critical Reasoning questions you'll see on the GMAT. The same practices that we have used on these questions—deciding an approach for each question, paraphrasing portions of the argument we're analyzing, making predictions, eliminating answer choices—will ensure that you do the best possible on these questions on the GMAT. Or, possibly, you're not through this book yet, but you are looking ahead (or looking for a break!). Either way, here are some directions for additional study:

- Your purchase of this book comes with a free download, the ▯▯▯▯▯▯▯▯▯▯▯▯▯▯▯▯▯ ▯▯▯▯▯ You can get the download at www.gmatfree.com/CR-Strategy-Sheets.

- For more GMAT Prep resources, see our "GMAT Prep" page at www.gmatfree.com/gmat-prep/, which includes links to important resources such as GMATPrep, the software from the test maker.

- Review these questions! It's worth reviewing every GMAT question you do at least two more times. Further reviews help you view the question more strategically and ingrain in yourself the practices that you want to replicate when you sit for the test.

Good luck. To be in touch with us, you can find us at www.gmatfree.com/contact-us/.

Warm regards,

Andrew Mitchell
Chief Freedom Officer
GMAT Free, LLC

>> Download the free
CR Strategy Sheets
GMATFree.com/CR-Strategy-Sheets

Index of Questions

3D Printer Use	147
Aggressive Loans	143
Alternative Plants	7
Author X's Novel	235
Auto Body	27
Automobiles in Bordland	219
Balbonia's Vice Tax	93
Bean Exports	141
Beginning Negotiations	181
Blindsight Denial	125
BSE and Beef Customers	69
Buyers' Commitment	179
Calendar Causes	153
Calendrical Pyramid	225
Caller Complaints	23
Car Dealer Credit	177
Car Review	39
Cattle Cost	163
Cause of Disease X	167
Cell Phone Manufacture	209
Changing Rooms	89
Cheaper Subscription Product	205
Counterfeit DVDs	67
Cowbird Songs	51
Cranial Size	221
Crumbling Kingdom	149
Decline in Pickpockets	185
Decline of GMOs	139
Discount Hardship	121
Downloaded Ads	41
Drivers Over 30	3
Elderly Policy	113
Elephant Burials	115
Eliminating Fax Machines	215
Expert Virus	53
Expiring Meters	25
False Science	187
Foreign Direct Investment	203
Games and Literacy	91
Glowing Pigs	5

Gluten Increase	199
Gold Will Go Up	57
Graffiti Art	33
Haverbrook Hotels	79
Health Plan	43
Hervey Allen	207
Hidden GMOs	11
History of Slang	229
Impending Storm	85
Inside Information	145
Isolated Schizophrenics	99
Likely Tax Fraud	157
Local Bookstores	31
Loss Layer	17
Mark's Mask	117
Married Women's Sleep	237
Methods of Stimulation	87
Monotonous Counting Exercise	189
Mortgage Incentives	105
Moving Offshore	193
Neighboring Insurance	55
New DVD Standard	133
New Exercise System	95
Oil Projection	155
Old Sharks	29
Orctanian Health	109
Organic Fertilizer	97
Osprey Prey	9
Patented Clothing	245
Pirating Losses	77
Preserving Strength	111
Price Wars	73
R&D Investment	151
Rare Plasma	49
Recycled Plastic Lumber	183
Repairing Hubble	231
Reserve Usage	137
Restaurant Tables and Chairs	213
Right to Search	119
Ring of Commerce	21
Second Restaurant	47
Security Checkpoints	63
Self-Scheduled Exams	243

Shelbyville's New Dealership	211
Sheriff vs. Beer	71
Shipping Skills	15
Shorter Weeks	13
Skull 5	165
Small Robots	169
Smoking by Nation	59
Social Cuckoos	101
Sterilized Insects	61
Stock Fund Performance	191
Stock Predictions	201
Stopping Deforestation	131
Stories in Conflict	161
Straffkey's Project Guarantee	233
Subscription Plan	35
Subsidized Farmers	173
Sunday Delivery	45
Taaffeite, Painite & Co.	217
Tablets vs. Books	75
Taxes and Growth	19
Taxing Pollution	103
Text Passwords	107
Toba Supereruption	239
Topeka Flights	37
Touristic Impact	171
Travel Through Tubes	223
Troglotopia Cave	227
Turbine Pricing Model	195
Unemployment Trend	65
Unpasteurized Milk	197
Unusual Café	159
Vaccine Administration	83
Vanishing Cuis	123
Veteran Sales Staff	127
Vocal Shareholders	135
Weakened Competitor	129
White-Labelling	241
Wine Profits	81
Zeddifreddo's Acquisition	175

Printed in Poland
by Amazon Fulfillment
Poland Sp. z o.o., Wrocław